www.wadsworth.com

wadsworth.com is the World Wide Web site for
Wadsworth and is your direct source to dozens
of online resources.

At *wadsworth.com* you can find out about
supplements, demonstration software, and
student resources. You can also send e-mail to
many of our authors and preview new publications
and exciting new technologies.

wadsworth.com
Changing the way the world learns®

P9-CJK-026

THE WADSWORTH CONTEMPORARY ISSUES IN CRIME AND JUSTICE SERIES

Todd Clear, Series Editor

1995 Close/Meier: *Morality in Criminal Justice: An Introduction to Ethics*
Klofas/Stojkovic: *Crime and Justice in the Year 2010*
Silberman: *A World of Violence: Corrections in America*
Wooden: *Renegade Kids, Suburban Outlaws: From Youth Culture to Delinquency*

1996 Belknap: *The Invisible Woman: Gender, Crime, and Justice*
Friedrichs: *Trusted Criminals: White Collar Crime in Contemporary Society*
Johnson: *Hard Time: Understanding and Reforming the Prison,* Second Edition
Karmen: *Crime Victims: An Introduction to Victimology,* Third Edition
Walker/Spohn/DeLone: *The Color of Justice: Race, Ethnicity, and Crime in America*

1997 Golden: *Disposable Youth: America's Child Welfare System*
Hickey: *Serial Murderers and Their Victims,* Second Edition
Irwin/Austin: *It's About Time: America's Imprisonment Binge,* Second Edition
Messner/Rosenfeld: *Crime and the American Dream,* Second Edition
Shelden/Tracy/Brown: *Youth Gangs in American Society*

1998 Bailey/Hale: *Popular Culture, Crime, and Justice*
Chesney-Lind/Shelden: *Girls, Delinquency, and Juvenile Justice,* Second Edition
Johnson: *Death Work: A Study of the Modern Execution Process,* Second Edition
Pollock: *Ethics, Crime, and Justice: Dilemmas and Decisions,* Third Edition
Rosenbaum/Lurigio/Davis: *The Prevention of Crime: Social and Situational Strategies*
Surette: *Media, Crime, and Criminal Justice: Images and Realities,* Second Edition
Walker: *Sense and Nonsense About Crime and Drugs: A Policy Guide,* Fourth Edition
White: *Terrorism: An Introduction,* Second Edition

1999 Arrigo: *Social Justice/Criminal Justice: The Maturation of Critical Theory in Law, Crime, and Deviance*

2000 Walker/Spohn/DeLone: *The Color of Justice: Race, Ethnicity, and Crime in America,* Second Edition

2001 Austin/Irwin: *It's About Time: America's Imprisonment Binge,* Third Edition
Karmen: *Crime Victims: An Introduction to Victimology,* Fourth Edition
Shelden/Tracy/Brown: *Youth Gangs in American Society,* Second Edition
Pope/Lovell/Brandl: *Voices from the Field: Readings in Criminal Justice Research*
Walker: *Sense and Nonsense About Crime and Drugs: A Policy Guide,* Fifth Edition
Wooden/Blazak: *Renegade Kids, Suburban Outlaws: From Youth Culture to Delinquency,* Second Edition

It's About Time

America's Imprisonment Binge

Third Edition

JAMES AUSTIN
The George Washington University

JOHN IRWIN
Professor Emeritus, San Francisco State University

Wadsworth
Thomson Learning™

Australia • Canada • Denmark • Japan • Mexico • New Zealand • Philippines • Puerto Rico
Singapore • South Africa • Spain • United Kingdom • United States

Executive Editor, Criminal Justice: *Sabra Horne*
Developmental Editor: *Terri Edwards*
Assistant Editor: *Anne Tsai*
Editorial Assistant: *Cortney Bruggink*
Marketing Manager: *Jennifer Somerville*
Project Editor: *Susan Walters*
Print Buyer: *Karen Hunt*

Permissions Editor: *Joohee Lee*
Production Service: *Scott Rohr/ Gustafson Graphics*
Copy Editor: *Linda Ireland*
Cover Design and Image: *Sandra Kelch*
Compositor: *Gustafson Graphics*
Text and Cover Printer: *Webcom Limited*

For more information, contact
Wadsworth/Thomson Learning
10 Davis Drive
Belmont, CA 94002-3098
USA
http://www.wadsworth.com

International Headquarters
Thomson Learning
International Division
290 Harbor Drive, 2nd Floor
Stamford, CT 06902-7477
USA

UK/Europe/Middle East/South Africa
Thomson Learning
Berkshire House
168-173 High Holborn
London WC1V 7AA
United Kingdom

Asia
Thomson Learning
60 Albert Street, #15-01
Albert Complex
Singapore 189969

Canada
Nelson Thomson Learning
1120 Birchmount Road
Toronto, Ontario M1K 5G4
Canada

Library of Congress Cataloging-in-Publication Data

Austin, James, date.
    It's about time : America's imprisonment binge / James Austin, John Irwin.
—3rd ed.
        p.   cm.
    Irwin's name appears first on the earlier edition.
    Includes bibliographical references and index.
    ISBN 0-534-51498-7
        I. Irwin, John, date.   II. Title.
HV9471 .A969 2000
365'.973—dc21   00-035940

*Dedicated to those people
who have not given up the
struggle to make our criminal justice
system fair, rational, and humane*

Contents

Foreword   xi

Preface   xiii

1   Our Imprisonment Binge   1

America's Growing Correctional Industrial Complex   1

The Politics of the Fear of Crime   5

America's History of Warehousing Prisoners   9

What Has Been Accomplished
        by the Imprisonment Binge?   12

The Costs of the Imprisonment Binge   13

Notes   15

2   Who Goes to Prison?   17

Public Misperceptions About Who Goes to Prison   17

National Trends on Prison Admissions   19

A Closer Look at Who Goes to Prison   22

How Serious Are Their Crimes?   25

Patterns of Crime   31

Habitual Offenders   38

Conclusions   46

Notes   47

3   The Imprisonment of Children and Women   50

The Children's Imprisonment Binge   50

The Imprisonment Binge of Women   57

Notes   62

4   The Private Prison Binge   64

Background   64

Privatization of Corrections: A Historical Overview   67

The Debate   71

A Closer Look at State Prison Privatization   77

The Future of Privatization   85

Notes   86

5   Doing Time   90

Warehousing Prisoners   90

The Development of the Contemporary Prison   91

The Bureaucratic Prison   97

The Prisoner Experience   100

Coping with Violence   108

Crippled   109

Alienated   111

Notes   112

6 Super Max   117

What Is Super Max?   117

History of Administrative Segregation   119

The Official Program   120

The Reality of Lockup   121

Turmoil in Lockup   121

New Maximum-Security Prisons   125

A Closer Look at a Contemporary Lockup Unit: The Texas
      Administrative Segregation Population   129

The Consequences of Lockup   131

Notes   137

7 Release   139

The Growing Number of Prison Releases   139

The Rising Tide of Parole Failures   143

Obstacles to Making It After Release   146

Those Who Make It   151

Notes   157

8 The Correctional Treatment Industrial Complex   160

Introduction   160

Factors Related to Criminal Behavior   162

What Does Work?   165

Boot Camps   167

Prison Drug Treatment   169

Summary   179

Notes   180

9   The Three Strikes and You're Out Movement   184

Introduction   184

Diversity Among the States   186

Comparison of the New Laws with Preexisting
        Sentencing Provisions   191

Description and Legislative History
        of the California Law   195

Impact of California's Law on the Courts   197

Variation by Counties in the Application of the Law   201

Impact on State Prison Systems   202

Who Are the Strikers?   204

Impact on Correctional Costs in California   208

Impact on Crime Rates Within California   210

Impact on Crime Rates Among the States   212

Summary   213

Notes   214

10   It's About Time   219

The Financial Cost   220

The "Incarceration Reduces Crime" Debate   222

Voodoo Criminology   236

America's Farm System for Criminals   239

Our Prison System in the Twenty-First Century   240

It's About Time   244

Notes   249

Index   253

Foreword

We Americans are a patriotic people. Of course, we have a great deal to be proud of—the world envies our economic, religious, and political freedom. As Americans, we think of ourselves as a free people. And we think that our freedoms are central to what sets us apart from the rest of the world.

It is ironic, then, that in America more people are denied these freedoms by law than in any other western nation: we lock up more citizens per capita than any other nation that has bothered to count its prisoners. Perhaps some Americans are proud of this distinction, but most of us are left to wonder. What is it about America that leads to so many prisoners? Are we this kind of criminal society? What do we gain from this high level of imprisonment? What does it cost us?

In the Contemporary Issues in Crime and Justice Series, we offer studies of controversial, often misunderstood aspects of crime and justice by some of the most talented scholars in the field. For students interested in an in-depth understanding of particular problems in crime and justice, we provide volumes that address these questions in some depth. I am pleased to introduce the third edition of *It's About Time: America's Imprisonment Binge.* The first two editions proved an important addition to the books in our series, and we think students will find this third edition even more topical and useful. The data in this new edition are updated and the arguments extended to include recent state and federal crime policy reforms, such as "three strikes and you're out" legislation creating sentences of life without parole for repeat felons.

Irwin and Austin are perhaps two of the criminologists most qualified to write about imprisonment policy. Professor John Irwin wrote the classic study of the prison, *The Felon,* and James Austin is now associated with The George Washington University after 25 years with the National Council on Crime and Delinquency. They are also close friends who have collaborated on research for over a decade. Who would be more well-suited to write about imprisonment policy?

This is an important book. It confronts some of our most cherished myths about crime policy:

- Are most prisoners dangerous felons?
- Is America's enormous prison population necessary for community protection?
- What happens to prisoners; why do they return to prison so often?
- What are the impacts of the large prison system on our nation?

Ponder the dimensions of the problem. In 1973, a few short years before most readers of this volume were born, prisoners were less than 1 in 1,000 citizens. Today the growth has been so dramatic that prisoners are fully 1 for every 200 citizens. How did we become a nation of so many prisoners?

Wadsworth is proud to add the third edition of this book to its collection. This edition has an updated and improved collection of statistics, and it develops its most interesting themes with even more eloquence and logic. The result is a careful, thoughtful critique of crime policy in the United States. Every reader will find plenty in this volume that challenges carefully held perspectives and predispositions. For readers who open themselves to the arguments in this volume, there will be a profound challenge: how can we justify current crime policy in terms of its assumptions and effects?

There are some ominous numbers in this volume. The proportion of African-American males in prisons and jails on any given day is numbing. The startling number of petty offenders who occupy our expensive jails and prisons leads us to wonder about the wisdom of this enormous expenditure. The debilitating nature of the prison experience is troubling to all who would have our corrections system build better citizens. In short, this is a book that will make you think.

And that is the purpose of the Contemporary Issues in Crime and Justice Series—to help people think about the most difficult problems in crime and justice. Students will not always agree with the viewpoints expressed by authors in this series, but they will find the arguments authoritative and compelling. Most important, readers will, we hope, find their own viewpoints expanded and enriched by what they read.

This is a compelling study of crime and punishment in America. Enjoy it . . . and learn!

Todd Clear
Series Editor

Preface

For the last decades, we have been witnessing the national tragedy and disgrace of America's imprisonment binge. We, as sociologists/criminologists, have kept in close contact with America's prison systems, including their administrators, staffs, policy makers, and, most of all, clients—the prisoners. During the 1980s, we nervously listened to our political leaders (both Republicans and Democrats) and special interest groups advocate their simplistic but appealing message that to solve the crime problem we needed to escalate the use of imprisonment. We were equally dismayed to witness many of our colleagues pursue government-financed studies that would justify the conservative "war on crime" agenda. Then, we watched, incredulously, the unparalleled explosion of the prison populations.

Our education and experience regarding the relationship between crime and imprisonment had taught us that the ideas that were the conceptual building blocks of the conservative rhetoric on crime and its control were fallacious. The basic tenets of this political agenda can be summarized as follows:

- The War on Poverty, which sought to fight crime through education, job training, and rehabilitation in the 1960s and 1970s, was a total failure.

- Dangerous criminals repeatedly go free because of liberal judges or decisions made by the liberal Supreme Court that help the criminal but not the victim.

- Swift and certain punishment in the form of more and longer prison terms will reduce crime by incapacitating the hardened criminals and making potential law breakers think twice before they commit crimes.

- Most inmates are dangerous and cannot be safely placed in the community.

- It will be far cheaper to society in the long run to increase the use of imprisonment.

- Greater use of imprisonment since the 1980s is the most effective way for reducing crime.

It became increasingly apparent that nothing was working to dispel the conservative rhetoric on crime and that the prison populations were going to grow forever, or at least until the society created a veritable disaster. We, therefore, began conducting (privately financed) research to counter what we view as grossly misleading and often fallacious statements.

We first presented this research in a series of pamphlets—*It's About Time, Who Goes to Prison, and Does Imprisonment Reduce Crime?*—that was published and distributed by the National Council on Crime and Delinquency (NCCD) over five years. The appeal of the conservative rhetoric to the public and the size of prison populations have apparently not been reduced by our efforts or those of other critics of current criminal justice policies. However, there are glimmers of hope.

Many have finally begun to openly question the wisdom of lengthy mandatory prison terms for drug users. The huge costs of the imprisonment binge have led many states to reconsider prison construction programs. Governors and mayors openly state that they cannot afford to build another jail or prison. Some jurisdictions are actually reducing their prison terms and funding alternatives to prison.

We also take heart that some of the leading criminologists who have provided the intellectual fodder for the imprisonment binge (RAND's Peter Greenwood and Professor John DiIulio) now concede that their incapacitation theories were misguided and that we have built too many prisons. Indeed, no credible criminologist supports the notion that the imprisonment binge has or will in the future impact crime rates. Many other books and articles authored by respected scholars now echo the view that the imprisonment binge has gone on far too long. But not unlike Robert McNamara's public confession of his failed Vietnam policy, these admissions come far too late after far too much damage has been inflicted on millions of Americans, their families, and their communities. This is especially true for African-American males. Incredibly, those born today have a 30 percent chance of being sent to prison during their life.

Nonetheless, we still believe that one of the unique attributes of American democracy is its diversity—in both its citizenry and its ideas. For a democracy to exist, there must be a marketplace of ideas that often compete with one another. The current and dominant "imprisonment reduces crime" ideology has held a stranglehold on criminal justice policy. Studies designed to evaluate the effects of the conservative policy objectively or to look at alternatives were not requested or were denied funding. For these reasons, we felt it important that an alternative perspective be articulated—a perspective that we deeply believe will ultimately become accepted. So, we wrote this book.

Admittedly, we (like most social scientists) started off with a particular purpose. Clearly we believe that we are incarcerating far too many Americans. But the arguments and the analysis are honest, and they emerge directly from all the information and evidence we could accumulate.

In the third edition, we provide updated statistics on the crime rate, criminal justice expenditures, the growth of the prison system, and more. Along with a critical analysis of the whole prison system, the third edition covers relevant topics such as contemporary prison conditions; recent sentencing reform, including "three strikes and you're out"; truth in sentencing; private prisons; and the growing imprisonment binge of women and children. There is also more information on rehabilitation as well as alternative solutions to existing problems in the system. Our bottom line is that the length of prison sentences need to be significantly reduced. Only then will the imprisonment binge ease.

Many persons and organizations helped us finish the book. Over the course of our research, financial assistance was periodically provided by the Edna McConnell Clark Foundation, the Jessie Ball Dupont Religious, and the Charitable and Educational Fund. More recently we have continued to receive the support of the National Institute of Justice, the National Institute of Corrections, and the Bureau of Justice Assistance in conducting studies of "three strikes and you're out" and private prisons. We particularly would like to thank the various administrators associated with those agencies: Laurie Robinson, Jeremy Travis, Nancy Gist, Timothy Murray, Morris Thigpen, and Larry Solomon.

Chase Riveland, Michael Lane, Harry Singletary, and George Sumner, all of whom were directors of state prison systems at the time of our research, granted us permission and provided us with the necessary resources to conduct our inmate interviews in Washington, Nevada, Illinois, and Florida. In all four states, a number of prison guards and administrative staff—too many to mention here— assisted us in compiling inmate record data and providing access to the inmates.

We are grateful for suggestions made by the reviewers of this and previous editions: Paul Astone, Alabama State University; Stephen J. Bahr, Brigham Young University; Shannon Barton, Ferris State University; Paul V. Campbell, Wayne State College; Paul C. Friday, Research and Training Specialists; Michael Hallett, Middle Tennessee State University; Vincent Hoffman, Michigan State University; Edward Latessa, University of Cincinnati; Michael Lauderdale, The University of Texas at Austin; Bernard McCarthy, University of Central Florida; Robert D. Mendelsohn, South Dakota State University; William J. Miller, Ohio University; and Susan O. Reed, University of Wisconsin, Oshkosh.

Finally, we want to express our deep appreciation to the numerous inmates and parolees we interviewed and met in the course of doing this research. Although they represent a tiny subsample of the millions of Americans who are imprisoned each year, we hope that their life experiences, as represented in this book, will lead to a more enlightened and humane imprisonment policy.

IT'S ABOUT TIME
America's Imprisonment Binge

1

■

Our Imprisonment
Binge

AMERICA'S GROWING

CORRECTIONAL INDUSTRIAL COMPLEX

The United States has been engaged in an unprecedented imprisonment binge. Between 1980 and 1998, the prison population ballooned from 329,821 to 1,302,019—a rise of 295 percent.[1] The increase was so great that by 1998, the number of citizens incarcerated in state and federal prisons exceeded or approximated the resident populations of thirteen states and was larger than all of our major cities with the exceptions of Chicago, Houston, Los Angeles, New York, and Philadelphia.[2] The incarceration rate (number of persons in state and federal prison on any given day per 100,000 population) increased during the same time period from 138 to 461, as compared to only 26 in 1850 (see Figure 1-1). We now imprison at a higher rate than any nation in the world, having recently surpassed South Africa.

And there is little evidence that America's imprisonment campaign will end soon. Because so many states have adopted "truth in sentencing" and other mandatory sentencing policies advocated by both political parties, the prison population will likely mushroom to over 1.6 million by the end of the decade. Between 1990 and 1998, the prison population grew an average of 6 percent per year. In 1998, the annual rate of growth declined to 4.8 percent, which is the equivalent of requiring that 1,130 new prison beds be constructed each week.[3] As of 1998, 83,527 prison beds were under construction, and an additional 86,416 were being planned to be built over

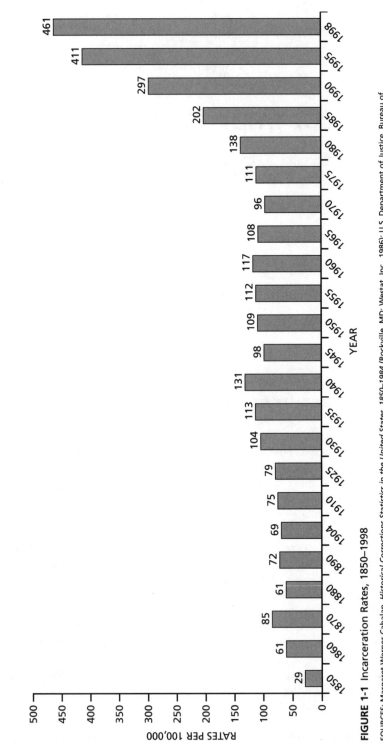

FIGURE 1-1 Incarceration Rates, 1850–1998

SOURCES: Margaret Werner Cahalan, *Historical Corrections Statistics in the United States, 1850–1984* (Rockville, MD: Westat, Inc., 1986); U.S. Department of Justice, Bureau of Justice Statistics, *Sourcebook of Criminal Justice Statiscs, 1997* (Washington, DC, 1995); U.S. Department of Justice, Bureau of Justice Statistics, *State and Federal Prisoners, June 30, 1998* (Washington, DC, 1998).

the next few years.[4] Yet even this massive construction program represents a futile effort to catch up with the increasing prison populations.

Most Americans are unaware that the adult prison population represents no more than one-fifth of the entire correctional industrial complex. There are another 585,000 people in jail. Furthermore, there are nearly 3.5 million on probation, and 705,000 on parole. In total, 6 million adults—about 1 of every 33 adults—were under some form of correctional supervision. In 1980 the ratio was 1 of every 91 adults.

In terms of growth, the rise in prison populations has been accompanied by equally large increases in these other forms of correctional supervision. Between 1980 and 1998, the probation, parole, and jail populations (facilities that typically house pretrial defendants and offenders sentenced to short jail terms of one year or less) grew almost as rapidly as the prison population (Table 1-1). Probation grew by 206 percent during the same time and has remained the dominant form of correctional supervision; over 3.4 million adults were on probation on any given day in 1998.

It should also be noted that more Americans experience jail time than any other form of correctional control. In 1994, the U.S. Department of Justice reported 9.8 million admissions to the nation's 3,300-plus jails.[5] Assuming that approximately 75 percent of these 9.8 million admissions represents mutually exclusive adults, this means that nearly 1 of every 25 adults in America goes to jail each year.

But even these staggering numbers do not account for all Americans caught up in the correctional system. Not counted in the 6-million figure are over 100,000 children incarcerated, and nearly 2,500 held by the military. Although there are no firm government estimates, there are several hundred thousand juveniles on probation or parole plus the same number of adults and juveniles on some form of pretrial supervision. Based on these estimates, one can safely assume that over 7 million Americans are caught up in the one of several correctional systems.

Those under the control of correctional authority do not represent a cross-section of the nation's population. They tend to be young African-American and Hispanic males who are uneducated, without jobs, or, at best, marginally employed in low-paying jobs. According to the most recent data from the U.S. Department of Justice, there are enormous disparities in incarceration rates by race and ethnicity. Blacks, Hispanics, and Native Americans have incarceration rates that are two to six times higher than whites (Tables 1-2 and 1-3). These disparities by race and ethnicity become even more troubling when age is factored into the analysis. In one recent study,[6] the average daily populations of those in prison, parole, probation, and jail revealed the following conclusions:

- Almost 1 of 3 (32.2 percent) African-American men in the age group 20-29 is either in prison, jail, probation, or parole on any given day.
- More than 1 of every 10 Hispanic men (12.3 percent) in the same age group is either in prison, jail, probation, or parole on any given day.
- For white men, the ratio is considerably lower: 1 in 15 (or 6.7 percent).

Table 1-1 Adult Correctional Populations,
Percentage Change, 1980–1998

	1980	1998	% Change
Probation	1,118,097	3,417,613	206%
Jails	163,994	592,462	261%
Prison	329,821	1,302,019	295%
Parole	220,438	704,964	220%
Totals	1,832,350	6,017,058	228%
Adult population	162.8 million	192.6 million	18%
Percentage of adults under supervision	1.1%	3.0%	173%
Adult arrests	6.1 million	8.6 million	41%
Reported index crimes	13.4 million	12.3 million	–8%

SOURCES: U.S. Department of Justice, Federal Bureau of Investigation, *Uniform Crime Reports: Crime in the United States, 1980 and 1997;* U.S. Department of Justice, Bureau of Justice Statistics, *Prisoners in 1998;* U.S. Department of Justice, Bureau of Justice Statistics, *Probation and Parole Populations in the United States, 1998.*

Table 1-2 Male Incarceration Rates per 100,000 Male Population
by Race and Ethnicity, 1990–1997

Year	All	White	Black	Hispanic	Native American
1990	564	338	2,234	1,016	516
1995	781	449	3,095	1,264	769
1996	810	468	3,164	1,279	850
1997	841	491	3,253	1,272	905
% Change	49%	45%	46%	25%	75%

SOURCE: U.S. Department of Justice, Bureau of Justice Statistics, *Prisoners in 1998* (Washington, DC, 1999).

Table 1-3 Female Incarceration Rates per 100,000 Female Population
by Race and Ethnicity, 1990–1997

Year	All	White	Black	Hispanic	Native American
1990	31	19	117	56	35
1995	47	27	176	64	72
1996	51	30	185	78	77
1997	53	32	192	87	80
% Change	71%	68%	64%	55%	129%

SOURCE: U.S. Department of Justice, Bureau of Justice Statistics, *Prisoners in 1998* (Washington, DC, 1999).

- Sixty years ago, less than one-fourth of prison admissions were nonwhite. Today, nearly three-fourths are nonwhite.

- African Americans and Hispanics constitute almost 90 percent of offenders sentenced to state prison for drug possession.

- African-American women have experienced the greatest increase in correctional supervision, rising by 78 percent from 1989 through 1994.

THE POLITICS OF THE FEAR OF CRIME

Several factors have fueled the imprisonment binge. The most powerful has been the public's growing fear of crime. Bill Chambliss has documented the well-orchestrated effort by powerful interest groups since the 1960s to make crime the most important issue on the public's mind. Chambliss points out that prior to the 1960s crime was never cited by the public as a major concern.[7] But led by a well-funded cartel of conservatives who were greatly concerned about the civil rights and anti-Vietnam movements, a "War on Crime" was formally launched by an increasingly defensive President Johnson. Part of the increasing concern regarding crime was fueled by a substantial increase in the major "index" crimes (homicides, assaults, rape, burglary, theft, and arson) reported to police in the late 1960s and early 1970s (see Figure 1-2). But despite massive increases in the amount of money being spent on law enforcement and corrections, and a tapering off in the crime rate, the public has continued to believe that crime has been increasing, and their fear of crime remains high.[8] The most recent national Gallup Poll shows that a majority of Americans believe that crime rates will continue to increase despite the well-publicized decline in serious crime.[9]

Through the 1980s, the fear of crime and drug abuse was elevated each election year by the attention that politicians (both Democrats and Republicans) and the media give to crime and drug problems. The first and most blatant example of these tactics was then Republican presidential candidate George Bush's successful effort to erase his opponent's (Michael Dukakis) early lead in the 1987 presidential campaign by blaming the tragic Willie Horton incident on liberal Democratic Party politics. Smarting from this poignant lesson in dirty politics, Democrats have fully embraced "get tough on crime" policies in an effort to outflank and neutralize what has traditionally been a Republican perspective.

It was under the democratically controlled Congress that the now infamous Federal Sentencing Guidelines, which mandated long prison terms for possession of crack cocaine, were adopted. And it was President Clinton's administration that endorsed the most expensive crime bill in the nation's history to fund 100,000 police officers and boot camps, and to help pay for prison construction for states willing to pass laws that would require long prison terms.

The public has shifted its focus (or more correctly has had its focus shifted by the media) on violent crime even as the crime rate has declined (see Chapter 6 on crime rate analysis). As we have suggested in an earlier publication:

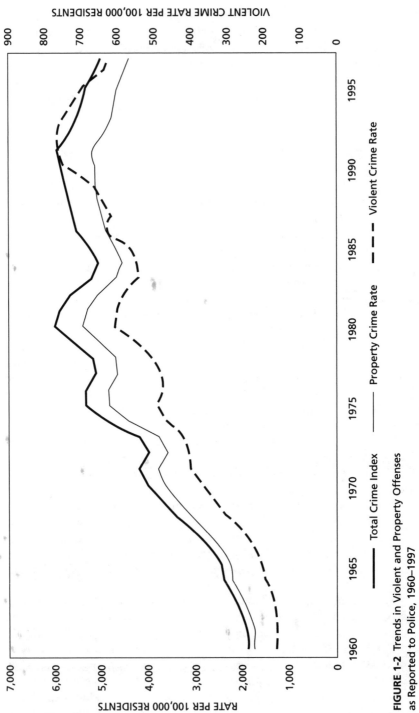

FIGURE 1-2 Trends in Violent and Property Offenses
as Reported to Police, 1960–1997

Politicians harangue on the street crime problem because it is a safe issue. It is easy to cast in simple terms of good versus evil and no powerful constituency is directly offended by a campaign against street crime. Some politicians also use street crime to divert attention away from other pressing social problems—such as the threat of nuclear war, unemployment, high living costs, and the economy—all of which persistently top the list of public concerns. Measures to solve these problems would require changes that would offend powerful interest groups.[10]

The public's concern over drug use has also been used as a political football to justify an ever-increasing use of imprisonment of drug users. As shown in Figure 1-3, the public's attention on drugs accelerated dramatically at the end of the 1980s, and then declined but rose again in 1997 and 1998 as Republicans and Democrats began to worry about modest increases in the use of marijuana by high school students. Marsha Rosenbaum, in her analysis of the nation's early rationale for the War on Drugs, states:

> The Reagan administration initiated a "War on Drugs" in the early 1980s. The Bush administration appointed a "Drug Czar," and recently offered a major plan to remove the "scourge" of drugs from the American landscape. The media have reported on the violence occurring in our inner cities and in cocaine-source nations like Colombia. The public is bombarded with news about drugs, like the drug death of sports figure Len Bias and the confessions of celebrities about personal struggles with substance abuse.[11]

The War on Drugs also spurred a movement toward more punitive sentencing policies for drug offenders. In addition, mandatory drug testing and a reduction in affordable publicly funded drug treatment programs have meant that more and more released felons are being returned to prison for use of illegal drugs.

Moreover, because this war is focused on crack cocaine, which is mainly sold and used in inner-city communities, it is increasing the already disproportionately high number of African-American and Hispanic prisoners. For example, in 1926, the first year that the race of prison admissions was recorded on a national basis, only 21 percent of all prison admissions were African American. By 1970, that figure had increased to 39 percent; by 1996, it had further grown to 51 percent.[12] In their steady and unrelenting harangues on the crime and drug problems, politicians have argued that steady and dramatic expansion of prison populations is absolutely necessary to maintain a safe society. They say that massive increases in imprisonment are positive signs—indications that the nation is increasingly intolerant of criminals and their antisocial and too often violent behavior. Moreover, they claim that increasing the use of imprisonment in particular and punishment in general has reduced crime. Former Attorney General William Barr restated this position well, indicating that the country had a "clear choice": either to build more prisons or to tolerate higher violent crime rates.[13]

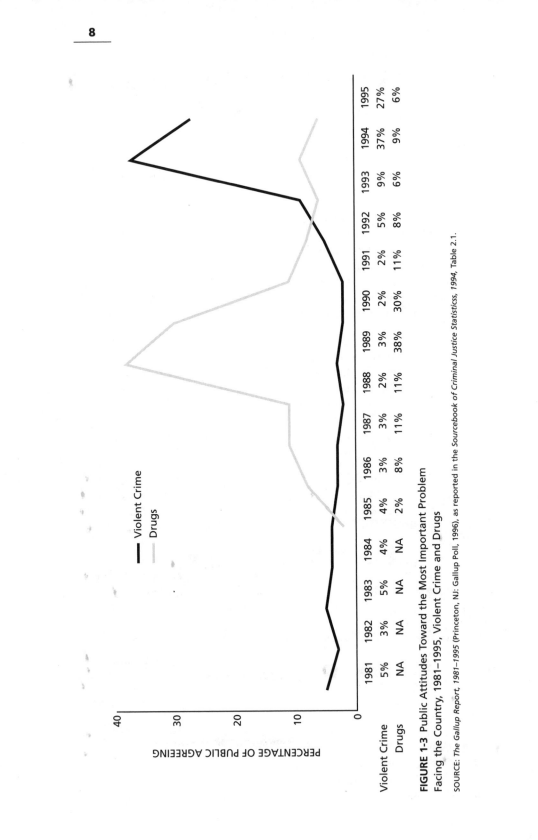

	1981	1982	1983	1984	1985	1986	1987	1988	1989	1990	1991	1992	1993	1994	1995
Violent Crime	5%	3%	5%	4%	4%	3%	3%	2%	3%	2%	2%	5%	9%	37%	27%
Drugs	NA	NA	NA	NA	2%	8%	11%	11%	38%	30%	11%	8%	6%	9%	6%

FIGURE 1-3 Public Attitudes Toward the Most Important Problem Facing the Country, 1981–1995, Violent Crime and Drugs

SOURCE: *The Gallup Report, 1981–1995* (Princeton, NJ: Gallup Poll, 1996), as reported in the *Sourcebook of Criminal Justice Statisticss, 1994*, Table 2.1.

AMERICA'S HISTORY
OF WAREHOUSING PRISONERS

Imprisonment as society's punishment for serious crime has been part of the American social fabric since the founding of this country. In colonial times, before the American Revolution, most felons were fined, whipped, branded, publicly shamed, or banished. A few were executed. The prison, a special location in which to place people for punishment for their crimes, was introduced soon after the revolution, ostensibly as a device to reform offenders. Americans, rejecting what they saw as excessively cruel measures employed in England and in the colonies under English rule, adopted the concept of the "penitentiary," where felons would "be kept in quiet solitude, reflecting penitently on their sins in order that they might cleanse and transform themselves."[14] After several decades of building and running penitentiaries, the states more or less gave up on reformation but continued to use the prison as the main form of punishment for serious crime.

During the nineteenth century, prisons became extremely cruel places in which convicts were kept under control through brutal forms of corporal punishment and were frequently used as cheap labor. Around 1900, federal legislation and emerging union power forced most convict labor out of the public sector. For the next fifty years, prisons were "big houses"—fortresslike institutions where prisoners did little more than "time." After World War II, many states returned to the reformative goal, with some new social scientific embellishments. Prisoners were to be "rehabilitated" through new scientific methods. This era lasted until evidence mounted that rehabilitative efforts were making no difference—that is, prisoners who were involved in treatment programs returned to prison at the same rate as those who were not.[15] This persistent finding of "no difference" convinced social scientists and then criminal justice policy makers that rehabilitation had been a mistake.[16] The social scientists argued that under rehabilitation, sentences were increased and many inhumane programs and routines were practiced.[17] Government policy makers believed that rehabilitation had been an expensive failure that led to higher crime rates. At this time, the general society entered a punitive period (1975), which continues today. Rehabilitation was abandoned, and now felons are sent to prison to receive their "just desserts" and to be deterred from committing crimes in the future.

In examining this history of shifting rationales for imprisonment, we clearly see that none of them accounts for our persistent and almost exclusive reliance on prison as the appropriate response to serious crime. What does explain it is the American people's strong desire to banish from their midst any population of people who are threatening, bothersome, and repulsive. As David Rothman points out in *The Discovery of the Asylum,* this is what was done from the outset with the insane, the feeble-minded, the poor, wayward children, and felons.[18] We continue to do it with the elderly poor, troublesome insane, street rabble, and felons.[19] The pattern is particularly clear in the latest upsurge in the use of the prison, which followed a period (1965–1970) during which there was considerable interest in finding other forms of punishment and actual success in significantly lowering prison populations.

Since that time, however, many unsettling developments have made Americans more fearful, conservative, and mean-spirited. The aforementioned perception of steady increases in crime is one contributing factor. But more fundamental are nationwide economic difficulties. Soaring inflation, high unemployment, and a decline in real wages of a significant proportion of the middle class have caused uncertainty about the economic future. Also, the proliferation of materialistic, ostentatious parvenus and the expansion of an underclass perceived as menacing have offended the public. These disturbing developments have been aggravated by the perception that, because of global, unmanageable economic processes, our society's economic problems are insoluble.

In terms of lowering our crime rate or of reducing the size and costs of corrections, the following social and economic trends offer little reason for optimism for the future:

- Between 1980 and 1996, the number of persons living in poverty rose from 29 million to 37 million (27 percent increase).
- Fourteen million children, or more than 1 of every 5 children, live in poverty.
- For minority children, the figures are even more desperate: 40 percent of African-American children and Hispanic children live in poverty.
- The number of single-parent families, predominantly headed by females, increased from 22 percent in 1980 to 32 percent by 1997.
- Between 1980 and 1995, the number of births to unmarried women increased from 666,000 to 1,254,000. Approximately 13 percent of all births are to unmarried teenagers. The rates of illegitimate births are highest among black and Hispanic women.[20]

Why are these disturbing trends emerging now? Part of the explanation lies in fundamental shifts in the distribution of wealth, as first documented by Kevin Phillips in his book *The Politics of Rich and Poor.*[21] Phillips, using a wide variety of official data, argued that the government economic policies of the past decade have improved the economic status of the rich at the expense of the lower and middle classes. Some of the more striking economic trends he identified for the 1980s are the following:

- In 1987, the income of the typical African-American family ($18,098) equaled just 56.1 percent of the typical white family's income, the lowest comparative ratio since the 1960s.
- Between 1979 and 1987, earnings for male high school graduates with one to five years of work experience declined by 18 percent.
- Between 1981 and 1987, the nation lost over 1 million manufacturing jobs.
- Between 1977 and 1988, the average after-tax family income of the lowest 10 percent, in current dollars, fell from $3,528 to $3,157 (a 10.5 percent

decline). Conversely, the income of the top 10 percent increased from $70,459 to $89,783 (a 24.4 percent increase), and the incomes of the top 1 percent increased from $174,498 to $303,900 (a 74 percent increase).

- Between 1981 and 1988, the total compensation of chief executives increased from $373,000 to $773,000 (an increase of 107 percent), and the number of millionaires and billionaires increased by more than 250 percent.[22]

These trends have continued to the present. Although the middle and upper class are now enjoying the prosperity of a booming U.S. economy, the data cited previously show that not all Americans are benefiting from the current economic situation. In economic terms, the United States is becoming a more fragmented and segregated society. These trends not only contribute to crime rates and other social problems but also fuel a growing public demand to fund criminal justice services. In particular, the number of those Americans who are uneducated and raised in impoverished conditions will continue to grow and justify the need to further expand the correctional system. As Phillips stated:

> For women, young people, and minorities the effect of economic polarization during the 1980's was largely negative. The nation as a whole also suffered as unemployable young people drove up the crime rate and expanded the drug trade. Broken families and unwed teenage mothers promised further welfare generations and expense. And none of it augured well for the future skills level and competitiveness of the U.S. work force.[23]

Our society faces an enormous public policy dilemma. On the one hand, we are expending a greater portion of our public dollars on incarcerating, punishing, treating, and controlling persons who are primarily from the lower economic classes in an effort to reduce crime. On the other hand, we have set in motion economic policies that serve to widen the gap between the rich and the poor, producing yet another generation of impoverished youths who will probably end up under the control of the correctional system. By escalating the size of the correctional system, we are also increasing the tax burden and diverting billions of dollars from those very public services (education, health, transportation, and economic development) that would reduce poverty, unemployment, crime, drug abuse, and mental illness.

Although we have become more punitive than at any other time in our history, the public still believes that America is soft on crime and wants legislators and the courts to "get tougher" on crime, especially in the face of what they believe are rising crime rates and a declining standard of living.[24] Edward Luttwak, in his analysis of the impact of U.S. economics on the middle class, argues that the growing insecurity of the middle class has translated into an almost "insatiable demand" for even more punitive sentencing practices:

The insecure majority does not realize that the economy too can be subject to the will of the majority . . . so it vents its anger and resentment by punishing, restricting, and prohibiting everything it can. The most blatant symptom is the insatiable demand for tougher criminal laws, longer prison terms, mandatory life sentences for repeat offenders, more and prompter executions, and harsher forms of detention (including, of late, chain gangs). Politicians, including President Clinton, have heard the people, and the result is a mass of new federal and state legislation that will greatly add to the staggering number of Americans already behind bars.[25]

In many ways, our current situation is similar to that of eighteenth-century England, which was passing through even more unsettling changes than we are today and was faced with unprecedented crime waves in its new, crowded, filthy, polluted, slum-encircled, rabble-ridden cities.[26] After experimenting with extraordinary punishments, particularly wholesale hanging and the use of prison barges, England turned to banishment as its primary penal measure. An important difference between eighteenth-century England and modern-day America, however, is that the world offered England locations to which it could send its felons—first America, and then Australia. Between 1787 and 1868, hundreds of thousands of convicts (over 100,000 in the first fleet) were transported to Australia.

America has had to construct its locations of banishment within its borders. This it is doing at a feverish pace. As was done in eighteenth-century England, we have tried using barges in New York City. Although we lack an Australia where we can set up prison colonies, we are increasingly building huge megaprison settlements in isolated rural locations where land is cheap and recession-starved communities are anxious for the economic benefits that a major prison will bring.

WHAT HAS BEEN ACCOMPLISHED
BY THE IMPRISONMENT BINGE?

Americans want several things accomplished by their support of our expensive imprisonment practices. Above all, they want to feel safer in their homes, in their neighborhoods, on the street, and in any public place. For this reason, they want menacing "street criminals" removed and placed in prison. They are also angry at criminals, particularly the types highlighted in the media and by politicians. Moreover, they want apprehended criminals punished harshly so that other potential or active criminals will think twice before committing a crime in the future. Finally, they want prisoners in prison to be given treatment and services that will result in their rehabilitation. For example, a 1996 national survey by Sam Houston University found that rehabilitation was the most important goal of prison. A similar finding was identified by the Public Agenda Foundation.[27]

Given the public perception of the crime problem, these are reasonable goals. But is the public view correct? Are persons sent to prison being given appropriate punishment for their crimes? Are potential criminals deterred by imprisonment? Are prisoners having their chances of returning to crime reduced by any programs or activities that occur in our new prisons? The evidence suggests otherwise. Although crime rates have begun to decline, these decreases cannot be directly linked to the imprisonment binge. In Chapter 10, we will address this question in much greater detail. For now, suffice it to say that most Americans agree that our crime problem has not been solved or even improved by the rise in imprisonment. If incarceration ever had a public safety benefit, it has apparently run its course.

THE COSTS OF THE IMPRISONMENT BINGE

As the size of the correctional complex has skyrocketed, so too has its costs. Annual spending on corrections rose from $9.1 billion in 1982 to nearly $40 billion in 1995, far outstripping any other segment of the criminal justice system (Figure 1-4). As of 1995, we were spending approximately $112 billion each year to operate the nation's entire criminal justice system. There are 2 million persons directly employed by criminal justice agencies, and this number does not include persons who perform services but are not directly working for these agencies. Over 650,000 people are employed by correctional agencies. Nationally, spending on corrections has become the fastest-growing item in state budgets. In 1995, state governments projected an 8 percent increase in correctional spending, while Medicaid was growing at 4.9 percent, higher education at 4.3 percent, and Aid to Families with Dependent Children at 2.1 percent. In California and New York, the booming prison population has resulted in these two states spending more on prisons than on their university systems.[28]

Significantly, the costs of crimes to victims are far below the costs of criminal justice. In 1992, the total costs of crimes to victims, as reported in the U.S. Department of Justice's National Crime Victim Survey (NCVS), were $17.6 billion, or about $500 per crime; the majority of crimes had value losses below $100.[29] These costs include economic losses from property theft or damage, cash losses, medical expenses, loss of pay caused by victimization, and other related costs. This figure, however, does not include the reimbursement of such losses by insurance companies or recovery by criminal justice agencies of stolen property. That recovery rate was estimated at 35 percent in 1986, which reduces the direct losses to $11.4 billion.

Given the enormous costs of aggressive imprisonment and its doubtful effectiveness on crime, one must question the wisdom of our current sentencing policies. More important, why is this draconian experiment failing so miserably? The answer lies in a better understanding of those being punished.

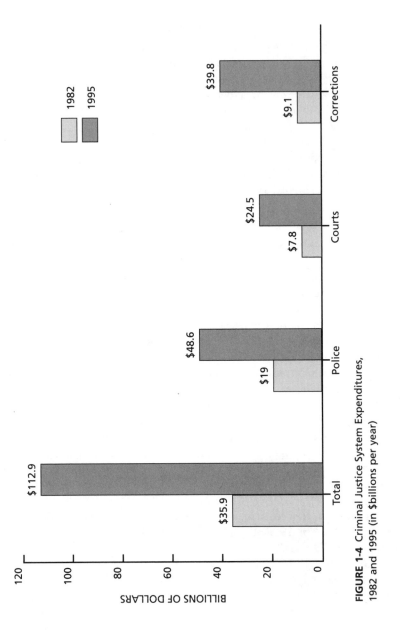

FIGURE 1-4 Criminal Justice System Expenditures, 1982 and 1995 (in $billions per year)

We will examine these people in the remaining chapters of this book. We will closely observe who is going to prison today and what happens to them in prison and immediately after their release. Then we will look at the other issues—the question of deterrence as well as the other costs, financial and social, of our imprisonment binge.

NOTES

1. U.S. Department of Justice, Bureau of Justice Statistics, *Prisoners in 1998* (Washington, DC: U.S. Government Printing Office, August 1999).

2. U.S. Department of Commerce, Bureau of the Census, *Statistical Abstract of the United States 1998* (Washington, DC: U.S. Government Printing Office, October 1998).

3. U.S. Department of Justice, Bureau of Justice Statistics, *Prisoners in 1998.*

4. Criminal Justice Institute, *The Corrections Yearbook 1998* (Middletown, CT: Criminal Justice Institute, 1999).

5. U.S. Department of Justice, Bureau of Justice Statistics, *Jails and Jail Inmates 1993–1994* (Washington, DC: U.S. Government Printing Office, 1994).

6. Marc Mauer and Tracy Huling, *Young Black Americans and the Criminal Justice System: Five Years Later* (Washington, DC: The Sentencing Project, October 1995).

7. William J. Chambliss, *Power, Politics, and Crime* (Boulder, CO: Westview Press, 1999).

8. Between 1972 and 1992, the monthly Gallup Poll showed that about half of the American public believed that crime was increasing, and only 20 percent believed it was declining; see George Gallup, Jr., *The Gallup Poll Monthly,* report no. 318 (Princeton, NJ: Gallup Poll, March 1992). In a 1987 study in Ohio, 86 percent of the respondents answered "true" to the statement "The crime rate has been going up steadily for the past 10 years." See Jeffrey J. Knowles, *Ohio Citizen Attitudes Concerning Crime and Criminal Justice* (Columbus, OH: Governor's Office of Criminal Justice Services, 1987). It is also noteworthy that the public is far more accepting of the notion of alternatives to prison and jail sanctions as they learn more details about the crime, the offender, and the relative costs of alternative sanctions. See John Doble and Josh Klein, *Punishing Criminals: The Public's View: An Alabama Survey* (New York: Edna McConnell Clark Foundation, 1989).

9. George Gallup, Jr., *Gallup Social and Economic Indicators* (Princeton, NJ: Gallup Poll, February 17, 1999).

10. John Irwin and James Austin, *It's About Time* (San Francisco: National Council on Crime and Delinquency, 1987).

11. Marsha Rosenbaum, *Just Say What?* (San Francisco: National Council on Crime and Delinquency, 1989), p. 1.

12. U.S. Department of Justice, Bureau of Justice Statistics, *Race of Prisoners Admitted to State and Federal Institutions, 1926–86; Sourcebook of Criminal Justice Statistics, 1989* (Washington, DC: U.S. Government Printing Office, 1991); and *National Corrections Reporting Program, 1996* (Washington, DC: U.S. Government Printing Office, February 1999).

13. William P. Barr, "Expanding Capacity for Serious Offenders," Attorney General's Summit on Corrections, Ritz Carlton Hotel, McLean, VA, April 27,1992.

14. John Irwin, *Prisons in Turmoil* (Boston: Little, Brown, 1980), p. 2.

15. The issue of whether rehabilitation is effective is controversial and will be taken up in Chapters 2 and 6.

16. In the late 1960s, a series of studies and reviews began to indicate that most of the "treatment" programs practiced in the 1950s and 1960s had no impact on recidivism. This was particularly true of the programs based on personality disorder theories. Even though a small number of programs, particularly those that pursued a learning or cognitive approach, seemed to show some reduction in recidivism, a general consensus formed at this time said that "nothing

worked." See particularly Robert Martinson, "What Works? Questions and Answers About Prison Reform," *Public Interest* 35 (April 1974): 22–54; and Douglas Lipton, Robert Martinson, and Judith Wilks, *The Effectiveness of Correctional Treatment: A Survey of Treatment Evaluation Studies* (New York: Praeger, 1975). Recently James Austin commented on the claim that some programs work, observing that well-designed and -administered treatment programs are the exception, not the rule.

17. These criticisms of rehabilitation on the part of social scientists and "liberal" prison reformers were first stated in the American Friends Service Committee, *The Struggle for Justice* (New York: Hill & Wang, 1971), which was followed by a series of books criticizing rehabilitation.

18. David Rothman, *The Discovery of the Asylum* (Boston: Little, Brown, 1971).

19. In his study of the county jail, *The Jail* (Berkeley: University of California Press, 1985), John Irwin discovered that it was intended as a device to help manage society's rabble—disorganized and disreputable people.

20. U.S. Department of Commerce, Bureau of the Census, *Statistical Abstract of the United States, 1998* (Washington, DC: U.S. Government Printing Office, September–October, 1998).

21. Kevin Phillips, *The Politics of Rich and Poor* (New York: Random House, 1991).

22. Ibid.

23. Ibid., p. 208.

24. In 1981, a Gallup Poll discovered that 70 percent of Americans had no confidence in the criminal court's ability to sentence and convict criminals.

More recently, a study in Alabama revealed the same lack of confidence in the courts: 69 percent agreed that Alabama needs more prisons (Doble and Klein, *Punishing Criminals*).

25. Edward Luttwak, "The Middle-Class Backlash," *Harper's* 292 (January 1996): pp. 15–16.

26. England was also experiencing its own drug problem, that of "killer gin." See Robert Hughes, *The Fatal Shore* (New York: Random House, 1988), Chapter 2, for an excellent discussion of threats from crime, the urban mobs," or the "dangerous classes" in England, which led to an expansion of transportation as a remedy.

27. A study by John Doble of the Public Agenda Foundation found that besides wanting criminals punished and incapacitated, Americans believe that criminals are produced by remedial circumstances and want prisons to rehabilitate prisoners into peaceful, productive citizens. See *Crime and Punishment: The Public's View* (New York: Edna McConnell Clark Foundation, 1987). Also see Survey Research Program, College of Criminal Justice, Sam Houston State University, 1996.

28. Justice Policy Institute, *Class Dismissed: Higher Education vs. Corrections During the Wilson Years* (September 1998); and *New York State of Mind? Higher Education vs. Prison Funding in the Empire State, 1988–1998* (Washington, DC: Justice Policy Institute, December 1998).

29. U.S. Department of Justice, Bureau of Justice Statistics, *Criminal Victimization in the United States, 1992* (Washington, DC: U.S. Government Printing Office, March 1994).

2

■

Who Goes to Prison?

PUBLIC MISPERCEPTIONS
ABOUT WHO GOES TO PRISON

The public reacts to crime with fear and intensity because they have been led to believe by the media and public officials that thousands of vicious, intractable street criminals menace innocent citizens. Actually, they have two slightly different images of the new street criminal. The "softer" version is that of a person who persists in committing property crimes even after repeated opportunities to live an honest life and after being arrested many times and serving numerous jail and prison sentences. The "harder" version is that of a violent criminal, equally intractable, who goes about his or her predatory crimes with no regard for other humans. When he snatches purses from old ladies, he bashes them in the head because he enjoys hurting people. When she robs a mom-and-pop grocery store, she executes her victims with a sneer on her face. Most Americans still believe that millions of these two slightly different types of street criminals stalk our streets; raid our homes; rape, assault, and murder innocent citizens; and generally menace and vilify our society.

For years, criminologists debunked the "evil person" theory of crime and instead attributed the crime problem to social and economic conditions. But recently, many researchers, perhaps swayed by the general conservative shift or lured by government incentives in the form of grants, jobs, and recognition, have resurrected old theories of the "criminal type" (now most often labeled the "career criminal") and have searched for methods to identify such career criminals.

This trend started in 1970, when Marvin E. Wolfgang, Robert M. Figlio, and Thorsten Sellin examined the arrest records of all youths born in Philadelphia in 1945 and discovered that 6 percent of the youth in that "birth cohort" accounted for more than half of all the arrests or police contacts of the entire cohort. The idea that a few criminals commit most of the crime—along with the hope that there was some way to identify these persons before they embarked on their criminal careers—evolved from this study.[1]

In the early 1980s, Peter Greenwood and his colleagues at the Rand Corporation set out to identify "high-rate" offenders in samples of incarcerated burglars and robbers in Texas, Michigan, and California. Greenwood and Alan Abrahamse asked these prisoners how much crime they had committed in the months before incarceration. Ten percent of their sample stood out from the rest in the number of crimes they reported, and a set of characteristics distinguished this subgroup of high-rate offenders from the other robbers and burglars.[2] Even though Greenwood and his associate at Rand Corporation, Susan Turner, discovered later that persons identified by these same characteristics actually did not continue to commit crimes of the type and at the rate expected of high-rate offenders (a finding that caused Greenwood to recant his earlier claims), the idea of the high-rate offender or career criminal had taken hold. Even today, the concept of the career criminal continues to drive America's imprisonment binge.[3]

In a series of longitudinal studies, Alfred Blumstein, along with various coauthors, examined forty-one different "criminal careers," which they offer as a category independent of that of career criminal.[4] (All persons who are arrested have a criminal career even if they commit one crime, which would constitute their entire criminal career.) Blumstein and his colleagues located subgroups of male offenders who, instead of maturing out of crime like the vast majority of offenders, continued to commit crime at the same rate throughout a relatively extended criminal career, that is, until they were past 35 years old. Blumstein abstained from calling these persons either high-rate offenders (actually, the frequency with which they committed crimes was relatively low) or career criminals. He recognized instead that the idea of career criminal implies that certain individuals have significant differences from other offenders and these differences, whatever they are, propel them toward a career in crime. This is particularly essential in employing the concept of career criminal in criminal justice decisions, because there must be some way to distinguish career criminals early in their careers from the majority of offenders who do not persist in crime.

Blumstein's "persisters," it turned out, were not identified until far along on their criminal careers, and he and his associates could not locate "background" characteristics that separated them from many other male offenders who had less enduring criminal careers. In estimating the effect of Blumstein's articles, however, David Greenberg points out that there is a tendency for "laypersons to oversimplify, misunderstand, or lose sight of distinctions and qualifications criminologists make," and to see in these studies the positive identification of the career criminal. And this misperception definitely occurred, particularly among criminal justice policy makers. Characterizing the search as fruitless, Michael Gottfredson and Travis Hirschi note:

> On March 26, 1982, 14 leading members of the criminology community in the United States met in Washington, D.C. to discuss the future of criminal justice research in this country. The priority area for future research listed first by this panel was "criminal careers." . . . Four years later the criminal career notion so dominates discussion of criminal justice policy and so controls expenditure of federal research funds that it may now be said that criminal justice research in this country is indeed centrally planned.[5]

Fear of crime and these new images of the criminal have encouraged politicians and judges to change sentencing laws and practices, a practice that has multiplied prison populations. But are popular images and the social scientists' ideas about contemporary criminals accurate? We think not, for the simple reason that most of these popular images of crime and criminals are shaped by the media, and media depiction consists mostly of selective attention on sensational crimes, politicians' rhetoric, and studies of career criminals funded by the federal government.

In these studies, social scientists have formed most of their ideas "in armchairs" (or now, more accurately, at computer desks), using evidence that is unreliable and skimpy—police arrest records, prison files, and convicts' penciled-in answers to questionnaires—which they study to discover the elusive traits of the career criminal. Very few of these criminologists have spent any significant time observing or talking to their subjects, the prisoners, something that is absolutely necessary to develop an accurate understanding of offenders' motives and criminal practices.

To discover who is actually going to prison, the extent of their criminal involvement, the seriousness of their crimes, and the "danger" they pose to society, we pursued a broad research methodology. In addition to examining the official records, we conducted lengthy interviews of persons sentenced to prison. This is not to say that we ignored the records and available statistics, but we went beyond the so-called hard data and sought a more accurate and comprehensive understanding of a complex social issue.

NATIONAL TRENDS
ON PRISON ADMISSIONS

There are three basic ways one can be admitted to prison. First, you can be convicted of a felony-level crime and be directly sent to prison. Second, you can be convicted of the same crime but sentenced to a term of probation in lieu of a prison term. Should you fail to complete the probation term for any

Table 2-1 The Number of Persons
Going to State Prison, 1990 and 1997

Year	State Prison Population	Total Prison Admissions	New Commitments	Average Time to Serve	Parole Violators
1990	689,577	460,739	323,069	40 months	137,670
1997	1,100,850	540,748	326,547	42 months	214,201
% Change	59.6%	17.4%	1.1%	5.0%	55.6%

SOURCE: U.S. Department of Justice, Bureau of Justice Statistics, *Special Report. Truth in Sentencing in State Prisons* (January 1999).

of a variety of reasons (for example, you are convicted of another crime, fail to meet the terms of probation supervision, and so on), your probation status can be revoked by the judge, and you can be sentenced to prison. Third, if paroled from prison, you can be readmitted to prison as a parole violator if you fail to complete the conditions of parole supervision.

In 1997, the last year that aggregate national-level data are available, it was reported that an estimated 540,748 persons were admitted to state prisons (see Table 2-1). As shown in the table, most of these admissions were new court commitments, although the total number of these admissions has virtually remained unchanged. Despite the lack of increases in new court commitments, the daily prison population has increased by nearly 60 percent since 1990. This increase in the prison population has occurred for two reasons—namely, the number of parole violations has increased, as has the length of prison terms. The proportion of new admissions that are parole violators has increased from 23 percent to nearly 35 percent. Furthermore, the projected length of stay in prison has increased from 40 months to 42 months.

The estimated time to serve for new prison admissions differs dramatically from the U.S. Department of Justice's reported figure of 25 months served by inmates released from prison in 1996. This is due to several factors. First, the figure does not include the estimated 5 to 6 months one waits in jail before being transferred to the state prison or the amount of time parole violators spend in jail and prison until they are released again. Nor does it include the impact of recently adopted sentencing reforms such as mandatory minimums and the "truth in sentencing" laws that are designed to greatly lengthen prison terms. Nor do the data include the growing number of prisoners who have been sentenced to life. In 1996, approximately 1.2 percent of all prison sentences were life sentences (Bureau of Justice Assistance, May 1999). Because these inmates must die in prison, it will be many years before the effects of these sentences are factored into the release data.

The total amount of time an offender is actually incarcerated is a subject we will address in greater detail in Chapters 6 and 8. But it is clear that the current practice is not to send more people to prison but to reincarcerate them more often and/or keep them incarcerated for longer periods of time.

Table 2-2 Proportion of Convicted Offenders Sentenced
to Prison and Jail for Serious Crimes, 1996

Offense	Arrests	Felony Convictions	Jail or Prison	Prison Only	% of Convictions Incarcerated
Murder	16,161	11,430	10,833	10,505	94.8%
Robbery	106,178	42,831	37,382	31,195	87.3%
Aggravated assault	445,005	69,522	49,852	29,042	71.7%
Burglary	229,745	93,197	66,101	42,252	70.9%
Motor vehicle theft	102,578	17,794	13,242	5,919	74.4%
Drug trafficking	322,393	212,504	154,977	83,913	72.9%
Totals	1,222,060	447,278	332,387	202,826	74.3%

SOURCE: U.S. Department of Justice, Bureau of Justice Statistics, *Felony Sentences in the United States, 1996* (July 1999).

Another misperception of the public is that most persons convicted for serious crimes are infrequently imprisoned. Using national data, we can see that this perception is profoundly inaccurate (Table 2-2). Contrary to popular perceptions, the vast majority of these offenders who are convicted of a felony are incarcerated, with 69 percent sentenced to prison or jail. For those convicted of the most serious crimes, the rates are even higher, with three out of four convictions resulting in prison or jail.[6] Most offenders sentenced to prison were admitted for either nonviolent crimes or no crimes at all. As shown in Table 2-3, the vast majority has been originally sentenced for property, drug, and public order crimes.

But these data provide very little information on such important items as the number of prior prison terms or prior felony convictions. However, a few states have been able to report on these key attributes. Texas completed an exhaustive study of its felony sentencing patterns with special attention to the attributes of offenders sentenced to state prison.[7] That study reported the following sentencing patterns:

- Forty-nine percent of convicted felons were sentenced to prison. Twenty-four percent of the convicted felons sentenced to prison had no prior felony convictions.

- The most frequent crime resulting in a prison sentence was drug possession (22 percent) followed by burglary (20 percent), theft and fraud (20 percent), and drug delivery (15 percent). These four nonviolent crimes constituted 77 percent of all prison admissions.

- Fifty-three percent of all drug offenders (possession and trafficking) sentenced to prison were convicted for possession of one gram or less of the illegal substance.

The Texas data, like those for many states, reflect the growing use of prison for incarcerating drug offenders. As shown in Table 2-3, over 30 percent of all

Table 2-3 Type of Offense for 1996 Prison Admissions
New Court Commitments and Parole Violators

Most Serious Offense	New Court Commitments	Parole Violators
Violent Crimes	29.5%	24.5%
Murder/manslaughter	2.7%	1.4%
Rape	1.9%	1.4%
Other sexual assault	4.1%	2.4%
Robbery	9.1%	10.9%
Assault	8.7%	6.7%
Property Crimes	29.0%	35.1%
Burglary	12.0%	15.7%
Larceny/theft	7.5%	9.7%
Motor vehicle theft	2.1%	3.7%
Drug Crimes	30.2%	31.0%
Possession	8.0%	7.0%
Trafficking	17.2%	16.1%
Public Order	10.6%	8.1%

SOURCE: U.S. Department of Justice, Bureau of Justice Statistics, *Special Report, Truth in Sentencing in State Prisons* (January 1999).

prison sentences in 1996 were for drug crimes, with one-third being for simple possession. In 1960, the proportion of prison admissions for drug crimes was only 5 percent; in 1981, the percentage was only 9 percent (Figure 2-1).[8] It is also no coincidence that as the proportion of prison admissions for drug crimes has increased, so have the proportions of nonwhites being sent to prison. Since 1960, this proportion has increased from 32 percent to 55 percent.

These quantitative studies suggest that a significant number of persons are being sentenced to prison for relatively minor crimes. This is not to say that there are not offenders who are highly dangerous and need to be incarcerated for long periods of time. But what proportion of these half-million prisoners are truly dangerous and require long-term confinement? To answer this question, we undertook a more detailed analysis of who goes to prison.

A CLOSER LOOK
AT WHO GOES TO PRISON

Although the data cited earlier suggest a far less violent population serving lengthy periods of imprisonment, they are unable to paint a complete picture of the criminal lifestyles or the types of crimes committed by the present prison population. To fill in these blanks, we conducted an ethnographic study of 154 males sentenced to prison, randomly selected from the intake populations of three states (Washington, Nevada, and Illinois).[9] Although these cases were

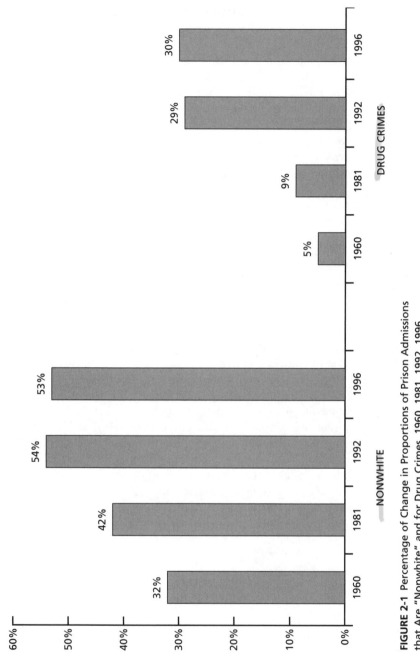

FIGURE 2-1 Percentage of Change in Proportions of Prison Admissions that Are "Nonwhite" and for Drug Crimes, 1960, 1981, 1992, 1996

drawn from studies conducted in the early 1990s, they are reflective of inmates who continue to be incarcerated and remain incarcerated due to the recently enacted sentencing reforms discussed earlier. We emphasize intake population because most studies of prison populations—such as the survey conducted every five years by the Bureau of Justice Statistics—are designed to answer the question "Who is in prison at a particular time?" Surveys of the daily inmate population provide a distorted picture of who is going to prison because those prisoners with longer sentences, usually sentenced for more serious crimes, stack up in the prison population and are overrepresented in one-day surveys.

The states we selected for our study varied in their sentencing structures, population sizes, rates of imprisonment, and lengths of imprisonment at the time of our research (Table 2-4). Illinois uses a determinate sentencing structure in which release occurs after a prisoner serves a significant proportion of the original sentence. Although a parole board exists, it has no authority to grant release. At the time of the study, Illinois had a large prison population (nearly 25,000 inmates) but a moderate rate of incarceration compared to other states (226 per 100,000 in 1989 versus the national average of 274 per 100,000). Although Illinois's determinate sentencing law eliminated discretionary release by the parole board, the vast majority of inmates must serve some period of parole supervision. Washington adopted sentencing guidelines with the specific goal of increasing lengths of stay for inmates convicted of violent crimes. It had a smaller prison population (approximately 7,000) and a low incarceration rate (144 per 100,000). Because Washington eliminated parole as part of its sentencing guidelines reform act, very few inmates were released to parole or violators returned to prison. Nevada had a relatively smaller inmate population but the highest incarceration rate (473 per 100,000). It uses an indeterminate sentencing scheme that allows inmates to be released by a parole board after serving approximately 20 percent of the original sentence.

In selecting inmates to be interviewed for the study, we received lists of inmates admitted to reception centers during the prior two weeks. We then separated the names on these intake lists into the following five categories based on the most serious crime of conviction:

1. Violent crimes (murder, rape, assault, and so forth)

2. Robbery (armed and unarmed)

3. Other theft (burglary, larceny, and so forth)

4. Drug crimes (possession and trafficking)

5. All others

Our sample does not include women or persons readmitted to prison for parole violation who were convicted of no new felony. The exclusion of these two groups means that our sample is biased toward those persons who have committed the most serious crimes. In most cases, a parole violation is triggered by arrests for misdemeanor crimes or violations of supervision, such as failure to appear for office visits with parole agents or failure to attend a prescribed treatment program. Female prisoners tend to be convicted of less serious crimes.

Table 2-4 Key Characteristics of Three State Prison Systems

Inmate Characteristic	Nevada	Illinois	Washington
I. Sentencing structure	Indeterminate	Determinate	Guidelines
II. Inmate population (1989)	5,112	4,712	6,928
III. Annual admissions (1989)	3,052	14,567	4,155
A. New court commitments	2,514	10,732	3,543
B. Parole violators	509	3,693	401
C. Returned escapees	34	102	199
D. Other	0	40	12
IV. Incarceration rate (1989)	473	226	144
V. Releases (1989)			
Total	2,826	10,936	3,043
Parole/conditional	1,472	9,802	966
Unconditional	1,293	841	1,907
Other	61	293	170

SOURCES: Nevada Department of Prisons, Illinois Department of Corrections, and Washington Department of Corrections.

For each state, we then randomly drew 10 persons from each of the five categories, for a total sample of 154.[10] We interviewed these persons in lengthy open interviews, covering their social histories, criminal activities in the period before the current arrest, and the full circumstances of their arrests. The information gathered from the interviews was verified and augmented by the arrest records along with police and probation office reports.

HOW SERIOUS ARE THEIR CRIMES?

An essential part of the public conception of street crime is that growing numbers of persons are engaged in very serious crime. To evaluate the severity of the crimes committed by inmates in our samples, we used an objective measure of seriousness from the public's perspective based on data gathered in 1980 by the Center for Studies in Criminology and Criminal Law at the University of Pennsylvania. In the center's survey of crime seriousness, a national survey asked 52,000 Americans to assign a numerical score to a short description of 204 criminal acts, which reflected the respondents' perceptions of the crimes' seriousness. For example, two of the acts described were "A person, using force, steals property worth $10 from outside a building" and "A person, using force, robs a victim of $1,000. No physical harm occurs." The center reduced these raw scores into "ratio scores," which indicated the relative severity of each crime.

We observed that if the acts involved minor injury, the threat of injury, theft over $1,000, the use of a weapon, use of heroin, or the selling of marijuana, they received a score of more than 5 on the center's scale. We labeled these "moderate" crimes. If they involved theft of over $10,000, serious injury, attempted murder, sales of heroin, or the smuggling of narcotics, they received a score of more than 10. We considered these "serious" crimes. If they involved rape, manslaughter, homicide, a child victim, or kidnapping, they received a score of more than 15. We labeled these "very serious" crimes. Crimes that lacked any of these characteristics received a score of less than 5. We called these "petty" crimes. Two such acts from the survey were: "A person breaks into a department store and steals merchandise worth $10" and "A person smokes marijuana."

We sorted the crimes of our sample into the categories "petty," "moderate," "serious," and "very serious" according to these characteristics. Figure 2-2 summarizes the results of this distribution. In this figure, we have adjusted our stratified samples so that they reflect the offense distribution for the nation as shown in Table 2-3.[11]

As Figure 2-2 reveals, most of the crimes for which persons are sent to prison (52.6 percent) fall into the petty category. This finding is wholly consistent with inmate classification studies that have repeatedly found that most prisoners are committed to prison for nonviolent property or drug crimes, with the result that the majority (50 to 70 percent) are classified as minimum-custody inmates.[12]

The distribution on crime seriousness was somewhat different in the three states, as shown in Figure 2-3. Washington, which has the lowest rate of incarceration of the three states, also had the lowest proportion of petty felonies and the highest proportion of serious crimes. This is to be expected, as Washington recently enacted sentencing guidelines that purposely restrict the use of prison for nonviolent and property crimes.[13] Illinois, which has a medium rate, did not differ very much from the total sample. Nevada, which has the highest rate of the three states and the highest rate in the nation, predictably had the lowest proportion of serious and very serious crimes.

Our research indicates that over half the persons being sent to prison are being sent for petty crimes, which are crimes with no aggravating features—that is, no significant amount of money, no injury, or any other feature that would cause ordinary citizens to view the crime as particularly serious. The following are narrative descriptions of three typical petty crimes from our sample.

> George, a 17-year-old black youth, was arrested for possession of a stolen vehicle. He had been kicked out of school in the ninth grade. Since then, he had worked at a couple of jobs—a small soul food restaurant and a small garage fixing cars. He had not been working for a while. He had been arrested a few times before, once for curfew, another for shoplifting. A couple of months before this arrest, he was arrested for "busting a car window." "A man tried to hit me with his car, and I swung at him and broke his window. I got three months' supervision." On the current arrest he was caught inside a car trying to steal the radio. "They said I busted the window, but it weren't locked. He [the policeman] took the screwdriver I was using and put it in the lock and said I was stealing the car." He was sentenced to three years in prison.

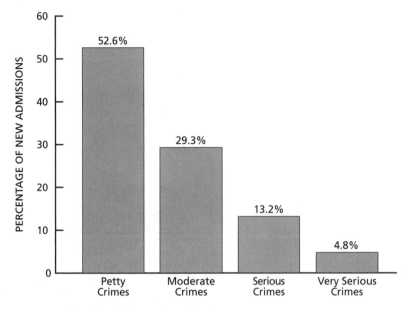

FIGURE 2-2 Severity of Crimes Committed by Persons Admitted to Prison (National Estimate)

Jimmy, a 26-year-old black man, dropped out of high school in the tenth grade. He worked at several unskilled jobs as a teenager but started getting into trouble when he was 17. After several arrests, he was sent to prison for aggravated assault against a relative. He served three years and then another year and a half for violation of parole. He had been out for two months when he was arrested this time. He was living with his grandmother, "trying to stay out of trouble." He was not able to find a job and was living on general assistance. He was caught in an abandoned school where he and some other young men were looking for junk metal that they intended to sell for "some loose change." The school had been abandoned for six years, and local people had been stealing from it repeatedly. He received seven years for burglary.

Edmond was a 50-year-old white carpenter who worked in Florida in the winter and Seattle in the summer. He had been arrested once 22 years before for receiving stolen property. He was passing through Las Vegas on his way to Seattle and said he found a billfold with $100 on a bar where he was drinking and gambling. The owner, who suspected him of taking it, turned him in. He was charged with grand larceny and received three years.

Twenty-nine percent of our sample fell into the moderate category, but many of these were aggravated because the charges involved possession or sales of heroin or cocaine. Acts in the 1980 national public opinion survey with heroin involved had a score of seven or more. We assumed that cocaine, which

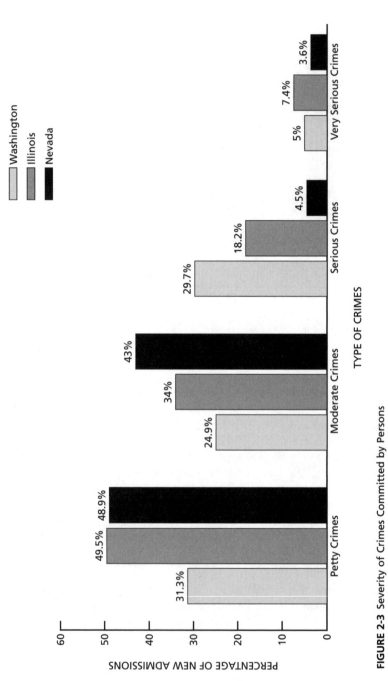

FIGURE 2-3 Severity of Crimes Committed by Persons Admitted to Prison in Washington, Illinois, and Nevada

was not mentioned in the survey, would be given approximately the same value today. However, most of our sample's heroin or cocaine crimes involved only very small amounts of the drugs, and the persons, if they were dealers, were small-fry, as the following cases indicate.

Luis, a 29-year-old Puerto Rican raised in Chicago, had never been arrested before. He had been a member of Latin gangs but in recent years had less and less contact with them. He used cocaine occasionally and hung around with a lot of guys who dealt cocaine. He was riding with a friend on a motorcycle, and the police pulled them over because they were not wearing helmets. The police found a packet of cocaine on his friend and several on the ground around them. He and his friend were charged with possession of cocaine. Luis was sentenced to three years.

Felix had been in trouble on the West Side of Chicago since he was 10 years old. He had dropped out of school in the eighth grade and was arrested several times before he was 18. He had served three prison terms since then. At 26, he was living at home with his mother, "taking little side jobs," and hustling a little. He said he wanted "an average job and to go home after it and enjoy life." On the present arrest, he was riding with his girlfriend, and the police stopped them. The police said they had a report that a man and a woman were selling drugs out of a car in that neighborhood. They found one bag of cocaine (0.5 grams) on his girl-friend's side of the car and arrested him. He was sentenced to two years.

Robberies were considered at least moderate crimes because the public, officials, and criminologists invariably view robbery as a serious crime and a violent crime (government agencies that compile statistics on crimes always place robbery in their "violent" category). In actuality, however, many robberies differ from the public's perception of them. The following accounts, for example, do not seem to fit the image, and many citizens, perhaps a majority, would not consider them serious or violent crimes.

Darryl was a 21-year-old black man raised on the South Side of Chicago in housing projects. He had dropped out of school in the tenth grade and had been working on and off at minimum-wage jobs. He had been arrested three times for minor crimes (battery, disorderly conduct, and marijuana) and had no convictions. In this case, he had gone to a neigh-borhood drug dealer to borrow some money on his girlfriend's watch because his "brother was coming to town and I wanted to have some money to do things with him." The dealer offered him $60 but only gave him $20, telling him that he would give him $40 later. Darryl did not see the dealer for two weeks, and when he finally encountered him and asked him for the money, the dealer said he did not have any and offered Darryl drugs. When he was showing him the drugs, Darryl saw the watch and grabbed for it. They fought and the drug dealer was "whip-ping" him. Darryl's brother jumped in and helped him. Then the dealer gave Darryl the watch. Three days later, the police came to his apartment and arrested him for robbery and assault. He was bailed out and later went to a jury trial. The jury found him not guilty on aggravated assault and was hung on the robbery. However, Darryl had run from the court while they were deliberating. He later turned himself in, bail was set at $150,000, and the public defender talked him into pleading guilty to robbery. He was sentenced to prison for three years.

Richard graduated from high school in Seattle and went into the armed services. After being discharged, he went to cosmetology school and worked for 13 years as a cosmetologist. Three years ago he began learning a new trade and worked part time in a print shop. He had started using marijuana and heroin in high school. When he was working as a cosmetologist, he and his wife "got into coke, heavy." He had several arrests for driving while under the influence and one for child molesting. "That was a mistake. I was drunk and high and I just got carried away with this young girl." After this last arrest, he and his wife decided to change their lives and quit all drugs. "I became responsible and became manager of Super Cuts. But after a while, I got bored and started hanging around with my old friends. They were freebasing and pretty soon I was back into drugs heavy. I left my wife and moved in with a friend. I couldn't believe that I had let my life get so fucked up again, so I went into a drug program, but I didn't get along with the director. After three weeks I tried coke again. And I was right back into the same lifestyle. I needed money, so I decided to rob some stores. I robbed the same store three times, a convenience store like 7-Eleven. I got about $50 each time. I tucked a BB gun in my belt and went in, showed the clerk the gun in my belt, and asked for the money. In court the clerk said I was polite." He was sentenced to five years.

There were many serious and some very serious crimes in our samples. Two were very serious armed robberies (they involved larger amounts of money and persons were threatened during the robberies). There were seven first-degree homicides (2 percent of our adjusted samples), and three were gang-related. The following is one:

Parnell, a 20-year-old member of the Disciples, had dropped out of school and hung around with his neighborhood branch of the gang since he was 15. He had never held a job and was arrested fourteen or fifteen times for activities related to "gang banging," mostly possession of weapons.[14] He was arrested once for robbery when he was 17. "The guy I was walking with strong-armed some guy. But I wasn't into robbing, just gang banging." The night of the murder, he and some of his gang were at a skating rink, which was the location of many altercations between rival gangs. His group saw a guy from another gang who they thought had robbed one of their buddies. They chased him, and one of them beat him with a baseball bat. He died a week later. Parnell was the only one convicted because "I was the only one a witness identified." He received twenty-five years.

Two of the homicides occurred during drug robberies. This is one of them:

> Anthony, a 24-year-old black man, was sent to prison when he was 17 for aggravated battery. "Some guy broke out the windows of a neighbor of mine. I went to court, and after the court a fight broke out and they arrested all of us." After serving eighteen months, he completed two years in community college and had been working for five years as a roofer. He says he was living a clean life in the suburbs of Chicago—working, playing basketball, and taking care of his common-law wife and her son. "They said I went to this house, kicked in the door and demanded drugs and money, and then shot the man. The woman in the house identified me. The police had received an anonymous phone call and they arrested me. They said I searched the house, but they didn't find any fingerprints. The description she gave the police didn't fit me."

In two of the homicide cases, persons were convicted of killing their girl-friends. In one, a 33-year-old Cuban man who had never been in trouble before and who had worked steadily was convicted of killing his girlfriend:

> It was an accident. I was fighting with my girlfriend. She bothered me a lot. I had a son with her, and she was wanting me to leave my wife. We had been drinking and we got into a fight. I hit her with my fist and killed her.

Most of the serious crimes (53 percent) were sex crimes. These ranged from child molesting to rape, and most were acts committed against family members or close associates. These are serious crimes, but it should be noted again that most of them depart from the popular images of crime and criminals in which a menacing stranger is the perpetrator. The other serious crimes were robberies (17 percent), attempted murders (8 percent), manslaughters (12 percent), and drug charges (10 percent). Several of the robberies and drug crimes do approach the popular image: that is, they involved larger amounts of money, threats or injuries to victims, or larger amounts of cocaine or heroin.

PATTERNS OF CRIME

As we suggested earlier, the public and many officials believe that most street criminals are "career criminals" or "high-rate offenders" who, if free, will commit many felonies. Some public officials and criminologists have recommended that these high-rate offenders be "incapacitated" through long prison terms.

Today, the concept of the career is entrenched in criminal justice—a dramatic rethinking of policy and practice. Now research is examining ways to identify those offenders more accurately, moving toward the recommendation of one recent study that concluded that public safety would clearly benefit from incarcerating a larger proportion of high-risk probationers and prisoners, and for longer periods of time. Though no specific program to do this has been introduced in the United States, legislators, judges, and prosecutors have

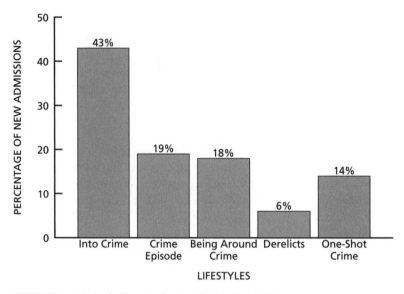

FIGURE 2-4 Criminal Lifestyles for Newly Admitted Prisoners

passed laws to extend sentences, have recommended longer sentences, or have granted longer sentences because they hold this belief in the prevalence of high-rate offenders. The habitual offender and three strikes laws are examples of this.[15] (See Chapter 9 for an assessment of these laws and their impact on crime and incarceration rates.)

To test the validity of the "career criminal" viewpoint, we focused on patterns of offending among our surveyed convicts. We discovered five distinct patterns—"into crime," "crime episode," "one-shot crime," "being around crime," and "dereliction"—that are defined and summarized here. Figure 2-4 indicates the proportion of our sample that corresponds to each crime pattern.

Into Crime

Persons into crime (43 percent) call themselves thieves, "hustlers," "dope fiends," or "gang bangers," which they understand as identities within particular criminal systems. They also follow the patterns of crime consistent with these identities and criminal systems—that is, they attempt to steal large amounts of money through burglaries and robberies; they "hustle" on the streets, making money any way they can; they maintain drug habits by selling drugs and stealing; or they hang out with their fellow "homeboys," wear their gang's colors, steal, and fight with other gangs. Parnell, described earlier, was a gang banger into crime. Bertram, a thief, and Donald, a dope fiend, were into crime:

> Bertram says he "started a life of crime" when he was in high school. When he was 17, every weekday, he and older friends walked from their neighborhood on the South Side of Chicago to Hyde Park, a middle-class racially mixed neighborhood, and burglarized some houses. They

took TVs, jewelry, and any other thing they could sell. "It was like a job." They were caught in one house and arrested. Bertram was sentenced to three years in prison. When he got out of prison, his brother and sisters were living alone, and his younger brother was selling cocaine. Bertram stopped him, but he had to supply them with money. So he started burglarizing houses and trucks on the West Side at night. Then he and his "rappies" pulled sixteen armed robberies of gas stations and convenience stores. In one week, he says, they made $7,000 apiece. After the last robbery, they were pulled over by the police, who found guns in their car. He received a ten-year sentence.

Donald started using heroin and cocaine when he was 19. He was convicted of burglary when he was 25 and served six months in the county jail. He was convicted of possession of drugs when he was 29 and received a year in the state prison. As soon as he got out, he was arrested again for burglary and served four years. He says he did not want to go back to drugs, but he met a friend right after getting out and got high with him. He was quickly addicted and stealing again. He says he was pulling one or two burglaries a day. He could not sell drugs because the police knew him too well. In his last arrest, he was caught trying to pry open a door of a construction business and was convicted of two attempted burglaries. At 33, he says he wants to stop using drugs, but he does not know how. He says he is getting tired.

Since they were committing crime regularly, it is accurate to view the 43 percent of our sample who were into crime as high-rate offenders. Of these high-rate offenders, more than half (57 percent) had served a prior prison sentence, and 32 percent a juvenile sentence. However, most of the active offenders (59 percent) were convicted of petty crimes. All of our data strongly suggest that, rather than being vicious predators, most were disorganized, unskilled, undisciplined petty criminals who very seldom engaged in violence or made any significant amount of money from their criminal acts.

Crime Episode

These inmates (19 percent) had engaged in a crime episode or spree. Many had committed crimes in some earlier period; some had even been into crime. Unlike the into-crime group, these offenders had less severe histories of prior incarcerations, either as adults (33 percent had a prior prison term) or as juveniles (26 percent had a prior record). But for an extended period, perhaps after a jail or prison sentence, they had lived a relatively conventional life.

Joe joined a Latin gang when he was 13. By his 18th year he had been arrested three times in activities with his "homeboys" (the Latin Kings). For the last, a residential burglary, he served a county jail sentence and was placed on probation for two years. After that, he pulled back from gang banging but was still hanging around with some of his old friends. "We hung around the corner drinking, but we didn't think of ourselves as a gang. We thought of ourselves as an organization. We tried to protect all the old people, to stop the blacks from robbing them." He was working steadily at the Golden Grain packing house making $7 an hour. "I was going to work there the rest of my life." He had a car and a girlfriend, and they were buying furniture—a bedroom set. The crime he was convicted of occurred early on a Sunday morning. He had been partying at a house with his friend—"smoking, drinking, and snorting." Someone borrowed his car and did not bring it back to the house. He was angry about this. A friend gave him a ride home, and on the way, he said, "Someone said, 'Let's go rob someone.' I guess I said, 'Let's go, I'll do it.' I don't remember much about it. A white guy was stabbed in the stomach and neck. For all I know, the other guy in the car did it. It was stupid. I blacked out from the time I got home until the police came." He received six years for attempted murder.

Richard was one of the few black students in his high school in Montana and the star football player. He was also selling drugs. "I scored five touchdowns on Friday and was busted on Monday. I was hanging around white kids trying to prove myself. They wouldn't let me play football after that." His father put him out of the house, so he left for Oklahoma with some friends. He returned to Montana but could not find a job. He began hanging around some of the black guys who were "going to discos and being cool." He was arrested for a house burglary and received two years' probation. He went to California with a friend who was in the air force. He joined the army, got married, and had two kids. He had broken up with his wife by the time he was discharged from the army. He stayed in Fort Lewis, Washington, and worked part time in construction, living across the street from a corner where drugs were being sold. "One night I walked over there, and a guy asked me if I wanted to make some money. So I started selling drugs. I sold to the police. They wanted me to set up my supplier, so I went back to the corner, but the word had got out, so the other dealers told me to get out of town." He went back to California and went back to his wife. They both used cocaine heavily. He turned himself into a drug program, but she continued to use cocaine. He went back to the house and found her in bed with another man. He kicked the man out and took his son. He was charged with kidnapping his child and served two years in a California prison. He was transferred to Washington upon release and charged with unlawful delivery of drugs for the earlier arrest. He received fifteen months.

Being Around Crime

About one-fifth (18 percent) of our sample were "corner boys," men who were raised and lived in lower-class neighborhoods in which street crime is a prominent feature. Many in these neighborhoods, particularly young males, regularly commit crimes. Most other young males avoid regular participation in crime but accept it as a normal feature of life around them. Many of the males, particularly younger ones, though they avoid regular involvement in crime and do not think of themselves as criminals, are at risk of being arrested because they are on the streets for many hours and police regularly patrol these neighborhoods looking for street criminals. When confronted by police, these corner boys also frequently exhibit macho behavior that provokes hostile reactions from the police. Finally, corner boys are often present at crimes being committed by friends or relatives, and, under special circumstances—such as when they are in the company of more criminally oriented acquaintances, saving face in front of peers, intoxicated, or trying to take advantage of an opportunity for a financial gain—they are drawn into the commission of a crime.

Once arrested, their corner boy or lower-class identity makes it very likely that police, district attorneys, and judges will treat these young men as if they were more criminally involved than they actually were. Sixty-eight percent of our corner boys were convicted of petty crimes. Only a small minority had adult prior terms (8 percent) and/or juvenile terms (15 percent). The cases of Darryl and Robert described in the section on crime seriousness are examples of this pattern. The following are two more:

> Maurice is an 18-year-old black youth raised on the South Side of Chicago. He was in the Disciples from ages 12 to 16, but he dropped out. "My grandmother told me to get out of the gang. They hate it when you pull out, so they were right at my door waiting for me." He dropped out of high school in the tenth grade. He had gotten into a little trouble before— some fights and the theft of a moped, for which he received two years' probation. "A guy let me ride it. I didn't know he had stole it." At the time of this arrest, he was staying off the streets. "I had a girlfriend with two kids. She lived with her father. I would go over to her house and stay all day. We'd sit around and watch TV, clean the house, help with the kids." On the day of this arrest, he was going to his grandmother's to get something and a policeman who worked in that area stopped him to question him. "There's a guy around there that looks like me. He would get into a few things. The police asked what was I doing over there. I wrestled with him and his gun fell out of his holster. I kicked it and ran. They got me later. They found out I didn't do nothing so they charged me with taking his gun." He received five years for disarming a police officer.

> Eddie is a 32-year-old black man who was raised in Little Rock, Arkansas. His mother supported the family of six kids. She worked as a cook in a motel, and they lived in a housing project. He quit school in the ninth grade and went to work as a busboy in the motel. He worked there for seven years, ending up as a cook. He got married in Little Rock to a woman with a daughter. They moved to Seattle, where he worked at several jobs, the last one as a supervisor of a janitorial crew in a federal building. Years before, the police had arrested him in an apartment he managed. The charge was dismissed. This was his only prior arrest. In Seattle he spent a lot of time playing basketball. He was on a team sponsored by the Mormons. He was the top player and scored 36 points in one game. He

started hanging around one of the other players who was using a lot of cocaine. Eddie says he "sort of took this guy under his wing." He started using cocaine with him. His wife objected to this, so Eddie stopped. He says he was trying to get his friend to stop also. One night he took his friend to his friend's apartment to collect some money from his roommate. Eddie stayed in the car. The friend and the roommate got into a fight over the money, and the friend ended up stabbing the roommate. The roommate accused both of them of robbing him, and Eddie was arrested for robbery. He was released on his own recognizance, but after a week the supervisor said she did not want to supervise him. He was held in the county jail for five months, and finally he pleaded guilty. The public defender told him since he had admitted being there he would not be able to win a trial. "I decided I was going ahead and get it over with and get on with my life." He received five years for robbery.

Dereliction

These men (6 percent) had completely lost the capacity to live in organized society. Some had teetered on the edge of physical survival. All had been incarcerated a lot in early life, and most used drugs and alcohol, usually from their early teens. Though they tried to avoid committing serious crimes (to avoid returning to prison), they occasionally robbed, burgled, or committed some other felony (for example, arson, assault, sexual deviations) and were arrested. Though their crimes were invariably very petty, their repulsive disreputability and former records resulted in imprisonment. This small group had the highest prior prison record (91 percent), with 71 percent incarcerated as juveniles.[16] The following are two examples of their crimes and lifestyles:

> Leonard is a 32-year-old black who grew up on the South Side of Chicago. His father died when he was small, and his mother raised seven children on welfare. He dropped out of school in the ninth grade and never had a steady job. He was a Disciple until his early 20s. He started to drink heavily when he was a teenager. He was first arrested when he was 15 and again when he was 17. Both times he was sent to youth institutions. He was arrested for robbery and auto theft as an adult and served two prison terms. He lived with his mother and says all he did was drink. Three years ago it was discovered that he had cirrhosis of the liver. Two years before this imprisonment, he and a friend robbed another black man on the street. This man lived in the neighborhood and knew them. His friend had a stick, and they were charged with robbery. Leonard received probation, but he quit reporting, and they arrested him and sentenced him to five years.

> Charles and his three sisters were raised by his nurse mother on the South Side of Chicago. He "got to drinking and smoking reefer at about 10." He was hanging around with the "bad kids" and not going to school. He started getting into trouble with the police, and then "they started harassing me." He was in a small local gang, and they got into a lot of fights.

Later he joined the Gangster Disciples, a splinter group of the Disciples. He has never held a steady job. He was arrested when he was 16 for not going to school and was sent to a boys' school. He ran away and was sent to another youth institution. When he was 17, he was arrested for robbery and was sent to Stateville (Illinois State Prison) for six months. When he was 22, he was convicted of another robbery and sent back to prison for five years. For the last five years, he has been a derelict. He stays high or drunk most of the time. "I been stealing petty things, anything you can take from a store. I quit robbery. Made a believer out of me. I been 'carrying a stick' [had no residence and slept anywhere he could]." Some days before this arrest, he went to the house of a girlfriend and a man came to the door. "I asked him for my girlfriend, and he said, 'Fuck you, punk.' I went to his car and hit it with a water-meter cover I picked up off the street. He came after me with a hatchet and hit me in the head. I went to the hospital, and when I got out, I went over and smashed his car. Then a week later, I started a fire in a old building next to his house. My old girlfriend told them who did it. I was drunk at the time." He received four years for attempted arson.

One-Shot Crime

A significant number of our sample (14 percent) had never been involved in serious crime before the current arrest. Something about the crime—its seriousness or an associated mandatory sentence—resulted in their receiving a prison sentence. The following are two of these crimes.

Jose was born in Puerto Rico, and his father sent for him to come to Massachusetts when Jose was 10. He quit high school when he was a junior. He joined the army when he was 20 "to get a GED" and was discharged three years later. He worked as a baker for the next ten years for Nabisco. He quit this job to help a friend run a grocery store. Then he worked for five years with Sanco, until the firm moved to Philadelphia in 1983, four years before. He had not found a steady job since. He had been married for twenty years and had four daughters. At 46 he had no steady job and was drinking a lot. He had a friend who dealt in cocaine. A narcotics undercover officer who had been trying to set up his friend repeatedly asked Jose to buy some cocaine for him. He finally did and was arrested. He was out on bail for two and a half years before sentencing, but the sentence was mandatory.

Donald was raised on a farm in Iowa. Two years after graduating from high school, he went into business for himself, leasing livestock. At 30, he changed businesses and had been selling mobile home running gear ever since. He was married for ten years but separated five years before. He had been arrested for failure to pay child support, but nothing else. He was drinking heavily in the last year of his marriage but had about quit drinking. All he was doing was "work[ing] my ass off in my business. I have been working seven days a week. Most of the time I am on the road with two helpers, delivering mobile home running gear." Three years ago, he and two employees were making a delivery with a large truck and trailer. After dinner, they picked up a six-pack, and a little later they stopped on the side of the road in a rural area of Illinois to urinate. He and one of the employees got back into the cab of the truck. He says he thought the other employee, a 16-year-old (who had told Donald he was 18) was also in the cab, but he was not, and he was run over by the truck when Donald pulled out onto the highway. "He might have been trying to get on the trailer and fell under the wheels." They accused him of being drunk, although he says he only had a couple of beers. "They never ran a test on me, and the officer who arrested me testified that I didn't have alcohol on my breath." Donald was convicted of reckless homicide and sent to prison for a year.

HABITUAL OFFENDERS

Many persons being sentenced to long prison terms depart from the public image of the vicious or serious criminal. This should be taken very seriously because their numbers are increasing. Though most offenders are sent to prison for less than serious felonies and for short sentences (for instance, twenty-four months), a growing number receive very long sentences, many life. This is mainly because virtually all states and the federal government have passed laws that mandate that certain offenders be sentenced to prison under "habitual offender," "mandatory," or "three strikes" sentence laws, which require inmates to spend a minimum of ten years or longer, or to be sentenced to life without the possibility of parole (that is, they must die in prison).

According to the Criminal Justice Institute, as of January 1998, there were 23,758 inmates serving "natural" life sentences, 72,352 serving life with the possibility of parole, and 177,197 serving sentences of twenty years or longer.[17] In other words, nearly 275,000 of the 1.3 million state and federal prisoners in 1998 were serving extremely long sentences. An unknown but probably high percentage of these were serving time under these restrictive laws. One would expect that these laws are reserved for only the most vicious and dangerous offenders, but recent studies suggest otherwise.

The Correctional Association of New York Study

One study completed by the Correctional Association of New York reported on the types of inmates who were serving mandatory prison sentences for drug offenses, repeat felony convictions, and violent crimes.[18] In the 1970s, the New York Legislature passed a number of laws that mandated a prison term for persons convicted of certain drug crimes, violent offenses (robbery, assault, murder, manslaughter, rape), or persons who had prior felony convictions. At the time of this study, nearly two-thirds of all prisoners were sentenced under one of these three laws (8 percent drug, 14.5 percent repeat felony, and 41.5 percent violent offender laws).

The research consisted of selecting a small (21) but representative sample of inmates who were sentenced via these mandatory sentencing laws and developing detailed case histories of the crimes they had committed and also of their life circumstances. In the report, the researchers concluded that many of these inmates, though "not Boy Scouts," did not deserve the type of sentences they had received. What follows are two examples.

Bernice Lane—Mandatory Drug Sentence—15 Years to Life—Criminal Sale of Controlled Substance in the First Degree

In November 1977, Bernice Lane was found guilty after trial of criminal sale of a controlled substance in the first degree and conspiracy in the first degree. According to the district attorney's office, Lane, a hotel manager who lived with her mother, had sold a total of 2.9 ounces of heroin to undercover officers in Manhattan in two separate transactions in 1976.

It was Lane's first conviction but not her first arrest. In 1966, drug possession charges were filed against her but were later dropped when authorities arranged a guilty plea with her codefendant, a known drug dealer. Eight years later, conspiracy charges were filed but also dropped after authorities failed to produce an informant who, they said, could have linked Lane to a major drug ring.

The judge at Lane's trial, former Supreme (now Appellate) Court Judge Ernst H. Rosenberger said that had the law not prevented him, he would have ordered a more lenient sentence than fifteen years to life, the minimum required in Lane's case. "I do not feel that the acts of the defendant warrant a life imprisonment," Rosenberger stated. Lane was also sentenced to zero to seven years for conspiracy; the sentences were to run concurrently.

Lane was 46 when she entered Bedford Hills Correctional Facility. She lived on the honor floor and took part in both the Long Termers and the Pre-Release committees. She helped design a Career Awareness Program to prepare inmates for work after release. One professional associated with the prison called Lane "a mature and capable woman who is held in high regard by both peers and staff."

Almost four and a half years later, Judge Rosenberger ruled on a motion from Lane's new attorney that Lane had been the victim of ineffective counsel. The judge vacated Lane's conviction and dismissed the indictment.

Freed without supervision on February 12, 1982, Lane returned home to care for her aging mother. She soon found work as a rental assistant with a property management company in the South Bronx. There, according to one of her supervisors, she was granted two pay raises and given the responsibility of opening the office with her own set of keys. "She gave more time than necessary," said Dialis Romero, manager of Two Trees Management Inc. Another supervisor said that Lane showed "concern and compassion" in her work.

Lane also did volunteer work. According to Rosemary O'Regan, executive director of Tender Loving Crafts, a business that sells inmate crafts, Lane worked "tirelessly and enthusiastically" in her spare time for the nonprofit company. Lane also sat on the board of directors of the nursing home where she helped serve lunch every day. "[Lane] is loved and adored here," reported Doris Terry, founder of the center. "She is an asset to the community."

But on April 12, 1983, the Appellate Division unanimously reversed Rosenberger's decision. The court ruled that Lane had not been denied effective assistance of counsel, reinstated the original conviction, and ordered her to return to prison.

Supporters were stunned. "She lived at home with her mother, she had a good job, and she was a taxpayer," stated Doris Terry. "She was rehabilitated. Isn't that what the criminal justice system is all about?" On November 14, 1983, after all appeals failed, Lane traveled to Bedford Hills unescorted and turned herself in.

Today, Bernice Lane, 54, still takes part in the Long Termers Committee and the Career Awareness Program. She is also taking courses in data processing. Her prison counselor calls her "an excellent human being who . . . just doesn't belong here."

Lane's mother now lives by herself. Friends say she is growing frail. She is visited once a week by a staff member from the center where Lane did volunteer work. Lane was denied clemency in 1984. She will be eligible for parole release when she is almost 65.

Henry Barker—Mandatory Violent Felony Law— 15 Years to Life—Felony Murder

When two New York City Department of Corrections bounty hunters arrested Henry Barker in 1978, they believed they had captured a dangerous criminal. A convicted murderer, Barker had escaped to Miami, where he lived undetected for almost three years. By the time they returned to New York, the bounty hunters, Steven Levy and Marvin Badler, had become Barker's supporters. "Under unbelievable circumstances, Henry Barker has straightened himself out, rehabilitated himself, and has become a benefit to society," Badler told the *New York Times*.

Raised in the Bay Ridge section of Brooklyn, Barker graduated from Fort Hamilton High School and found a job as a runner on Wall Street. He drifted into handyman work, and in 1974, he ended up painting tenements for a landlord, Samuel Richards. Richards later laid Barker off and, Barker claimed, withheld $200 owed him in back wages.

Barker made plans to retrieve the money by theft. He stood watch on the street while, inside Richards's apartment building, a friend attempted to steal the 76-year-old man's wallet. Richards was fatally stabbed in a scuffle. Barker tried to save him, placing a pillow under his head, putting an ice pack on his chest, and calling an ambulance. Cooperating with police, Barker was arrested a few days later and was subsequently indicted on charges of intentional murder and felony murder.[19] Barker had only one previous conviction: carrying a concealed weapon (a knife), for which he had served three months' probation.

Barker claimed that the violence was never intended and that he did not know about his friend's knife. The presentence report stated that Barker was a "sincere, somewhat misguided youth who did not impress this writer as a dangerous individual." Nevertheless, his court-appointed lawyer persuaded Barker to plead guilty to felony murder and accept the mandatory minimum sentence of fifteen years to life—a better fate, the lawyer argued, than going to trial and facing a possible maximum of twenty-five years to life. Two months after being sentenced, Barker fled Riker's Island.

In Miami, he built a life for himself, often working three jobs at once. Using the name Tommy Prendergast, he won the affection of merchants, neighbors, and employers—many of whom called him "Our Tommy" in letters now in Barker's file. "In a very short time, we and most other[s] were treating him as if he was our son," reported one woman for whom Barker had worked. A man for whom Barker had provided housing and found a job wrote, "There should be a world full of human beings like him." At the time of this capture, he was working full time as a motel maintenance man and supporting his female companion and her three teenage daughters.

Employed as a hospital dietitian at Green Haven Correctional Facility, Barker, now 35, is performing work that supervisors say is "over and above" the basic requirements. In August 1984 he graduated with a degree in psychology from Marist College with a B-plus average. Seven officers from the honor block at Great Meadow Correctional Facility, his first assignment, wrote letters of support for his unsuccessful commutation application. One called him a "respectable guy, a sincere person who cares about the people around him."

The judge in Barker's case, Leonard Scholnick, has written, "After careful consideration, it is my opinion that neither he [Barker] nor society would benefit from any further incarceration." Under mandatory sentencing statutes, however, Barker must serve the full fifteen-year minimum before being considered for parole.

Evaluation of Florida's Habitual Sentencing Law

A second and more recent study was conducted by James Austin to evaluate the effects of Florida's habitual sentencing laws.[20] In Florida, two situations may trigger the court's decision to apply the habitual offender statute. The most common occurs for offenders who have two or more prior felony convictions. However, another provision, called the violent habitual statute, permits an offender who has a prior felony conviction for a violent offense to be "habitualized." Habituals will serve approximately ten years before they will be released with no parole supervision.

The decision to apply the statute rests with the state attorney. As it turns out, only about one-fifth of all cases that meet the criteria for habitualization actually have the statute applied. The study found that this high degree of discretion results in significant racial bias in the application of the law. An analysis comparing the attributes of offenders who were habitualized versus those who were not found that black inmates were nearly twice as likely to receive a habitual sentence even when controlling for the offender's offense and prior criminal record.

A sample of 90 male and female inmates sentenced under the habitual offender sentencing laws in September and November 1992 was drawn at random at four prison facilities, and the inmates were interviewed. They are characterized in the following manner:

- They tend to be not married (74 percent), with at least one child (69 percent), employed full time (54 percent) or part time (13 percent) but in a low-paying occupation.

- A significant number (43 percent) have not completed their high school diploma, with very few advancing to college (8 percent).

- A small but sizeable number reported having histories of sexual abuse as a child or as an adult (27 percent) and/or histories of mental illness (16 percent).

- The vast majority were convicted of either a property crime (44 percent) or a drug crime (24 percent).

- Within the drug category, virtually all of the crimes were related to crack cocaine.

- Nearly two-thirds were using drugs at the time the crime was committed (64 percent).

- In one-fifth of the crimes (usually drug crimes), there were no victims. The majority of the crimes where a victim was identified were inflicted on strangers, businesses, or law enforcement personnel (resisting arrest, assault, and so forth).

- In 87 percent of the crimes, there was no injury to the victim.

- In those instances where a property loss was suffered by the victim, the median loss was $300.

Using these data, each inmate was classified according to a criminal career typology reflecting their criminal lifestyle, including both the official data contained in the inmate's file and data from our interviews. The basic categories that were developed are discussed later, as is the proportion of cases that fell into these categories (Figure 2-5):

1. *Crack-heads (36 percent).* These offenders were characterized by their severe addiction to crack cocaine. Daily use of crack was part of their lifestyle. They would do virtually anything to maintain their drug habits. Typically they were not employed, hung around other crack-heads, and engaged in a wide variety of petty property crimes or petty

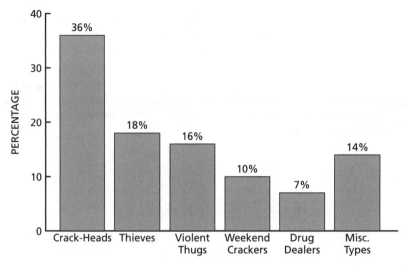

FIGURE 2-5 Proportion of Criminal Lifestyles of Interviewed Inmates Sentenced as Habitual Offenders

drug trafficking to support their drug habits. They probably represent the most difficult drug cases to treat.

2. *Weekend crack bingers (10 percent).* Unlike the crack-heads, these individuals used crack cocaine for recreational purposes—typically in the context of a weekend binge. They frequently were fully employed in blue-collar jobs and maintained relatively stable and normal outside interests. Because of their employability, they were frequently arrested through sting operations.

3. *Regular thieves (18 percent).* There were two types of thieves. The first were alcoholics who, when under the influence of the drug, attempted inept property crimes. They were incapable of holding a regular job or sustaining a marriage. The other type reflected skillful thieves who typified the predatory offender. These offenders were rarely involved in other forms of illicit drug use.

4. *Violent thugs (16 percent).* This group reflected the most dangerous group of offenders to public safety. They frequently were involved in violent activities as part of their criminal lifestyles and relied on violence and the use of weapons to commit their crimes.

5. *Drug dealers (7 percent).* This group consisted of inmates who did not abuse drugs but made a living selling drugs for profit. In almost all of our cases, these inmates would have to be considered small-time dealers who would make marginal profits by selling $244 rocks of cocaine to crack-heads or recreational drug users.

6. *Miscellaneous offenders (14 percent).* The last group was more difficult to classify, as they fit no particular pattern. Often these individuals had

associations with lower-class petty criminals, which allowed them to periodically become involved in situations that led to criminal activities and detection by law enforcement.

All these offenders had rather lengthy criminal records. Most had been arrested at least ten times and frequently sentenced to jail, probation, or prison. In this respect, they accurately represented the habitual offender label. On the other hand, with the noted exception of the violent thugs category, their crimes were petty and pathetic. These are drunken car thieves falling asleep in their victim's car, shoplifters being caught in a clumsy attempt to brazenly walk out of a store with a shopping cart filled with stolen goods, and crack-heads selling $2 rocks to undercover agents. They are, in many respects, aging offenders who know no other way to live.

The following five case studies represent a sampling of these offenders. For each, the inmate's offense and sentence are presented, along with an estimate of how much money Florida will spend on each individual at today's cost of incarceration ($15,700 per year).

Alcoholic—Alex B.—Fraud, Grand Theft, and Burglary—5.5-Year Sentence—Incarceration Costs of $64,763

Alex is a 46-year-old white male who is spending his first term in prison, although he has seven prior arrests and one prior jail term. One of his prior arrests and convictions was for assault; the other crimes were nonviolent. He has no prior juvenile crime record. He is currently serving three concurrent sentences for fraud (attempting to pass a bad check worth $20) and entering a person's home wearing a mask and stealing a microwave oven and a TV. He later turned himself in to the police. There was no loss to the victim, as both items were returned. The victim testified in court that, before the offense, Alex had been helping out with various errands and moving furniture. For this crime, he received a five-year, six-month sentence for grand theft and burglary. The worthless check crime resulted in a one-year probation term running concurrently with the burglary and robbery charges. He is also required to pay $200 in restitution to the victim when he is released from prison.

Drug Dealer—Toni G.—Trafficking Cocaine—Life Sentence—Incarceration Costs of $565,200

Toni is a 35-year-old African American serving her third and last time in prison. Under her sentence, she must die behind bars. She was caught selling rock cocaine to an undercover police officer in Broward County. There was no violence or injury associated with the crime. Toni has been arrested ten times as an adult, with seven prior jail sentences. She also has a prior commitment to the juvenile system for being truant. She has no violence in her record. She has four children (ages 16, 13, 12, and 2) who now live with her mother. While on the streets, she was unemployed and made her money running drugs. She completed the tenth grade and has some training as a beautician. Although she has tried marijuana, she denied ever using hard drugs. Because of her sentence, she is classified as close custody but has not received any disciplinary reports since being imprisoned in April 1991.

Violent Thug—Cornelius A.—Arson—12-Year Sentence—Incarceration Costs of $141,300

Cornelius is a white 37-year-old male now serving his fourth prison term. Most of his prior arrests and convictions have been for assault. He has no prior juvenile record. The current offense involved an attempt to burn down his girlfriend's house as a result of a dispute. He had been drinking heavily at the time. Damage to the house was $1,000, and the only injury was to Cornelius, who burned his hand while starting the fire. He was not on probation or parole supervision at the time. Cornelius is not married but has four children (ages 3, 14, 16, and 17) who live with their natural mother (not his current girlfriend). He is functionally illiterate, having completed the fifth grade, and is just now learning to read. He was employed full time as a maintenance worker at his sister's truck rental business. Since being admitted to prison approximately one year ago, he has not been involved in any serious disciplinary incidents and has enrolled in a reading class. He is now classified as medium custody.

Crack-Head—Elaine D.—Burglary—15-Year Sentence—Incarceration Costs of $176,625

Elaine is a 32-year-old African American serving her second prison term. She has thirteen prior arrests for drug and property crimes and has been sentenced to jail six times in addition to her two prison terms. There has been no violence in her crimes. She was caught trying to break into an apartment but was apprehended by police after a neighbor called. No property loss or damage resulted. She was high on heroin at the time of the crime. Elaine has been using heroin for many years. She is married to a dope fiend. They have one child, an 8-year-old boy who lives with Tom's sister. At the time of her arrest, she was working full time as a nurse's assistant and X-ray technician. She has a simple work detail in the prison and has received two disciplinary reports for disobeying orders. She will be released from prison in the year 2003.

Crack-Head—Peter A.—Possession and Sale of Cocaine—10-Year Sentence—Incarceration Costs of $117,750

Peter is a 50-year-old white serving his fourth prison term. He has a very lengthy adult and juvenile arrest record, with three previous juvenile commitments and over fifty adult arrests. There are no violent crimes in his past. He is a drug addict who sells drugs and steals to support his drug habits. His current prison term resulted when police stopped him on the street and found a couple of $5 rocks of cocaine in his possession along with a pipe he used to smoke the crack. He was high on crack at the time of the arrest. He has been married for sixteen years and has three grown children (ages 18, 21, and 25). He is functionally illiterate, with a fifth-grade education. When not in prison, he finds part-time work as a mason tender or shrimper. Since being imprisoned in 1991, he has not received any disciplinary infractions and has been attending AA and a drug treatment program.

CONCLUSIONS

Our research indicates that most people being sent to prison today are very different than the specter of Willie Horton that fuels the public's fear of crime. Most crimes are much pettier than the popular images promoted by those who sensationalize the crime issue. More than half of the persons sent to prison committed crimes that lacked any of the features the public believes compose a serious crime.

Other recent research supports our findings. The original Rand Corporation studies on career criminals that greatly influenced the current imprisonment binge actually found that the vast majority of newly admitted inmates were low-rate offenders involved in petty crimes. When these same researchers studied people they labeled as "high-rate" and "predatory" offenders, their findings were similar to ours: that most in this group committed very unskilled and unprofitable crimes. As Greenwood and Turner note, many high-rate offenders "appeared to have taken foolish risks for very modest potential gains."[21]

The studies presented here revealed that the popular conception of criminal careers is also a distortion of reality. These data suggest that the majority (57 percent) of the persons sent to prison were not following criminal careers. Although 43 percent were into crime, most of these (60 percent) were sent to prison for petty crimes, and their dedication to criminal behavior did not appear to be as firm as the popular image suggests. In fact, the majority of them, as well as the majority of those following other patterns of crime (for example, one-shot, crime episodes, being around crime, or dereliction), indicated to us that they wanted to stop violating the law and were preparing themselves in prison for conventional careers. As Greenwood and Turner observe, "a much larger proportion of [career criminals] are not particularly successful at crime, but they periodically return to it because they are not good at anything else."[22]

Instead of a large, menacing horde of dangerous criminals, our inner cities actually contain a growing number of young men, mostly nonwhite, who become involved in unskilled, petty crime because of no avenues to a viable, satisfying conventional life. The majority (65 percent) of our prison samples had not finished high school, 64 percent had no job skills, over half had never been employed steadily, and 56 percent were not working at the time of arrest.

The same is not true of a small percentage of our sample—those who appeared to be committed to crime in spite of other options. In addition, a few were guilty of very serious crimes. However, the general picture is one quite different than the distorted images that have fueled our imprisonment binge.

In 1987, the Bureau of Justice Statistics reported on a national survey of 1,920 U.S. residents. Seventy-one percent had responded that a prison sentence was the most suitable penalty for a group of twenty-four specific crime scenarios, which included rape, robbery, assault, burglary, theft, property damage, drunk driving, and drug offenses. The authors of the report suggest that "the public wants long prison sentences for most crimes." The scenarios, however, did not reflect the reality of street crime and imprisonment in America. In the robbery scenario from the study, for example, $1,000 was taken, the offender brandished a gun, and the victim was hospitalized. Our study discovered that less than 5 percent of the people being sent to prison committed a crime of this magnitude, which we would classify as very serious.[23]

A number of other studies have also discovered that when respondents are given scenarios that are closer to the actual crimes of most people sent to prison, the majority recommend some punishment other than imprisonment. A national poll taken by the Wirthlin Group in 1991 found that four of five Americans favored a nonprison sentence for offenders who are not dangerous. A 1991 California poll found that three-fourths of Californians felt that the state should find ways of punishing offenders that are less expensive than prison. In Alabama and Delaware, a focus-group analysis conducted by the Public Agenda Foundation found that when citizens were given detailed data about the crimes committed and the relative costs of various sanctions available to the courts, the public strongly supported nonprison sentences for inmates convicted of nonviolent crimes (who represent the vast majority of prisoners).[24] Collectively, these polls show that a majority of citizens would not recommend imprisonment for most of the people being sent to prison if they knew more about the offenders' crimes and life circumstances.

NOTES

1. Marvin E. Wolfgang, Robert M. Figlio, and Thomas Sellin, *Delinquency in a Birth Cohort* (Chicago: University of Chicago Press, 1972).

2. Peter Greenwood and Alan Abrahamse, *Selective Incapacitation* (Santa Monica, CA: Rand Corporation, 1982).

3. Peter Greenwood and Susan Turner, *Selective Incapacitation Revisited: Why the High-Rate Offenders Are Hard to Predict* (Santa Monica, CA: Rand Corporation, 1987).

4. See Alfred Blumstein, Jacqueline Cohen, and David P. Farrington, "Criminal Career Research: Its Value for Criminology," *Criminology* 26, 1 (February 1988): 1–35, for a summary of their work on criminal careers.

5. Michael Gottfredson and Travis Hirschi, "The True Value of Lambda Would Appear to Be Zero: An Essay on Career Criminals, Criminal Careers, Selective Incapacitation, Cohort Studies, and Related Topics," *Criminology* 24, 2 (1986): 213.

6. U.S. Department of Justice, Bureau of Justice Statistics, *Felony Sentences in the United States, 1996* (Washington, DC: U.S. Department of Justice, July 1999).

7. Tony Fabello, *Sentencing Dynamics Study* (Austin, TX: Criminal Justice Policy Council, January 1993).

8. U.S. Department of Justice, Bureau of Justice Statistics, *Historical Corrections Statistics in the United States, 1850–1984* (Washington, DC: U.S. Government Printing Office, December 1986).

9. The main reason for choosing these states was access. We wanted to include California, but the then director of corrections refused our request. Among those states we had access to, we selected these three on the grounds that they represented a spread on several variables—urban/rural, small population/large population, West/Midwest, and particularly on rates on incarceration.

10. Each selected inmate was informed of the purpose of the interview and told that participation was voluntary. Only three inmates refused to participate. In those instances in which an inmate declined to participate, that inmate's name was replaced with another from the same crime category list. Each person was visited twice, and twenty-five persons were selected each time. This was done to spread the sampling over a longer time period and thereby avoid any particular skewing of the samples by temporal variables. Also, we mistakenly selected and interviewed four persons over the fifty total in Washington. We left them in our study because we eventually adjusted our stratified sample so that our percentages of different time categories—for instance, robbery, violent crimes, other theft, drug-related crimes, sex crimes, and miscellaneous crimes—corresponded to national percentages. Consequently, the four extra interviews did not introduce any distortion.

11. It will be recalled that our original samples were stratified so that each crime category had an equivalent number of prisoners to be interviewed. Given that the vast majority of persons admitted are convicted of property and, increasingly, drug crimes, our samples had disproportionate numbers of violent crimes and robberies and needed to be statistically adjusted to reflect a true intake population. This was done by re-weighting the sampled cases consistent with their observed proportions in the national admission data. For example, offenders convicted of robbery represent 11 percent of prison admissions as compared to the 20 percent representation in our sample. To make our sample nationally representative of robbers, we reweighted the robbery cases by a factor of 0.55 so that they constitute 11 percent of the adjusted sample.

12. For a review of these evaluations, see Jack Alexander and James Austin, *Handbook for Evaluating Objective Prison Classification Systems* (San Francisco: National Council on Crime and Delinquency, 1991).

13. When we adjusted the total sample, we used the national data on percentages of the crime categories. For these state distributions, we adjusted our samples according to each state's offense distribution. Consequently, comparisons between the national estimates and the state-specific estimates are somewhat inconsistent. For example, none of the three states has as big a percentage of petty crimes as the total sample. This slight discrepancy is simply the result of the inconsistency of the intake offense distribution of the three states with the national offense intake distribution.

14. *Gang banging* is the term gang members use for engaging in gang violence against other gangs and more generally for belonging to a gang and participating in gang activities.

15. James K. Stewart, director, National Institute of Justice, U.S. Department of Justice, *NIJ Reports* (Washington, DC: National Institute of Justice, 1987), p. iii.

16. The number of these cases is so small (six) that little can be made of these descriptive statistics.

17. Criminal Justice Institute, *The Corrections Yearbook: 1998* (Middletown, CT: Criminal Justice Institute, 1999).

18. Correctional Association of New York, *Do They Belong in Prison? The Impact of New York's Mandatory Sentencing Laws on the Administration of Justice* (New York: Correctional Association of New York, 1985).

19. Under New York state law, felony murder applies to situations in which, during the course of certain designated felonies such as robbery or burglary, the offender's actions result in someone's death. The person charged with felony murder participated in the crime but did not directly cause the death.

20. James Austin, *Reforming Florida's Unjust, Costly, and Ineffective Sentencing Laws* (San Francisco: National Council on Crime and Delinquency, 1993).

21. Peter Greenwood and Susan Turner, *Selective Incapacitation Revisited: Why High-Rate Offenders Are Hard to Predict* (Los Angeles: Rand Corporation, 1987), p. 36.

22. Ibid.

23. Press release from the Department of Justice, Bureau of Justice Statistics, Sunday, November 8, 1987. Actually, the Bureau of Statistics was well aware that the scenarios were atypical because an earlier study it had conducted discovered, for example, that the median loss in a robbery was $195 and that 75 percent of all robberies involved less than $700. See J. Frederick Shenk and Patsy A. Klaus, *The Economic Cost of Crime to Victims: Special Report* (Washington, DC: Bureau of Justice Statistics, 1984).

24. See *Americans Behind Bars* (New York: Edna McConnell Clark Foundation, March 1992); and John Doble and Josh Klein, *Punishing Criminals: The Public's View: An Alabama Survey* (New York: Edna McConnell Clark Foundation, 1989).

3

■

The Imprisonment
of Children and Women*

THE CHILDREN'S IMPRISONMENT BINGE

The History of the Juvenile Correctional System

The development of a distinct justice system specifically tailored to recognize the many mitigating factors associated with juvenile crime is generally recognized as one of the most progressive developments in the evolution of criminal justice in the United States. Until this century, no formal differentiation had been made in society's response to crimes committed by juveniles versus crimes committed by adults. Beginning in Illinois in 1899, juvenile court systems were instituted throughout the United States to provide greater emphasis upon the welfare and rehabilitation of youth in the justice system. Specialized detention centers, training schools, and youth centers were developed to confine and treat delinquent youth apart from adult offenders. These facilities were intended to provide a structured, rehabilitative environment where the individual educational, psychological, and vocational needs of youthful offenders could be effectively addressed. Although system crowding and funding shortfalls have frequently compromised the achievement of these objectives in many jurisdictions, the goals of the juvenile court system have remained focused on protecting the welfare of youthful offenders.

This vision of a distinct justice system for juveniles focused upon treatment has come under attack in recent years. Beginning in the late 1980s, communities around the nation began to experience dramatically increased rates of juvenile crime. As shown in Figure 3-1, the arrest rate for violent

Arrests per 100,000 juveniles ages 10–17

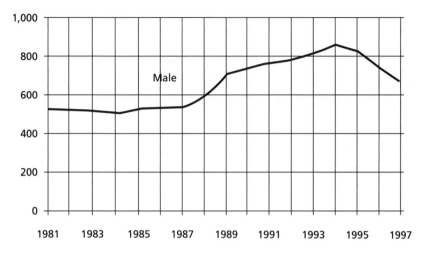

Arrests per 100,000 juveniles ages 10–17

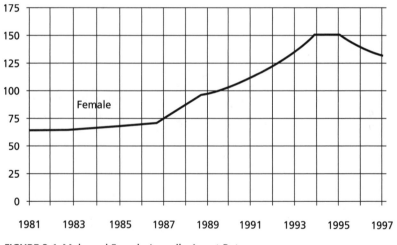

FIGURE 3-1 Male and Female Juvenile Arrest Rates
for Violent Crime Index Offenses, 1981–1997

Note: The Violent Crime Index includes the offenses of murder and nonnegligent
manslaughter, forcible rape, robbery, and aggravated assault.

SOURCE: Howard Snyder, "Male and Female Juvenile Arrest Rates for Violent Crime Index
Offenses, 1981–1997," *OJJDP Statistical Briefing Book* (December 10, 1998). Online. Available:
http://ojjdp.ncjrs.org/ojstatbb/qa004.html.

crimes for both males and females began to increase in 1987 and continued to escalate until the mid-1990s. Although this trend appears to have reversed itself, rates of serious crimes by juveniles remain well above historical levels.[1]

The increasing incidence and severity of crimes committed by juveniles have led many to question the efficacy of the juvenile court system and to call for a harsher response to juvenile crime. Juvenile delinquency, at least for more serious offenses, has come to be viewed more as a criminal rather than a behavioral problem, resulting in a substantial shift in public responses to the management of juvenile offenders. Researchers have noted this shift in trends toward more arrests, longer periods of incarceration, fewer opportunities for rehabilitation, and most significantly in the increasing transfer of juveniles to the adult criminal justice system.

Now there is a trend to place increasing numbers of juveniles in adult correctional facilities. Concerned that the juvenile justice system may be ill-equipped to handle youth charged with serious crimes and that the juvenile court may be too lenient in its ability to punish and control such youth, many states have initiated the process of amending their criminal codes so that youth charged with certain crimes can be waived into the adult court, and tried and sentenced as adults. All states now have the authority to try some juveniles as adults in criminal court under a number of mechanisms and circumstances (usually determined by the youth's age and type of crime committed).[2] Subsequent to conviction, youth are often sentenced to serve time in an adult correctional facility (either a jail or prison).

Conditions of Confinement

One of the concerns regarding the jailing of kids is their safety in such facilities. For example, a study completed in 1980 found that the juvenile suicide rate in jails is five times higher than the rate in the general youth population and eight times higher than the rate for adolescents in juvenile detention facilities.[3]

According to a study completed in 1989, juveniles were found to be more likely to be violently victimized in adult prisons than in juvenile correctional facilities.[4] Although property crime victimization rates are about the same for the two groups (over half of the inmates), 37 percent of the juveniles in training schools versus 47 percent of juvenile prison inmates suffer violent victimization, including violence at the hands of staff. Sexual assault is five times more likely in prison, beatings by staff nearly twice as likely, and attacks with weapons almost 50 percent more common. These data suggest that the increased use of adult facilities to house juveniles may pose unique problems for the adult corrections system, including development of treatment and reintegrative services, and protection from predatory inmates.

It was for these reasons that Congress passed the Juvenile Justice and Delinquency Prevention Act in 1973. In 1980, the act was amended by Congress to require states to remove all juveniles from jails within a five-year period. However, the current Congress is now recommending that such restrictions be removed to permit more children to be jailed.

Table 3-1 Juveniles in Juvenile Private and Public Facilities, 1997

Age	Totals	Males	Females
Under age 13	2,164	1,782	382
13 years	4,627	3,639	968
14 years	11,584	9,160	2,424
15 years	21,251	17,568	3,683
16 years	28,284	24,455	3,829
17 years	24,754	22,355	2,399
18 years and above	13,126	12,512	614
Totals	105,790	91,471	14,319

SOURCE: Melissa Sickmund, "One Day Count of Juveniles in Public or Private Custody Facilities," *Children in Custody Census of Public and Private Juvenile Detention, Correctional, and Shelter Facilities* (Office of Juvenile Justice and Delinquency Prevention, September 1998).

Trends in the Number
of Youth Confined in Adult Facilities

Most youth are housed in facilities that are designed to hold only youthful offenders. As of 1997, the total number of youth in these facilities was 105,790. As shown in Table 3-1, the vast majority of these youth are males aged 15 and higher.

In addition to these youth, many adult jails now hold juveniles despite the efforts of Congress to eliminate this practice (Table 3-2). Since 1983, there has been a sharp increase in those persons under age 18 (from 1,736 to 8,090). Table 3-2 also shows the huge increases in the female population—a topic we will examine more fully later in this chapter.

Similar time series data do not exist for the nation's prison system. In order to obtain a more current and accurate enumeration of the extent of confinement of juveniles in prison, a national survey of prison systems was recently completed by the Institute on Crime, Justice and Corrections (ICJC) at George Washington University. That survey, which was conducted in 1996, found that the number of juveniles housed in state prisons totaled 4,775, with 158 of these inmates being females (Table 3-3). Thus, there are a total of approximately 120,000 children incarcerated on any given day in America.

"Adult Crime, Adult Time"—Waivers to Adult Court

A major reason for the increases noted in the previous section has been the adoption of laws that allow youth charged with felony-level crimes to be waived to adult courts and to be tried as adults. During the past decade, most states have adopted legislation that allows for youth to be transferred from the juvenile court to the adult court to be tried as adults. Usually these laws target very serious crimes and allow the age of jurisdiction to be lowered. Relative to the issue of juveniles in adult correctional facilities, these laws often become the basis for

Table 3-2 Juveniles in Adult Jails, 1983–1998

Year	Totals	Males	Females	Juveniles
1983	221,815	206,163	15,652	1,736
1984	233,018	216,275	16,743	1,482
1985	254,986	235,909	19,077	1,629
1986	272,736	251,235	21,501	1,708
1987	294,092	270,172	23,920	1,781
1988	341,893	311,594	30,299	1,676
1989	393,303	356,050	37,198	2,250
1990	403,019	365,821	37,198	2,301
1991	424,129	384,628	39,501	2,350
1992	441,780	401,106	40,674	2,804
1993	455,500	411,500	44,100	4,300
1994	479,800	431,300	48,500	6,700
1995	499,300	448,000	51,300	7,800
1996	510,400	454,700	55,700	8,100
1997	557,974	498,678	59,296	9,105
1998	584,372	520,581	63,791	8,090
% Change	163%	153%	308%	366%

SOURCE: U.S. Department of Justice, Bureau of Justice Statistics, *Sourcebook of Criminal Justice Statistics 1998* (Washington, DC: Office of Justice Programs, 1999), p. 481.

Table 3-3 Summary of Juveniles Incarcerated

Type of Facility	Number	%
Juvenile facilities	105,790	89%
Jails	8,090	7%
Prisons	4,775	4%
Totals	118,655	100%

a juvenile to be housed in a jail (if charged and awaiting court disposition) or within a prison if the juvenile has been convicted and sentenced.

Perhaps the most striking example of this practice is the recent case of Nathaniel Abraham who was tried in Michigan's court after being charged with murder at age 11. He is believed to be the youngest defendant to ever be tried as an adult for first-degree murder. This was possible in Michigan, which had passed legislation that set no age limit for waiving juvenile offenders to the adult court. As Governor Engler stated to the media in response to the case, "adult crime, adult time."[5]

Between 1992 and 1996, forty-four of the fifty-one state legislatures (including the District of Columbia) made substantive changes to their laws

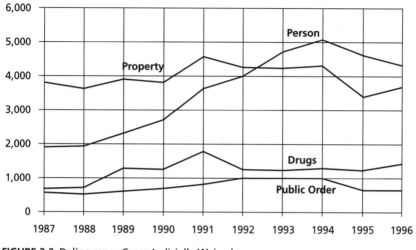

FIGURE 3-2 Delinquency Cases Judicially Waived
to Criminal Court, 1987–1996

SOURCE: Adapted from Anne Stahl, "Delinquency Cases Judicially Waived to Criminal Court,
1987–1996," *OJJDP Statistical Briefing Book* (July 1 , 1999). Online. Available:
http://www.ojjdp.ncjrs.org/ojstatbb/qa084.html.

targeting juveniles who commit violent or serious crimes.[6] All but ten states
adopted or modified laws making it easier to prosecute juveniles in criminal
court. Nearly half of the states (twenty-four) added crimes to the list of
excluded offenses, and thirty-six states and the District of Columbia excluded
certain categories of juveniles from juvenile court jurisdiction. The list of
offenses considered serious enough for transfer as young as age 14 included
murder, aggravated assault, armed robbery, and rape; but the list also included
less serious and violent offenses such as aggravated stalking, lewd and lascivi-
ous assault or other acts in the presence of a child, violation of drug laws near
a school or park, sodomy, and oral copulation. Since 1992, thirteen states and
the District of Columbia have added or modified statutes that provide for a
mandatory minimum period of incarceration for juveniles adjudicated delinquent for certain serious and violent crimes.

   A legal method used to try a youth as an adult is accomplished by lowering the age of jurisdiction. For example, seven states (Georgia, Illinois,
Louisiana, Massachusetts, Michigan, South Carolina, and Texas) set their age of
jurisdiction at 16, while New York, Connecticut, and North Carolina have
lowered the age to 15 years. Missouri lowered the age for transfer to criminal
court to 12 for any felony.

   In all but two states (Nebraska and New York), a juvenile court judge
can waive jurisdiction over a case and transfer youth to the adult court for
certain crimes and at certain age limits. The number of juvenile court cases
transferred to criminal court increased from approximately 7,200 in 1985 to

a high of nearly 12,300 in 1994. The numbers then declined to approximately 10,000 by 1996.[7]

Although the legal basis for waiver varies from state to state, the clear trend across the country is to rapidly expand the use of waivers. This is being accomplished by casting wider nets in criteria for waiver by lowering the age of adult jurisdiction or by adding to the list of applicable crimes, and by adopting more procedures by which youth can be transferred to adult court (for example, either through the discretion of the prosecutor or through legislative mandate). Currently, waiver provisions are often applied to nonviolent offenders, and in some states, running away from a juvenile institution is grounds for prosecution in adult courts. Although crimes against the person is now the most frequent offense related to the waiver, the majority of cases are charged with property, drugs, and public order offenses (see Figure 3-2).[8]

A Closer Look at Juveniles in Prison

The survey conducted by The George Washington University collected data that allows us to look at those youth housed in prisons as compared to adult inmates (Table 3-4). Although youth placed in adult facilities are more likely to be convicted or charged with crimes against the person, a significant number are there for nonviolent and drug-related offenses. Approximately 60 percent of the youth incarcerated in these facilities have been either convicted or charged with a crime of violence as compared to 46 percent of the adult population. More significantly, 45 percent of the youth have been convicted of a serious violent offense such as murder, non-negligent manslaughter, forcible rape, robbery, and aggravated assault as compared to 26 percent of the adult prison population. Property offenders comprised 20 percent of the youthful inmates population, and 10 percent of the youthful offender population are being held for a drug-related offense compared with 21 percent of the adult offender population. Another 2 percent were parole or probation violators.

In terms of ethnic background, these youth are more likely to be African Americans, with black youth making up 55 percent of the youthful offender population compared to 48 percent of the adult offender population (see Table 3-5). The proportion of the population with a Hispanic background is virtually the same for both the youthful and adult population (14-15 percent).

The age distribution of the youthful offender population is heavily skewed toward 17-year-olds (Table 3-6). Nearly 78 percent of the reported youthful offender population is 17, with another 20 percent in the 16-year-old category. It should be noted that in a number of states such as Michigan, Illinois, and New York, 17-year-olds are considered adults. Accordingly, the presence of 17-year-old offenders in these states' populations does not necessarily reflect a policy of juvenile transfers, but could instead simply be a function of normal prosecution of adult crimes. Offenders below the age of 16 are very rare in adult correctional facilities; the youngest reported age of a youthful offender was 11.

Table 3-4 State Prison Populations, Adult and Juvenile, 1998

State	Youth	Adult	State	Youth	Adult
Alabama	104	20,488	Montana	81	2,714
Alaska	24	2,897	Nebraska	29	3,532
Arizona	140	25,154	Nevada	36	9,164
Arkansas	89	10,677	New Jersey	35	23,989
California	163	161,466	New Mexico	9	5,031
Colorado	23	13,773	New York	316	69,499
Connecticut	505	15,778	North Carolina	369	32,118
Delaware	20	18	Ohio	158	48,972
District of Columbia	26	6,719	Oklahoma	46	14,603
Florida	572	66,117	Oregon	25	8,253
Georgia	152	39,347	Pennsylvania	98	35,765
Hawaii	2	4,009	Rhode Island	0	3,657
Idaho	10	3,545	South Carolina	200	20,916
Illinois	162	42,292	South Dakota	N/R	2,359
Indiana	89	18,830	Tennessee	37	15,554
Iowa	9	7,3341	Texas	272	129,661
Louisiana	87	33,572	Utah	21	5,084
Maryland	76	22,566	Vermont	15	1,198
Massachusetts	13	11,224	Virginia	84	26,578
Michigan	208	38,927	Washington	104	13,866
Minnesota	32	5,562	Wisconsin	22	166
Mississippi	164	16,291	Wyoming	37	1,233
Missouri	111	25,493	Totals	4,775	1,130,599

THE IMPRISONMENT BINGE OF WOMEN

Beyond the unprecedented growth of the total prison and jail population and the increased incarceration of juveniles, there is another, hidden crisis—the growing incarceration of women. Between 1983 and 1998, the number of women entering the nation's state and federal prisons increased by 344 percent compared to a 207 percent increase in the number of men entering prison. By the end of 1998, the women prisoner population reached 84,427. And there are another 63,791 women in the jail for a total of nearly 150,000 incarcerated women on any given day (Table 3-7).

Although the image most commonly evoked by the word *prisoner* is that of a minority male, the reality is that the faces of prisoners also increasingly belong to women, especially women of color. When Marc Mauer and Tracy Huling of the Sentencing Project released their 1995 report "Young Black Americans and the Criminal Justice System," the finding that gained the most national attention was that one in three young black men nationally was under some form of criminal justice control. However, the same study revealed

Table 3-5 Characteristics of State Prison Inmate Offense Charge, Demographics and Housing Patterns, 1998

Offense Charge	Youth	%	Adult	%	Totals
Crime against persons	2,722	59.7%	473,821	45.0%	476,544
Property crimes	974	21.4%	216,756	20.6%	217,730
Alcohol related	135	3.0%	20,457	1.9%	20,592
Drug related	467	10.2%	210,975	20.0%	211,442
Public order	185	4.1%	40,468	3.8%	42,325
Probation and parole violators	79	1.7%	90,260	8.6%	90,339
Unknown	92	2.0%	5,676	0.5%	5,768
Other	85	1.9%	13,327	1.3%	13,412
Totals	4,562	100%	1,052,737	100%	1,058,972
Race/Ethnicity					
Asian	65	1.3%	11,056	1.1%	11,121
African American	2,706	54.7%	497,343	48.3%	500,050
Caucasian	1,309	26.5%	355,960	34.5%	357,269
Hispanic	689	13.9%	156,782	15.2%	157,471
Native American	176	3.56%	9,421	0.9%	9,597
Totals	4,945	100%	1,030,562	100%	1,035,508
Housing Type					
Single cell	1,019	29.6%	120,221	21.8%	120,221
Double cell	670	19.4%	193,754	35.1%	193,754
Dormitory	1,757	51.0%	237,801	43.1%	239,558
Totals	3,446	100%	551,776	100%	553,534

Note: These housing pattern statistics only reflect data reported by 21 states that house juveniles in adult correctional facilities.

Table 3-6 Age of Youthful Offender Population

Age of Youthful Offender	Female	Male	Totals
13 years old	0	1	1
14 years old	0	11	11
15 years old	9	117	126
16 years old	32	782	814
17 years old	135	3,532	3,667
Totals	176	4,443	4,619

Table 3-7 Jail and Prison Populations by Gender, 1983–1998

	JAIL		PRISON	
Year	Males	Females	Males	Females
1983	206,163	15,652	396,021	19,020
1984	216,275	16,743	441,208	20,794
1985	235,909	19,077	479,359	23,148
1986	251,235	21,501	518,441	26,531
1987	270,172	23,920	555,961	29,123
1988	311,594	30,299	594,996	32,604
1989	356,050	37,198	671,752	40,612
1990	365,821	37,198	729,840	44,079
1991	384,628	39,501	777,908	47,651
1992	401,106	40,674	832,093	50,407
1993	411,500	44,100	911,044	58,257
1994	431,300	48,500	990,306	64,396
1995	448,000	51,300	1,057,406	68,468
1996	454,700	55,700	1,069,257	69,727
1997	498,678	59,296	1,123,478	74,112
1998	520,581	63,791	1,217,592	84,427
% Change	153%	308%	207%	344%

SOURCES: U.S. Department of Justice, Bureau of Justice Statistics, *Sourcebook of Criminal Justice Statistics, 1997* (Washington, DC: Office of Justice Programs, 1999), Table 6.35; U.S. Department of Justice, Bureau of Justice Statistics, *Prisoners in 1998* (Washington, DC: Office of Justice Programs, 1999).

another equally striking finding: that due to the War on Drugs legislation and other factors, "African American women have experienced the greatest increase in criminal justice supervision."[9]

Descriptions of the Female Inmate

Lorraine Fowler describes the "typical" female inmate as follows: probably minority, aged 25 to 29, unmarried but has one to three children, a likely victim of sexual abuse as a child, a victim of physical abuse, has current alcohol and drug abuse problems, has had multiple arrests, first arrested around 15, a high school dropout, on welfare, has low skills, and has held mainly low-wage jobs.[10] James Austin similarly describes female inmates as having very high needs for educational programs, job training, and health and mental health counseling; as having drug problems and job problems; and as having poor parenting skills and continued responsibility for children.[11]

1. Current Offense and Prior Record Women have less violence in their current or prior criminal record than men, and are more generally convicted of minor crimes.[12] They have fewer prior convictions than men, usually for minor or nonviolent crimes—for example, fraud, larceny, theft, or drug offenses. Although national data suggest an increasing number of women are charged with serious crimes, they are generally accessories and not the instigator or leader.[13]

Furthermore, many of women's violent crimes occur in a specific long-term relationship and are unlikely to generalize to the public at large. Mary Morash, citing 1991 BJS statistics, notes that more female offenders relative to male offenders were incarcerated for killing a family member, spouse, or other close intimate (25 percent versus 6 percent).[14]

2. Institutional Conduct Women's institutional behavior appears substantially better than that of male inmates.[15] They exhibit less escape or escape attempts, less violence, and about half as many formal misbehavior reports as males. Austin concluded that females "almost uniformly" pose lower institutional risks as indicated by lower severity of current crimes, lower criminal histories, lower levels of disciplinary infractions, and lower escape activities. Austin notes that most disciplinary infractions by women tend to be nonviolent (for example, refusal to obey an order, unauthorized possession of money, and so on).

In contrast, male infractions involve more fights and assaults. Correctional staff describe female inmates as being more socially adjusted and positive in their attitudes than males.[16] Peggy Burke and Linda Adams found that many correctional staff felt that women were more sensitive, more demanding, needed more daily attention, were more concerned with personal problems, and had higher expectations that staff listen and care about their problems. While less violent and risky, staff felt that females were "more trouble" than male prisoners.[17]

3. Children and Family Relationships An intense need that primarily characterizes women inmates is the maintenance of bonding with children and family. Austin described this need as the foremost difficulty women inmates experience, with many of them hoping to resume their maternal role following release.[18] Considerable stress and anxiety occur among female inmates if this bond is threatened. The staff have noted that this anxiety has a very negative impact on women's adjustment to incarceration.

A majority of female inmates have children, most have primary responsibility for child rearing, and most have legal custody. Morash reported that about 66 percent of women in prison had children under 18 years of age.[19] Austin reported slightly different statistics—but reached the same general conclusions. More than 80 percent of their female inmates had at least one child, and close to 70 percent had children under 18 years of age.[20]

Additionally, the effects of the increasing incarceration of women are reaching into the next generation. Close to 80 percent of women in prison are mothers, a majority of whom are single caretakers of minor children. These children are routinely left without a parent, without a coordinated system of care, and without the supports guaranteed to other children in America in 1980 by the Federal Adoption Assistance and Child Welfare Act (PL 96-272, a federal law mandating services primarily to promote the preservation of families). While the traumatic effects on children of losing their mothers to prison or jail have been well documented, the children themselves have remained largely invisible. They have not yet become part of the equation when policy makers evaluate the costs of incarcerating women.

4. Medical Needs The medical needs of female inmates include several special issues: pregnancy, abortions, birth control, birth, child custody, and so on. Classification is crucial in detecting these needs and referring the female inmate for appropriate care. Female inmates overall have a higher demand for both medical and psychiatric services than males.[21] Failures to properly assess or adequately treat such needs would have a disparate impact on the welfare of the female inmate.

5. Vocational, Educational, and Economic Needs Women inmates have more severe social, educational, and economic risk factors than male inmates. The few statistical reports of the early 1990s suggest that most are uneducated, unskilled, poor, unemployed, or hold minimum-wage jobs; that about 20 percent have not attained functional literacy; and that about 60 percent are on public assistance.[22] Unfortunately, alleviating these social needs is *not* prioritized in prisons and jails, and such problems are ignored or not addressed due to lack of resources. This low priority regarding rehabilitation has been vigorously attacked. Burke and Adams, for example, criticize the low emphasis on "habitation" relative to security.[23] Fowler argues that cost-effective solutions in corrections must emphasize prevention by placing a higher emphasis on alleviating social needs.[24]

Abuse of Women Inmates

Finally, there have increasing reports of female inmates (and staff as well) being sexually abused by male guards. In 1999, Amnesty International released a study of the level of abuse occurring in the nation's jails and prisons. Abuse occurs because many guards working in female prisons are males. In the U.S. federal prisons, approximately 70 percent of the guards are male, while in Canada only 9 percent are male. When performing normal activities, male guards are allowed to touch a prisoner's breasts and genitals during routine pat-down and strip searches and watch women as they shower and dress. There have even been reports of selling women inmates to male inmates for sex. Some of the examples cited in the study, as reported by *The Washington Post,* are as follows:

A female prisoner was raped and impregnated by a guard at a Washington state prison.

The Federal Bureau of Prisons agreed to pay $500,000 to settle a lawsuit filed by three female inmates who said they had been sexually abused at the Federal Detention Center in Pleasanton, California. One of the women, Robin Lucas, stated she was housed in a men's facility where she was attacked by a male inmate who was allowed in her cell by the staff. When she complained, she claims the guard retaliated by allowing three men in her cell where she was handcuffed, beaten, and raped.

Florence Krell committed suicide by hanging herself after she had written numerous letters to her mother and a judge complaining about mistreatment, including being observed by male guards when she was left naked in her cell.

In 1994, a federal judge ruled that the D.C. Department of Corrections had violated the constitutional rights of thirteen female inmates by allowing male guards to fondle and rape them.

The Arlington County jail, based on its own internal investigation, found that female inmates were being sexually abused by male guards over a six-month period.

Currently, there are twelve states where it is not a crime for guards to have sex with an inmate.[25]

These and other atrocities have led many to recommend that male guards be removed completely from prisons that house women. Although such a personnel policy may not pass constitutional muster, it is clear that if left unattended, this dark side of the prison experience will emotionally scar thousands of women who are exposed to such repugnant behavior.

NOTES

* The survey data presented in this chapter on children in adult facilities was supported by a grant funded by the U.S. Department of Justice, Bureau of Justice Assistance which is a component of the Office of Justice Programs. Points of view or opinions in this chapter are those of the authors and do not represent necessarily the official position or point of view of the U.S. Department of Justice.

1. Howard Snyder, "Male and Female Juvenile Arrest Rates for Violent Crime Index Offenses, 1981–1997," *OJJDP Statistical Briefing Book* (December 10, 1998).

2. Melissa Sickmund, *How Juveniles Get to Criminal Court* (Washington, DC: U.S. Department of Justice, Office of Juvenile Justice and Delinquency Prevention, May 1994).

3. Community Research Center, *Juvenile Suicides in Adult Jails* (Washington, DC: U.S. Department of Justice, OJJDP, Juvenile Justice Transfer Series, 1980).

4. M. Forst, J. Fagan, and T. S. Vivona, "Youth in Prisons and State Training Schools," *Juvenile and Family Court Journal* 39 (1989): 1–14.

5. "13-Year-Old Convicted in Shooting," *The Washington Post,* November 17, 1999, p. A3.

6. P. Torbet, R. Gable, H. Hurst, I. Montgomery, L. Szymanski, and D. Thomas, *State Responses to Serious and Violent Juvenile Crime* (Washington, DC: U.S. Department of Justice, OJJDP, 1996).

7. Anne Stahl, "Delinquency Cases Judicially Waived to Criminal Court, 1987–1996." *OJJDP Briefing Book* (July 1, 1999).

8. See C. Shauffer, S. Burrell, M. Ramiu, and M. Soler, "Children in Adult Custody: A Concept Paper on Waiver of Juvenile Court Jurisdiction" (San Francisco, CA: Youth Law Center, 1993).

9. Marc Maurer and Tracy Huling, *Young Black Americans and the Criminal Justice System* (Washington, DC: The Sentencing Project, 1995).

10. Lorraine T. Fowler, "What Classification for Women?" in *Classification: A Tool for Managing Today's Offenders* (American Correctional Association, 1993).

11. James Austin, *Women Classification Study—Indiana Department of Corrections* (San Francisco, CA: National Council on Crime and Delinquency, 1993).

12. Lorraine T. Fowler, "What Classification for Women?"; James Austin, *Women Classification Study—Indiana Department of Corrections.*

13. Charlotte Nesbitt, *The Female Offender in the 1990's Is Getting an Overdose of Parity* (Longmont, CO: U.S. Department of Justice, National Institute of Corrections Information Center, Unpublished paper, 1994).

14. Mary Morash, *Identifying Effective Strategies for Managing Female Offenders* (Longmont, CO: U.S. Department of Justice, National Institute of Corrections Information Center, 1992).

15. James Austin, *Women Classification Study—Indiana Department of Cor-*

rections; Charlotte Nesbitt, *The Female Offender in the 1990's Is Getting an Overdose of Parity;* Jack Alexander and Elaine Humphrey, *Initial Security Classification Guidelines for Females* (Longmont, CO: NY State Department of Correctional Services, National Institute of Corrections Information Center, 1988).

16. Charlotte Nesbitt, *The Female Offender in the 1990's Is Getting an Overdose of Parity;* Jack Alexander and Elaine Humphrey, *Initial Security Classification Guidelines for Females.*

17. Peggy Burke and Linda Adams, *Classification for Women Offenders in State Correctional Facilities: A Handbook for Practitioners* (Washington, DC: National Institute of Corrections, 1991).

18. James Austin, *Women Classification Study—Indiana Department of Corrections.*

19. Mary Morash, *Identifying Effective Strategies for Managing Female Offenders.*

20. James Austin, *Women Classification Study—Indiana Department of Corrections.*

21. Peggy Burke and Linda Adams, *Classification for Women Offenders in State Correctional Facilities: A Handbook for Practitioners.*

22. James Austin, *Women Classification Study—Indiana Department of Corrections;* Barbara Owen and Barbara Bloom, *Profiling the Needs of California's Female Prisoners: A Needs Assessment* (U.S. Department of Justice, National Institute of Corrections, 1995).

23. Peggy Burke and Linda Adams, *Classification for Women Offenders in State Correctional Facilities: A Handbook for Practitioners.*

24. Lorraine T. Fowler, "What Classification for Women?"

25. "Abuse of Female Prisoners in U.S. Is Routine, Rights Report Says," *The Washington Post,* March 4, 1999, p. A11.

4

■

The Private Prison Binge*

BACKGROUND

As noted in Chapter 1, prison and jail crowding is one of the most burdensome problems plaguing the U.S. criminal justice system. It has also been a major catalyst for the relatively recent growth in private prisons. Compounding the problems created by the growing demand for prison space and funding is the lack of public confidence in the quality of correctional services provided by federal, state, and municipal governments. Programs designed to rehabilitate offenders have not demonstrated a reduction in crime or recidivism and have thus lost credibility with the public and policy makers. In short, there is an increasing belief that government is not equipped to meet the challenges of contemporary, institutional confinement. In the 1980s, many saw private prisons and jails as part of the solution to meet the increasing pressure for prison bed space, at a time when taxpayers were reluctant to pay for correctional services and were not supportive of divestiture of resources from other areas of state responsibilities and services.[1] As a means of confronting escalating prison populations and costs, policy makers are now turning to the private sector for assistance.

"Privatization" is commonly defined as a contract process that shifts public functions, responsibilities, and capital assets, in whole or in part, from the public to the private sector. Privatization in correctional services can assume a number of institutional characteristics. For instance, the most common form of privatization in corrections is the contracting-out (or out-sourcing) of specific services, which entails a competition among private bidders to perform governmental activities. Over the past two decades, the practice of state and local correctional agencies contracting with private entities for medical, mental health, education, food services, maintenance, and administrative office security functions has risen sharply. Under these circumstances, the correctional agency remains the financier and continues to manage and maintain policy control over the type and quality of services provided.

A more radical approach occurs when government transfers ownership of assets, commercial enterprises, and management responsibilities to the private sector. This is called an "asset sale," leaving the government with a limited or nonexistent role in the financial support, management, and oversight of the sold asset.[2] This form of privatization is more radical and, until the 1980s, was not adopted by government in operating correctional facilities.

There is no doubt there has been a dramatic increase in the use of private correctional facilities, initially in the United States, and more recently in the United Kingdom, Australia, Scotland, and now South Africa (see Tables 4-1 and 4-2). We use the term *correctional facilities,* as many of the so-called private prisons are actually jails and detention centers that do not house state or federal prisoners.

In 1987, the total number of inmates in privately operated prisons and jails worldwide was approximately 3,100. By 1998, that number had increased to over 132,000. Although 14 private correctional facility firms exist at the time of the writing of this book, two companies (Corrections Corporation of America and Wackenhut) account for over three-fourths of the entire worldwide market. The total amount of revenues now allocated to private prisons and jails is estimated at $1 billion.[3]

Despite the rapid increases in the presence of private correctional facilities, they represent only a small share of the entire correctional population market. Private prisons have captured only a minor share of the correctional market, at least within the United States. With a total jail and prison population of approximately 1.7 million in the United States, the estimated 116,626-bed capacity in the United States reflects less than 7 percent of the U.S. market. The recently completed Abt Associates report found that with regard to privately operated prisons, less than 5 percent (or 52,370 inmates) of the total 1.2 million prisoner population was housed in private prisons.

In terms of prison facilities, the Abt study identified no more than 65 facilities that could be classified as housing state prisons, which is a small percentage of the more than 1,500 prisons in the United States.[4] Very few of these facilities have been studied (Table 4-3). Furthermore, there are some indications that growth in the use of privatization may be losing steam and has reached a plateau. For example, there has been no increase in the private facility bed capacity since January 1, 1998.[5] The stock prices for most of the major firms have dropped substantially in the past year, and there have been a number of highly publicized management problems with several privately operated facilities in Texas, Ohio, and New Mexico.

Table 4-1 Private Adult Correctional Firms, December 31, 1998

Management Firm	U.S. Capacity	Outside U.S. Capacity	Total Capacity	%
Alternative Programs, Inc.	340	0	340	0.3%
Avalon Community Services, Inc.*	350	0	350	0.3%
The Bobby Ross Group	464	0	464	0.4%
CiviGenics, Inc.	3,563	0	3,563	2.7%
Cornell Corrections, Inc.*	5,794	0	5,794	4.4%
Correctional Services Corp.*	6,727	0	6,727	5.1%
Corrections Corp. of America*	65,748	2,244	67,992	51.4%
Correctional Systems, Inc.*	272	0	272	0.2%
The Group 4 Prison Services Ltd.	0	4,510	4,510	3.4%
The GRW Group	362	0	362	0.3%
Management and Training Corp.	7,465	0	7,465	5.6%
Maranatha Production Company	500	0	500	0.4%
Securicor	0	800	800	0.6%
Wackenhut Corrections Corp.*	25,041	8,166	33,207	25.1%
Totals	116,626	15,720	132,346	100.0%

SOURCE: Charles W. Thomas, *Private Prisons Project* (Gainesville, FL: Center for Studies in Criminology and Law, University of Florida, http:web.crim.ufl.ed/pcp, 1998).

Table 4-2 Geographic Location of Private Management Firms Outside the United States as of December 31, 1998

Management Firm	Design Capacity by Firm	%
Wackenhut	8,166	51.9%
Group 4 Prison Services, Ltd	4,510	28.7%
CCA	2,244	14.3%
Securicor	800	5.1%

Country	Facilities	Design Capacity by County	%
South Africa	2	3,000	19.1%
Scotland	2	1,300	8.3%
U.K.	10	6,761	43.0%
Australia	12	4,659	29.6%
Totals	26	15,720	100.0%

SOURCE: Charles W. Thomas, *Private Prisons Project* (Gainesville, FL: Center for Studies in Criminology and Law, University of Florida, http:web.crim.ufl.ed/pcp, 1998).

Table 4-3 Private Prison Market Share of Prison Facilities

U. S. Prison Facilities	N	%
Total prison facilities	1,515	100.0%
Total publicly operated prisons	1,450	95.7%
Privately operated prisons	65	4.3%
Privately operated prisons evaluated	13	0.9%

SOURCE: D. McDonald, E. Fournier, M. Russell-Einhorn, and S. Crawford, "Chapter 2: An Overview of the Private Imprisonment Industry, Past and Present." Pp. 12–29 in *Private Prisons in the United States: An Assessment of Current Practice* (Boston: Abt Associates Inc., 1998).

PRIVATIZATION OF CORRECTIONS: A HISTORICAL OVERVIEW

Private enterprise in the United States has an extensive history of involvement in the provision of correctional services. According to Feeley, the involvement of the private sector in corrections stems, in part, from an Anglo-American political culture that is somewhat skeptical of governmental authority yet promotes private initiative.[6] Feeley traces the private sector involvement back to shortly after the first colonists arrived in Virginia in 1607. The colonists were followed by a handful of convicted felons transported by private entrepreneurs to America as a condition of pardon to be sold into servitude.[7]

The overseas transportation of these felons was organized by private entrepreneurs. Merchants transported convicts in exchange for the privilege of selling them as indentured servants.[8] Transporting convicts to America (and later many more to Australia following the American Revolution) was an innovation that radically transformed the administration of criminal justice. This innovation expanded the sanctioning power of the state without the need to increase its administrative structure. In other words, the policy of transportation multiplied the state's penal capacity at a low cost to the government.

During the eighteenth century, the modern prison emerged in America as a viable alternative to servitude or the death penalty. Also during this time, the use of privately operated facilities became popular. In the colonies, criminal justice procedures were copied from English custom, which had a long history of private involvement in operating jails. Privately operated jails date back to medieval England.[9]

For a fixed fee, states allowed private contractors to supervise prisoners inside prison walls.[10] Although appointed by government, a head jailer was considered an independent operator of a profit-making enterprise functioning as a government contractor. Often, jailers provided employment for prisoners.[11] In privately operated facilities, inmates were often engaged as laborers and craftsmen in private sector activities. Early American jails may be characterized as exploitative. Clair Cripe describes the conditions as follows:

There was seldom any separation of types of prisoners—women and children were often confined with hardened criminals. Many jails were very crowded; most were unsanitary. Payments were extracted for special services, such as better meals or other privileges. Some money was given to the jailer (often the sheriff) for basic services. But it was widely accepted that jailers could charge additional money for virtually any type of special benefit.[12]

By 1885, thirteen states had contracts with private enterprises to lease out prison labor.[13] One of the more interesting situations occurred in California in which San Quentin prison was first constructed and operated under a private provider in the 1850s. Private entrepreneurs persuaded state officials that the facility could best be operated under a long-term lease arrangement with an entity with experience in law enforcement. Even back then the debate centered on costs, with the argument made that the private sector would be less expensive and less corrupt than government. However, after a number of major scandals surrounding the mismanagement of the facility by the private provider, the state decided to turn the facility over to the control of state government. Eventually, government turned out to be as ineffective and corrupt as the private provider.[14]

As the year [1856] went on it became increasingly clear to more and more people that, regardless how much money it might save the taxpayers, a private contract was no way to run the state prison. The Bulletin was not alone when it demanded that, whatever it cost, a final end had to be put to the system of farming out the management of the state convicts. . . . After the final ejection of [Warden] McCauley, however, the prison fell into the hands of men who were primarily professional politicians rather than pirates. The distinction is a nice one, and the change was more a matter of style than of substance. The prison remained a rich piece of political spoils, but the looting was now carried on more in line with the ancient traditions of American state politics.

Even back then, private contractors claimed they could both manage prisons and employ convicts in labor, arguing that the practice would be both rehabilitative as well as financially rewarding.[15] Prison models of convict labor took various forms. At some, companies outside the prison provided raw materials that were refined in prison workshops and later sold by private companies. At others, prisons leased out their inmates to private farms or other businesses if they could not produce saleable items within the prison. In a number of states, contractors paid the prison a fee or percentage of profits for the right to employ convicts. For example, in the 1860s the Texas legislature directed state correctional administrators to contract out inmate labor to the private sector. Even when prisons were not operated entirely by private entrepreneurs, inmates were used as a cheap source of labor supply. Prisoners often worked on farms, for railroads, and in mines, in addition to other public work programs.[16]

For most of the correctional history of the United States, prison labor was expected to generate a profit for the institution. If generating a profit was not feasible, it was incumbent upon the prisoner to pay the costs of incarceration and become self-supporting. The "managers" of early detention facilities charged their inmates for food and clothing, while providing substandard service. The income generated by inmate labor, however, was not sufficient to cover the high costs of operating correctional systems, despite persistent and intense efforts to make the system pay for itself.[17] Without independent oversight and monitoring, the convict labor system eventually succumbed to bribery and corruption.

Moreover, there was strong opposition to the convict lease system from organized labor, manufacturers, and farmers. This broad constituency opposed what was considered as unfair competition and pressed for legislation restricting the use of convict labor and convict-produced goods. Public opposition was also mobilized by reformers and religious groups who protested about the scandalous conditions found at many of the privately run facilities and in labor lease systems. State legislatures began investigating alleged incidents of mismanagement and cruelty within privatized institutions, resulting in modifications to the leasing system.[18]

An Executive Order signed by President Theodore Roosevelt in 1905 prohibited the use of convict labor on federal projects. In 1929 Congress passed the Hawes–Cooper Act permitting states to ban the importation of inmate products from other states.[19] Congress and state legislatures also passed laws during the Depression that further curtailed the use of inmates in private enterprise.

By the 1920s, the prevailing practice in American correctional agencies was to increase governmental involvement. The subsequent demise of the convict lease system eventually gave way to state-run institutions. Their operations and administrative functions were delegated to governmental agencies, authorized by statute, staffed by government employees, and funded solely by government.[20]

Since the early twentieth century and until more recently, the custom in all American correctional agencies has been to provide virtually all correctional services as governmental functions in institutions constructed and maintained at the government's expense.[21] In some program areas, rehabilitative services were provided by volunteer associations (religious and educational). Generally, private involvement in the provision of correctional services was diminished.

During the past thirty years, private enterprise again began to play an influential and expanded role in the functioning of the criminal justice system. In an attempt to manage escalating costs associated with supporting the many functions required to effectively run penal institutions, a trend gradually developed in the twentieth century for the contracting-out of prison services to both profit-making and not-for-profit firms. While prisons continued to contract out the provision of medical, dental, and psychological services, more services—such as food preparation, vocational training, and inmate transportation—were added. By the mid-1970s, federal, state, and municipal governments were again willing to expand their association with the private sector, moving beyond the conventional contractual relationship that became common in the early twentieth century. According to Alexis Durham, the 1970s ushered in a new phase in the development of private corrections, beginning with juvenile correctional operations:

> In 1976 RCA Services, a private company, assumed control of the Weaversville Intensive Treatment Unit located in North Hampton, Pennsylvania. This facility was designed to handle male delinquents. Although the private sector had long been involved in providing a wide range of correctional services . . . this was the first modern institution for serious offenders to be completely operated in what has become an increasingly lengthy line of such institutions in the American correctional system.[22]

The Weaversville Intensive Treatment Unit for Juvenile Delinquents is widely regarded as the first high-security institution that was entirely privately owned and operated under contract to the state. The second such institution did not appear until 1982, when the state of Florida turned over to the Eckerd Foundation the operation of the Okeechobee School for Boys.[23] The trend toward privately operated juvenile correctional facilities has continued, with over 40,000 youth now housed in privately operated juvenile facilities. It is noteworthy that these operations have not received nearly the level of scrutiny and criticism as have their adult counterparts. This may be due to the fact that some, but not all, are not-for-profit operations.

The U.S. Immigration and Naturalization Service (INS) was among the first governmental agencies to take advantage of the emerging market of private prison operators. At the end of 1984, the INS had contracts with two private companies for the detention of illegal aliens; by the end of 1988, the number of private INS detention facilities had grown to seven, housing roughly 800 of the 2,700 aliens in INS custody.[24] Also during this period, Corrections Corporations of America (CCA) was awarded a contract to manage the Hamilton County Jail in Chattanooga, Tennessee. This was followed by the first state-level contract award in 1985, when Kentucky contracted with the U.S. Corrections Corporation.

According to McDonald, these developments initially provoked little controversy or even notice, the likely reason being that private sector involvement in correctional management was still limited in size and scope.[25] The importance of these early contracts has been noted by Charles Thomas, a strong advocate of private prisons:

> The importance of these contract awards to the subsequent development of correctional privatization would be difficult to overestimate and the fact that all remain still in force today with the same management firms is not inconsequential for those who would be willing to accept this fact as at least an oblique performance indicator. Each provided a real world opportunity to test the hypothesis that contracting could yield meaningful benefits to government. Each also provided a valuable model that subsequent units of government could examine and improve upon in such critical areas as procurement strategies, the

formulation of sound contracts, and the creation of effective means of contract monitoring.[26]

Security adult institutions, once considered the near exclusive and inextricable preserve of government, emerged as one of the central issues debated among correctional agencies. Finally, in the last few years, governments have sought to contract out capital expenditure costs and operational services, including prison design, construction, and management.[27]

Thus, the pressure of increased incarceration rates combined with rising correctional costs enabled privatization of penal facilities to re-emerge as an acceptable political and correctional system operational concept. This re-emergence, however, has stirred considerable debate over the viability of privately operated prison facilities. The current enthusiasm for privatization is fueled by the prospect of more innovative, cost-effective prison management, including the anticipated private sector involvement in the financing of new prison construction. This enthusiasm is not shared by all. Much of the contention is reflected in the literature, especially with regard to the alleged advantages and disadvantages of private facility management.

THE DEBATE

There have been many claims by observers on the advantages and disadvantages of privatization. Dennis Cunningham has summarized the major reasons to either accept or reject the privatization concept (see Table 4-4).[28] These various reasons can be reduced to the overriding desire of many states and local governments to rapidly increase desperately needed prison bed capacity and to reduce prison operational costs. Others have raised the issue of whether private prisons can enhance the quality of care for inmates (including enhanced protection from harm for inmates and staff) and reduction in litigation. Thus far, there has been little need on the part of the private providers to argue that inmates incarcerated in privately operated prisons are more likely to be rehabilitated and less likely to recidivate, although such a claim was recently made in a Florida study.[29] Each of these claims that form the core of the debate on whether to privatize are discussed next.

Faster and Cheaper Bed Capacity

It is often cited that the major impetus behind the move toward privatization has been the dramatic increase in prison and jail population and the associated need to construct in a timely manner new and less costly prison and jail bed capacity. Contracting with the private sector allows prospective prisons to be financed, sited, and constructed more quickly and cheaply than government prisons. This flexibility is especially advantageous when a new facility is under consideration. Based on experience, it takes the government five to six years

Table 4-4 Public Strategies for Private Prisons

Reasons to Privatize

1. Private operators can provide construction financing options that allow the government client to pay only for capacity as needed in lieu of encumbering long-term debt.
2. Private companies offer modern state-of-the-art correctional facility designs that are staff-efficient to operate, built based upon value engineering specifications.
3. Private operators typically design and construct a new correctional facility in one-half the time of a comparable government construction project.
4. Private vendors provide government clients with the convenience and accountability of one entity for all compliance issues.
5. Private corrections management companies are able to mobilize rapidly and to specialize in unique facility missions.
6. Private corrections management companies provide economic development opportunities by hiring locally and, to the extent possible, purchasing locally.
7. Government can reduce or share its liability exposure by contracting with private corrections companies.
8. The government can retain flexibility by limiting the contract duration and by specifying facility mission.
9. Adding other service providers injects competition among the parties, both public and private organizations alike.

Reasons Not to Privatize

1. There are certain responsibilities that only the government should provide, such as public safety and environmental protection. There is a legal, political, and moral obligation of the government to provide incarceration. Major constitutional issues revolve around the deprivation of liberty, discipline, and preserving the constitutional rights of inmates. Related issues: use of force; loss of time credit; segregation.
2. Few companies available from which to choose.
3. Private operator inexperience with key corrections issues.
4. Operator may become a monopoly via political ingratiation, favoritism, and so on.
5. Government may lose the capability to perform the function over time.
6. The profit motive will inhibit the proper performance of duties. Private prisons have financial incentives to cut corners.
7. Procurement process is slow, inefficient, and open to risks.

SOURCE: Dennis Cunningham, Oklahoma Department of Corrections, Privatization Division, *Public Strategies for Private Prisons.* Paper presented at the Private Prison Workshop at the Institute on Criminal Justice, University of Minnesota Law School, January 1999.

to build a facility, while some private companies claim they can do it in two to three years (or less).

For example, the CCA built a 350-bed detention center in Houston for the Immigration and Naturalization Service (INS). CCA completed the project in five and a half months at a cost of $14,000 per bed. INS calculated construction to take two and a half years at a cost of $26,000 per bed.[30] In a comprehensive study of privatizing the District of Columbia's Department of Corrections, it was estimated that rebuilding several prison facilities would take the public sector five to six years while it would take the private sector only three to four years.[31]

Based on these and other reports, it seems clear that the private sector can add prison bed capacity faster and at less cost than most public entities. Cripe cited the numerous advantages advocates assert in support of private prison construction:

> Because private firms are not bound by governmental rules that tend to slow down prison construction, such as political pressures from unhappy neighbors, environmental hassles, and requirements of competed bidding and construction contracting, private firms have shown an ability to open new facilities more quickly. They claim they can also get the money to build new institutions more quickly from private investors or from lenders, while the government has to work more slowly, getting appropriations from the legislature or going through a bond issue process.[32]

On the other hand, Ira Robbins points out that privatization allows prisons to be built without the approval of the public.[33] For example, the construction costs of a privately operated facility can be lumped together in the state's prison operating budget as opposed to requiring the state to seek voter approval on a construction bond, as is usually the case. Contracting with the private sector allows prospective prisons to be financed, sited, and constructed more quickly and cheaply than government prisons. This flexibility is especially advantageous when a new facility is under consideration.

Reduced Operational Costs

Representatives of private sector firms assert they can save taxpayers more money by providing correctional services traditionally supplied by government at less cost. We have already noted that private entrepreneurs can build facilities faster and cheaper. However, the next claim is that they are also able to operate facilities more efficiently. This can be achieved by reducing the costs of labor associated with operational costs. Labor costs are controlled by reducing one or all three of the following personnel cost factors: (1) number of staff, (2) wages, and (3) fringe benefits. The private sector alleges that these costs can be contained or that, for the same dollar, more or at least better services can be provided.[34]

This point is the crux of the privatization movement. Prisons are extremely labor-intensive, with approximately 65 to 70 percent of the costs of operating a prison related to staff salaries, fringe benefits, and overtime. Controlling these costs is more difficult to achieve with unionized government workers. Private firms typically use nonunion labor, allowing for the lowest benefit packages. Overall, private firms claim that they can save 10 to 20 percent in prison operations largely due to efficiencies in labor costs.

Another, less powerful argument in favor of private contracting is that there is greater flexibility in the procurement process. It is argued that private sector contractors are not bound by the cumbersome and rigid government procurement system. Private vendors can purchase more quickly; maintain lower food, supplies, and equipment inventories; and negotiate better prices.[35]

It is by no means an uncontested fact that a private institution would be more cost-effective. It needs to be pointed out that the incentive to contain costs will be directly related to the type of contract structured:

> A public utilities or "pentagon" model reimbursement where a contractor receives costs plus a profit percentage would not necessarily provide an incentive to contain costs of service. On the other hand, a client charge may result in cost-overruns or even bankruptcy should the initial estimate prove wrong.[36]

One expense not normally included in the financial calculation of private firms is the cost to the government for monitoring contract performance. Constant monitoring of all aspects of internal performance is essential to a good contractual relationship, which may become expensive over time. If continual federal or state monitoring of private institutions is required for accountability purposes, the costs of monitoring will ultimately raise the price of privatized services. The potential costs of increased prison litigation are also rarely discussed by private prison advocates.

As a policy matter, opponents claim it is inappropriate to operate prisons based on a profit motive. In many instances, private prison operators are paid according to the number of inmates housed. Arguably, it is in the operator's financial interests to encourage lengthier sentences for inmates in order to keep bed spaces filled. If the private vendor enters into a contract based on a per-client charge, the profit margin and even the continued operation of the private facility is subsidized depending upon total population size. Firms driven by the profit motive could adversely influence prison population size by campaigning for longer sentences and stricter sentencing guidelines. Similarly, as private firms are in business to make a profit, high returns on their investments must be guaranteed. Critics of prison privatization argue that firms will cut corners, from using inferior construction materials to hiring inexperienced personnel, forsaking security and quality of service in the process.

Improved Quality of Service

In addition to the proposed cost savings and associated efficient services, one must also remember that the nation's prison and jail systems have been facing widespread allegations regarding the quality of care being afforded staff and inmates. In the 1980s and up to the present, most of the state prison systems as well the major urban jails have been under far-reaching consent decrees regarding medical, mental health, education, overcrowding, and protection from harm issues. There have also been major prison disturbances in New York, California, Illinois, and New Mexico, to name a few, that have added to the public perception that public prisons are not doing a good job in managing prisons.

However, one of the central concerns raised by critics of correctional privatization is that firms motivated by financial gain will make decisions that enhance profits at the expense of the rights and well-being of inmates.[37] History demonstrates that privately operated facilities have been plagued by problems associated with the quest for higher earnings. The profit motive produced such abominable conditions and exploitation that public agencies were forced to assume responsibility. The lack of contract supervision contributed to the squalid and inhumane conditions in privately run prisons. The current movement to reprivatize primary facility management assumes that modern entrepreneurs are somehow more benevolent and humanistic, so the exploitation of the past will not reoccur.[38] On the contrary, critics contend that privately managed facilities will bring new opportunities for corruption. Given poorly paid, undereducated, and inadequately trained staff, opponents question the professionalism and commitment privatized staff will bring to the job.

Proponents, on the other hand, suggest that present-day judicial activism provides control over private prison operations. The threat of inmate lawsuits and court-mandated consent decrees act as a deterrent to abusive behavior. Further arguments suggest that these kinds of abuses defeat the long-term interests of private contractors and can be avoided with careful monitoring mechanisms. Moreover, competition between firms will hold down costs and provide for superior service because contract renewals will depend on job performance. To date, the limited experience with privately managed prisons does not allow a thorough evaluation of public and private prisons in terms of overall quality of inmate services.

Legal Issues

Disagreements surrounding cost and efficiency may eventually be resolved with more complete data. Better contract monitoring and judicial oversight will curtail instances of exploitation and abuse of the inmate population. However, the legal ramifications of privatization pose challenging questions not easily rectified. Three complex issues stimulate heated debate on correctional privatization:

1. the propriety of private firms taking over state functions;
2. inmate rights and due process considerations; and
3. liability and accountability for state actions.

A fundamental issue is public responsibility for the well-being of society. It is often taken for granted that the apprehension and conviction of offenders is a public responsibility. Hence, the notion that convicted offenders should be the responsibility of private entrepreneurs motivated by profit seems contradictory.[39] The central question becomes whether government has the authority to contract away what is now widely regarded as a public function. Commenting on the issue, Durham states with some urgency that "if the transfer of responsibility to penal institutions is not carefully executed, the consequences may be disastrous. Beyond inconvenience and unanticipated costs, both public safety and inmate well-being may be at stake."[40]

At this time, it is clear the courts have decided that private prisons can be assigned the same management responsibilities as those undertaken by state and local government. This is not to say that government can wholly delegate its functions and duties to a private provider. Indeed, based on a number of recent incidents in private facilities, the courts will hold government responsible for actions taken by a private provider that violate an inmate's constitutional rights or put the prison staff, inmates, or surrounding community in harm's way.[41]

What has not yet been resolved is whether privatization will undermine or enhance prisoners' rights as compared to publicly operated systems.[42] The U.S. Constitution protects individuals against the violation of due process (Fifth and Fourteenth Amendments) as well as the related issue of cruel and unusual punishment (Eighth Amendment). The past few decades have witnessed a large volume of prison litigation concerning inmate rights and prison conditions that has resulted in most state correctional systems (or a facility within a state) operating under an imposed consent decree. The concern is whether private prisons operate in such a manner that the exposure to litigation against government is reduced.

There is a string of U.S. Supreme Court cases that have held that a person can only assert a denial of due process rights if that deprivation resulted from "state action."[43] The ultimate issue in determining whether an entity is subject to suit for violation of an individual's rights is whether the alleged infringement is attributable to the state.

A person acts under the "color of state law" only when exercising power possessed by virtue of state law, and made possible only because the wrongdoer is clothed with the authority of state law.[44] Federal civil rights law prohibits state officials or agencies from being named as defendants in their official capacities in civil suits if the plaintiffs seek monetary damages. The question remains whether the actions of private corrections facilities regulated by the state can be considered transformed into state actions.

Thus far, the courts have decided that persons who provide services to inmates under contract are not immune from litigation for constitutional violations.[45] What is yet to be settled is the propriety of private firms running entire correctional facilities and the broad legal or constitutional questions.[46]

The issues raised have practical implications in the day-to-day operations of a private correctional facility. Before entering into a contractual agreement with a private firm for the operation of a prison or jail, it would be necessary to identify whether the private company can be authorized to exercise force (even deadly force) to prevent escapes, to imprison citizens against their will, and to impose penalties on those who violate the regulations and rules of the institution. In the event private individuals are not allowed to enforce the rules and regulations of the institution, the likelihood of success of these corporations is obviously diminished. However, allowing a private prison to punish inmates who have violated institutional rules (which may differ from those of publicly operated facilities) without oversight by the state could be a denial of due process especially if the punishment entails the loss of good time that could serve to lengthen an inmate's period of imprisonment.

The other area of concern has to do with actual prison conditions, such as access to medical care, mental health services, work, and vocational and educational services; crowding; and protection from harm. A series of questions must be considered before full privatization of correctional facilities becomes commonplace.[47] They ask whether the contracting government agency will be liable for illegal actions of the contractor; who, if conditions in the contracted penal facility are found to violate constitutional requirements, will ultimately be responsible for their correction and held liable for damages; whether the contracting governmental agency can be rendered immune for not only the actions of the contractor but also for any negligence that results in the escape of prisoners or the financial mismanagement of the facility; and whether the contracting agency would be responsible for "bailing out" a bankrupt contractor. With no clear Supreme Court precedent on whether private prisons will come under the state action doctrine, prisoners' rights may ultimately depend on the nature of the contractual agreement between the state and the private operator.

A CLOSER LOOK
AT STATE PRISON PRIVATIZATION

Despite the level of debate in the United States, there is very little data on the cost-effectiveness of private prisons versus publicly operated facilities. To correct this lack of knowledge, a national survey was undertaken by the authors with funding from the U.S. Department of Justice's Bureau of Justice Assistance. The survey represents the first direct comparison of public and private prisons in the United States on a number of key dimensions.

Survey Methods

The survey methods were as follows. In late 1997, all known private correctional management firms were contacted and asked to participate in this survey. These firms were sent copies of the survey instrument and asked to distribute them among all their facilities.[48] The survey was based on a format used by the Bureau of Justice Statistics (BJS) for their five-year *Census of State and Federal Correctional Facilities.*[49] By mirroring the BJS 1995 survey, comparisons could be directly made between the public prison population as of 1995 and the private prison population as of December 31, 1997.

Information from privately operated state facilities was gathered during the first quarter of 1998. Survey respondents were asked to provide pertinent information compiled during calendar year 1997 and, in many instances, detailed facts from December 31, 1997. Ten private companies were identified as currently managing at least one state prison in operation. Three of the ten management firms chose not to participate in the survey.[50] Those three firms were operating a total of five state facilities. The seven management firms that responded were identified as having seventy-six state facilities either in operation or under construction. Of those seventy-six state prison facilities, four were not open during the time frame covered by the instrument; and seven facilities did not return the questionnaire before data collection and analysis commenced. Three international facilities were identified by their operators as adult confinement prisons and, therefore, were not included in the data analysis, bringing the final tally to seven operators of sixty-five private prisons. The Corrections Corporation of America and Wackenhut, together, manage forty-nine of the sixty-five private state facilities identified.

Inmate and Facility Characteristics

Table 4-5 summarizes inmate characteristics for the sixty-five private facilities included in the National Survey of State Prison Privatization. There were 46,120 inmates housed in privately operated state prisons on December 31, 1997. Over 90 percent of those inmates housed in private state prisons were male, a percentage comparable to the inmate population at federal and state public facilities at mid-year 1995. As in public facilities, over 60 percent of all persons held in private state facilities were black or Hispanic. A higher proportion of inmates housed at private state facilities were black (43.9 percent), followed by white (31.7 percent) and Hispanic (20.7 percent).

The private sector has yet to penetrate the market for housing maximum/close custody prisoners. Ninety-three percent of persons incarcerated at private state prisons were medium- and low-custody inmates (Table 4-5). Only two facilities out of sixty-five were identified as maximum-security institutions, with one located outside of the United States (Table 4-6).[51] Medium-security institutions accounted for the largest number of private state facilities sampled: thirty-eight of sixty-five (58 percent) were medium security, with twenty-five (38 percent) being minimum- or low-level security institutions. Approximately three out of four facilities housed exclusively male inmates; this is not surprising given the composition of the private prison populations. Seventeen percent of the private state facilities housed both sexes, with 8 percent holding females only. Approximately 84 percent of the male inmate population was housed in exclusively male facilities; the other 16 percent resided in facilities that housed both sexes. The female private prison population was split evenly between females-only institutions (50.6 percent) and mixed housing (49.4 percent).

Staffing and Employment

Private facilities reported a total of 13,444 regular and nonpayroll support staff (Table 4-7). Correctional officers accounted for 63 percent of employees at private facilities in 1997; a similar proportion was employed as security staff at public correctional facilities. Professional treatment staff accounted for 12 percent of private correctional employees, followed by clerical (8 percent), educational (6 percent), and maintenance and food service (5.5 percent).

Table 4-5 Inmate Characteristics at Public Facilities at Mid-Year 1995 and Private Facilities as of December 31, 1997

Inmate Characteristic	PUBLIC FACILITIES[a]		PRIVATE FACILITIES	
	N	%	N	%
Number of inmates	1,023,572	100.0	46,120	100.0
Totals				
Males	961,210	94.0	42,215	91.5
Females	62,362	6.0	3,905	8.5
Under age 18	5,309	0.5	180	0.4
Custody level				
Maximum/close/high	202,174	19.8	2,111	4.6
Medium	415,688	40.6	22,674	49.2
Minimum/low	366,277	35.8	20,379	44.2
Not classified	39,483	3.9	956	2.1
Race[b]				
White	363,918	35.5	14,620	31.7
Black	488,222	47.7	20,268	43.9
Hispanic	147,365	14.4	9,550	20.7
American Indian/Alaskan Natives	10,519	1.0	494	1.1
Asian/Pacific Islander	8,436	0.8	291	0.6
Not reported	5,112	0.5	897	1.9

[a]Data for mid-year 1995 includes federal and state correctional facilities.

[b]The number of inmates of Hispanic origin is underreported for public facilities. In 28 federal facilities, race but not Hispanic origin was reported for 21,563 inmates.

SOURCE: BJS, *Census of State and Federal Correctional Facilities, 1995* (1997).

Private state prisons have higher proportions of minority employees as compared to public prisons. Fifty-three percent of the staff at private facilities was white, while 32 percent of the inmate population was white. At public facilities, the corresponding figures in 1995 were 71 percent payroll staff to 36 percent inmate population. The racial composition of staff to inmates was similar for blacks at both types of facilities. Blacks comprised 22 percent of the staff and 44 percent of inmates at private state prisons versus 20 percent of staff and 47 percent of inmates at the public facilities.

Hispanics, on the other hand, comprised 14 percent of the inmate population at federal and state public facilities but only 6 percent of the correctional staff. Among the sixty-five private state facilities surveyed, Hispanics made up 21 percent of the inmate population and 18 percent of the staff (see Tables 4-5 and 4-7). When the three facilities located in Puerto Rico were excluded from the analysis, the private facilities still had a larger percentage of Hispanic staff (13 percent staff to 17 percent inmate population) than did the public facilities.[52]

TABLE 4-6 Characteristics of Private Facilities by Level of Security as of December 31, 1997

	NUMBER OF CONFINEMENT FACILITIES BY SECURITY LEVEL							
	TOTALS		MAXIMUM		MEDIUM		MINIMUM	
Facility Characteristic	N	%	N	%	N	%	N	%
All Facilities	65	100.0	2	3.1	38	58.5	25	38.5
Sex of Inmates Housed								
Males only	49	75.4	2	3.1	29	44.6	18	27.7
Females only	5	7.7	0	0.0	3	4.6	2	3.1
Both sexes	11	16.9	0	0.0	6	9.2	5	7.7
Function								
General adult population	54	83.1	1	1.5	37	56.9	16	24.6
Boot camp	0	0.0	0	0.0	0	0.0	0	0.0
Reception/diagnosis	5	7.7	0	0.0	3	4.6	2	3.1
Medical treatment	3	4.6	0	0.0	2	3.1	1	1.5
Alcohol/drug treatment	14	21.5	1	1.5	6	9.2	7	10.8
Youthful offenders	2	3.1	1	1.5	1	1.5	0	0.0
Work/prerelease	14	21.5	0	0.0	6	9.2	8	12.3
Returned to custody	12	18.5	0	0.0	6	9.2	7	10.8
Other[a]	5	7.7	1	1.5	3	4.6	1	1.5
Age of Facility[b]								
Less than 10 years	58	89.2	2	3.1	36	55.4	20	30.8
10–19 years	0	0.0	0	0.0	0	0.0	0	0.0
20–49 years	5	7.7	0	0.0	1	1.5	4	6.2
50–99 years	1	1.5	0	0.0	1	1.5	0	0.0
100 years or more[c]	1	1.5	0	0.0	0	0.0	1	1.5
Average Daily Population								
Less than 500 inmates	28	43.1	0	0.0	10	15.4	18	27.7
500–999 inmates	27	41.5	0	0.0	22	33.8	5	7.7
1,000–2,499 inmates	10	15.4	2	3.1	6	9.2	2	3.1
2,500 inmates or more	0	0.0	0	0.0	0	0.0	0	0.0

Note: Figures add to more than the total number of facilities because facilities may have more than one function.
[a]Includes U.S. Marshal Service, pretrial/posttrial federal offenders, prearraignment, and community service.
[b]Refers to the number of years between the date of original construction and the survey year.
[c]The oldest privately operated facility is operated by CiviGenics, which originally opened as a hospital in 1896.

Table 4-8 summarizes employee salary information and the number of employees hired, terminated, drug-tested, and unionized. The average salary for correctional officers ranged from $14,824 to $18,785. The starting salaries were not much lower ($12,958 to $16,640), suggesting that most of the private facility staff were new hires. By contrast, the average minimum starting salary in the public sector was $20,888.[53] Public correctional agencies in the South, where most of the private facilities were located, had an

TABLE 4-7 Persons Employed in Public Facilities at Mid-Year 1995 and at Private State Facilities as of December 31, 1997

Personnel Characteristic	PUBLIC		PRIVATE	
	N	%	N	%
All Facilities	347,320	100.0	13,344	100.0
Rate per 100 inmates	34		29	
All Staff[a]				
Administrative	9,509	2.8	554	4.2
Correctional/security	220,892	65.4	8,427	63.2
Clerical support	27,383	8.1	1,060	7.9
Educational	11,020	3.3	774	5.8
Professional treatment	45,291	13.4	1,604	12.0
Maintenance and food service	23,605	7.0	735	5.5
Other	0	0	190	1.4
Race[b]				
White	232,382	71.3	6,954	53.0
Black	65,513	20.0	2,932	22.4
Hispanic	20,702	6.3	2,364	18.0
Native American/other[c]	6,576	2.0	131	1.0
Asian/Pacific Islander	NA	NA	60	0.5
Not reported	974	0.3	669	5.1

[a]A total of 241 employees were not designated by employment category at 20 facilities.

[b]Includes only payroll staff for public facilities. Private facilities data include nonpayroll staff when given by private operator: 21 private facilities included a total of 200 nonpayroll staff in their racial breakdowns. Two facilities with 669 payroll staff could not provide a racial breakdown of staff.

[c]Figures for 1995 include American Indians, Alaskan Natives, Asians, and Pacific Islanders.

SOURCE: BJS, *Census of State and Federal Correctional Facilities, 1995* (1997).

average starting salary of $18,127, which was much higher than that of the private facilities.

Inmate Violations and Death

Table 4-9 compares the number of major infractions per 1,000 inmates, including assaults, riots, fires, and other disturbances at public and private institutions. The survey revealed a greater number of inmate-on-inmate assaults per 1,000 at private prisons (thirty-five) than at public facilities (twenty-five). Assaults resulting in inmate deaths were extremely rare at both types of institutions. Rates of staff assaults, riots, fires, and other disturbances were comparable for private and public facilities. A total of forty-five escapes occurred at fourteen private facilities between January 1, 1997, and December 31, 1997. The rate of escapes per 1,000 inmates for all of the sixty-five private facilities was 1.06. The 1995 *Census of State and Federal Correctional Facilities* reported that the number of inmate deaths rose from 2.4 per 1,000 state inmates in 1990 to 3.2 in 1995. The death

TABLE 4-8 Employee Characteristics of Private Facilities, January 1 to December 31, 1997

Contractor	Facilities	Starting Salary	Staff Hired	Staff Terminated	Facilities That Drug-Test	Employees Drug-Tested	Unionized Facilities
Cornell Corrections	3	min: $14,580 max: $16,598 avg: $15,537	58	33	1	125	0
Correctional Services Corporation	3	min: $14,040 max: $20,800 avg: $17,333	224	132	3	150[a]	0
Corrections Corporation of America	27	min: $13,200 max: $24,600 avg: $17,246	4,454[b]	1,327[c]	24	3,029[d]	1 (U.S.)
CiviGenics	2	min: $16,000 max: $16,000 avg: $16,000	9	0	0	0	0
Management Training Corporation	3	min: $16,640 max: $22,425 avg: $18,665	111	89	3	223	0
U.S. Corrections Corporation	5	min: $14,040 max: $17,200 avg: $14,824	271	257	4	342	0
Wackenhut Corporation	22	min: $12,958 max: $35,173 avg: $18,785[e]	3,022	1,750	20	2,735[f]	2 (Aus.) 1 (Eng.)

[a]Based on 2 facilities reporting.
[b]Based on 25 facilities reporting.
[c]Based on 24 facilities reporting.
[d]Based on 17 facilities reporting. Three facilities do not test; 7 facilities missing data.
[e]Based on 21 facilities reporting. One international facility reported data in British pounds.
[f]Based on 19 facilities reporting. Two facilities do not test; 1 facility missing data.

TABLE 4-9 Major Incidents in Public Facilities Between July 1, 1994, and June 30, 1995, and in Private Facilities During Calendar Year 1997

Inmate Violation	NUMBER OF VIOLATIONS		NUMBER OF VIOLATIONS PER 1,000 INMATES[a]	
	Public	Private	Public	Private
Totals	46,365	2,357	45.3	50.5
Assaults on inmates	25,948	1,617	25.4	35.1
Resulting inmate deaths	82	1	0.1	0.0
Assaults on staff	14,165	584	13.8	12.7
Resulting staff deaths	14	0	0.0	0.0
Riots[b]	317	12	0.3	0.3
Fires	816	29	0.8	0.6
Other disturbances	1,808	56	1.8	1.2
			0.0	0.0
Total deaths	3,311	30	3.2	0.7
Homicides by other inmates	82	1	0.1	0.0
Suicides	169	1	0.2	0.0
AIDS	1,111	4	1.1	0.1
Natural causes	1,186	21	1.2	0.5
Other causes	113	3	0.1	0.1

Note: Excludes tickets, official warnings, and other minor incidents.

[a]Based on average daily population.

[b]Includes only incidents that had five or more inmates participating, that required the intervention of additional or outside assistance, and that resulted in serious injury or significant property damage. Other causes include accidents, homicides, and other deaths.

SOURCE: BJS, *Census of State and Federal Correctional Facilities, 1995* (1997).

rate at privately operated prisons was considerably lower at 0.7 per 1,000 inmates.

None of these comparisons can be used to conclude that either private or public prisons are superior, as this analysis could not control for all the myriad of factors that influenced these performance measures. Later in this chapter, however, a reanalysis of the private and public facilities is conducted controlling for only facilities that are medium and minimum security.

The previous analysis does suggest that private facilities do not differ substantially from the publicly operated facilities with three possible exceptions. First, the number of staff assigned to private facilities per inmate population is approximately 15 percent lower than at public facilities (34 per 100 inmates in public versus 29 per 100 inmates in private facilities). Second, management information system (MIS) capabilities appear to be lacking. And third, there is a higher rate of major incidents at the private versus the public facilities.

Recognizing that the 1995 public facility survey included all types of facilities and that the private facilities were primarily medium- and minimum-security

TABLE 4-10 Major Incidents in Public and Private Medium
and Minimum Facilities

	NUMBER OF VIOLATIONS		RATE PER 1,000 INMATES[a]	
Types of Violations	Private 1997	Public 1995	Private 1997	Public 1995
Totals	2,103	18,710	48.0	29.6
Assaults on inmates	1,469	12,721	33.5	20.2
Resulting inmate deaths	1	29	0.0	0.0
Assaults on staff	537	5,182	12.2	8.2
Resulting staff deaths	0	12	0.0	0.0
Riots[b]	12	172	0.3	0.3
Fires	29	444	0.7	0.7
Other disturbances	56	150	1.3	0.2
Total deaths	29	1,711	0.7	2.7
Homicides by other inmates	1	31	0.0	0.0
Suicides	1	65	0.0	0.1
AIDS	4	565	0.1	0.9
Natural causes	20	1,001	0.5	1.7
Other causes	3	49	0.1	0.1

Note: Excludes tickets, official warnings, and other minor incidents.

[a]Based on average daily population.

[b]Includes only incidents that had five or more inmates participating, that required the intervention of additional or outside assistance, and that resulted in serious injury or significant property damage. Other causes include accidents, homicides, and other deaths.

SOURCE: BJS, *Census of State and Federal Correctional Facilities, 1995* (1997).

facilities, a better analysis would attempt to make direct comparisons between the medium- and minimum-security public facilities and the same type of private facilities.

Table 4-10 repeats the misconduct analysis but deletes surveys of public facilities that identified themselves as maximum- or higher-custody levels. In this comparison, the privately operated facilities have a much higher rate of inmate-on-staff and staff-on-staff assaults, and other disturbances. These differences may be related to other factors such as reporting standards or the fact that most correctional facilities experience management difficulties when they are newly opened. The CCA Youngstown facility is a good example of a facility with such difficulties.[54] However, one must also entertain the notion that insufficient training and the lack of qualified staff in key positions may be a valid explanation for these differences. This would be consistent with the claims of critics of privatization who charge that private prisons are inadequately staffed by inexperienced and poorly trained correctional officers, in which case, coupled with a lack of programs and work assignments, higher rates of misconduct would predictably occur. In any event, the notion that privately operated prisons are safer or better managed than publicly operated facilities is not supported by these results.

THE FUTURE OF PRIVATIZATION

Private facilities perform at the same level as public facilities. Although they tend to house a higher proportion of minimum-custody inmates in relatively new facilities, private facilities tend to have the same staffing patterns; provide the same levels of work, education, and counseling programs for inmates; and have the same rates of serious inmate misconduct as public facilities. The few credible impact studies also show few differences and more similarities between the two methods of operations. What seems to have evolved in the United States is a model that essentially mimics the public model but achieves modest cost savings, at least initially, by making modest reductions in staffing patterns, fringe benefits, and other labor-related costs. But there is no evidence that private prisons will have a dramatic impact on how prisons operate. The promise of 20 percent savings in operational costs has simply not materialized. Even if it had, the limited market share of less than 5 percent demands a limited impact on prison budgets.

For example, assume that 10 percent of a state's prison system becomes privatized and that each private prison produces a 10 percent savings in operational costs. Even at this level, the overall impact on the state prison budget would be only 1 percent (10 percent of 10 percent is 1 percent). This is not a number that will revolutionize modern correctional practices.

But it now appears that achieving even a 10 percent market share will prove to be increasingly difficult for the following reasons. First, there is a growing number of well-publicized stories of poor performance in Texas, Oregon, Colorado, Louisiana, and South Carolina. Most recently, the problems associated with the CCA-operated Northeast Ohio Corrections Center have dramatized how badly a privatized prison can be operated. In this facility, sixteen inmates were stabbed, two were murdered, and six escaped in less than a year of operations. Operational weaknesses were linked to inexperienced staff, inadequate training, and a willingness to accept inmates from the District of Columbia who should not have been transferred to the facility.[55] If nothing else, the private sector has shown that it is equally capable of mismanaging prisons as the public sector.

These recent problems suggest the "sales division" of the private sector may well be outstripping the "production division." It may be that private prisons will face increasing difficulties in expanding their market simply because they, like the public sector, are finding it more difficult to recruit competent staff.

Although promises of superiority of privatization as compared to the public sector have not been realized, the mere presence of private facilities has had a significant impact on traditional prison operations. Gerald Gaes and his colleagues acknowledge that privatization has been successful in that it has forced the public sector to re-examine how it does its business.[56] Certainly in those markets where the correctional officer salaries and fringe benefits have been excessive, privatization has fostered a re-examination of those costs that has often led to cost savings. In this sense, privatization has served as a catalyst for change by demonstrating other means for doing the business of corrections. But these cost savings innovations, as limited as they are, should not be the sole agenda.

It would be extremely interesting and productive for the private sector, in a partnership with the public sector, to become the vehicle for testing far more substantive changes in correctional policy in a number of areas—and not just in prisons and jails. For example, an extremely promising strategy would be for the private sector to test the long-term effects of state-of-the-art correctional programming in the areas of education, vocational training, and various forms of counseling—both in prison and after release—in reducing recidivism. The flexibility of the private sector would also allow for testing of the effects of reducing prison terms and other correctional policies on a limited basis. Finally, new management techniques, staff training, and facility designs could be tested by the private sector under controlled conditions. All such innovations would be directed at reducing the use and ineffectiveness of current correctional practices rather than producing a less expensive but just as ineffective system.

NOTES

* The survey data presented in this chapter was supported by a grant funded by the U.S. Department of Justice, Bureau of Justice Assistance, which is a component of the Office of Justice Programs (Grant No. 97-DD-BX-0026). Points of view or opinions in this chapter are those of the authors and do not necessarily represent the official position or policies of the United States Department of Justice.

1. Lawrence F. Travis III, Edward J. Latessa, and Gennaro F. Vito, "Private Enterprise and Institutional Corrections: A Call for Caution," *Federal Probation* 49, 4 (1985): 11–16.

2. General Accounting Office, *Privatization: Lessons Learned by State and Local Governments* (Washington, DC: GAO, 1997; GAO/GGD-97-48).

3. Douglas McDonald, Elizabeth Fournier, and Malcolm Russell-Einhorn, *Private Prison in the United States: An Assessment of Current Practice* (Cambridge, MA: Abt Associates, 1998).

4. McDonald et al., *Private Prison in the United States: An Assessment of Current Practice.*

5. Charles W. Thomas, *Private Prisons Project* (Gainesville, FL: Center for Studies in Criminology and Law, University of Florida, 1998). http://web.crim.ufl.ed/pcp.

6. Malcolm M. Feeley, "The privatization of Prisons in Historical Perspective," *Criminal Justice Research Bulletin* 6, 2, pp. 1–10.

7. During the North American phase of transportation, some 50,000 convicts were shipped across the Atlantic, where they were sold as agricultural laborers.

8. David Ammons, Richard Campbell, and Sandra Somoza, *The Option of Prison Privatization: A Guide for Community Deliberations* (Athens, GA: University of Georgia, 1992).

9. R. B. Pugh, *Imprisonment in Medieval England* (Cambridge, UK: Cambridge University Press, 1968).

10. Philip A. Ethridge and James W. Marquart, "Private Prisons in Texas: The New Penology for Profit," *Justice Quarterly* 10, 1.

11. Robert D. McCrie, "Private Correction: The Delicate Balance," in Gary Bowman et al., *Privatizing Correctional Institutions* (New Brunswick, NJ: Transaction Publishers, 1993).

12. Clair A. Cripe, *Legal Aspects of Correctional Management* (Gaithersburg, MD: Aspen Publications, 1997), p. 378.

13. Robert D. McCrie, "Private Correction: The Delicate Balance," p. 24.

14. Kenneth Lamott, *Chronicles of San Quentin: The Biography of a Prison* (New York: David McKay Co., 1961), pp. 74, 78.

15. The modern "penitentiary," based on the ideas of Jeremy Bentham in England, was first established in Philadelphia and New York in the United States. It became the prototype of prison reform efforts in the late eighteenth and early nineteenth centuries. Solitary confinement for personal reflection combined with hard labor became the cornerstones of this new approach.

16. Ethridge and Marquart identify other forms of private inmate labor such as the piece-rate system and public account system. Under the piece-rate system, inmates worked inside prison walls under the supervision of state employees. In the public account system, prisoners worked under state supervision and produced goods for state institutions. However, the convict lease system was considered the most profitable, and the most brutal and corrupt, of all inmate labor systems.

17. Malcolm M. Feeley, "The Privatization of Prisons in Historical Perspective."

18. Robert McCrie, in "Private Correction: The Delicate Balance," refers to the case of the privatized Huntsville prison in Texas, which was the subject of a legislative investigation into prison conditions. The investiga-

tion resulted in modifications to the leasing system in which the state maintained control of the penitentiary and convicts but continued contracting arrangements with private interests beginning in 1883.

19. Ammons et al., *The Option of Prison Privatization: A Guide for Community Deliberations,* pp. 4–5.

20. Clair A. Cripe, *Legal Aspects of Correctional Management,* p. 380.

21. Health services was the exception. Smaller jails and prisons could not economically provide the full range of specialized care by competing for staff in the health-care market. These services were usually contracted out with local hospitals.

22. Alexis M. Durham III, "The Future of Correctional Privatization: Lessons from the Past," in Gary Bowman et al., *Privatizing Correctional Institutions* (New Brunswick, NJ: Transaction Publishers, 1993), p. 33.

23. Charles Logan and Sharla Rausch, "Punishment for Profit: The Emergence of Private Enterprise Prisons," *Justice Quarterly* 2, 3 (1985): 303–318.

24. Douglas C. McDonald, "Public Imprisonment by Private Means: The Re-emergence of Private Prisons and Jails in the United States, the United Kingdom, and Australia," *British Journal of Criminology* 34 (1994): 29–48.

25. In addition to juvenile and INS detention centers, private firms since the late 1960s have established early sites with various low-security facilities, and in the "less visible" regions of the adult and juvenile penal systems, such as operations of community treatment centers and halfway houses. See Douglas C. McDonald, "Public Imprisonment by Private Means: The Re-emergence of Private Prisons and Jails in the United States, the United Kingdom, and Australia," p. 30.

26. Charles W. Thomas, Testimony Regarding Correctional Privatization, presented before The Little Hoover

Commission of the State of California, August 21, 1997.

27. David Yarden, "Prisons, Profits, and the Private Sector Solution," *American Journal of Criminal Law* 21, 1 (Fall 1993): 325–334.

28. Dennis Cunningham, *Public Strategies for Private Prisons.* Paper presented at the Private Prison Workshop at the Institute on Criminal Justice, University of Minnesota Law School, January 1999.

29. Charles W. Thomas, "Issues and Evidence from the U.S.," in Stephen T. Easton (ed.), *Privatizing Correctional Services* (British Columbia: Vancouver, 1998), pp. 15–61.

30. David Yarden, "Prisons, Profits, and the Private Sector Solution," p. 328.

31. James Austin, *District of Columbia Department of Corrections Long-Term Options Study* (Washington, DC: National Institute of Corrections, January 31, 1997).

32. Clair A. Cripe, *Legal Aspects of Correctional Management,* p. 384. Privately operated facilities for juveniles tend to be small and residential, with flexible programming catering to individual needs. See Robert D. McCrie, "Three Centuries of Criminal Justice Privatization in the United States," in Gary Bowman et al., *Privatizing the United States Justice System* (Jefferson, NC: McFarland & Co., 1992).

33. Ira P. Robbins, "The Case Against the Prison-Industrial Complex," *Public Interest Law Review* (Winter 1997): 23–44.

34. Travis et al., "Private Enterprise and Institutional Corrections: A Call for Caution," p. 13.

35. Ammons et al., *The Option of Prison Privatization: A Guide for Community Deliberations,* p. 10.

36. Travis et al., "Private Enterprise and Institutional Corrections: A Call for Caution," p. 14.

37. Alexis M. Durham III, *Crisis and Reform: Current Issues in American Punishment* (Boston: Little, Brown, 1994).

38. Donald B. Walker, "Privatization in Corrections," in Peter C. Kratcoski (ed.), *Correctional Counseling and Treatment* (Prospect Heights, IL: Waveland Press, 1994).

39. Ibid., p. 582.

40. Alexis M. Durham III, "The Future of Correctional Privatization: Lessons from the Past," p. 43.

41. John L. Clark, *Inspection and Review of the Northeast Ohio Correctional Center* (Washington, DC: Office of the Corrections Trustee for the District of Columbia, November 25, 1998); Eric Schosser, "The Prison-Industrial Complex," *The Atlantic Monthly* 283 (1998): 51–80.

42. Charles W. Thomas, "How Correctional Privatization Redefines the Legal Rights of Prisoners," *The Privatization Review* 6, 1 (Winter 1991): 38–55.

43. David Yarden, "Prisons, Profits, and the Private Sector Solution," p. 331.

44. Ira P. Robbins, "Privatization of Corrections: Defining the Issues," *Judicature* 69 (1987): 324–331, or *Federal Probation* 50 (1987): 24–30.

45. The leading case on this is *West v. Atkins,* 108 S. Ct. 2250 (1988). The case addresses the question of whether private persons under contract with the state can be sued under section 1983, or whether only public employees can be sued under this federal law. By deciding that such persons can be held liable and are acting under the "color of the law" when performing services, the court expanded the number and categories of individuals who may be sued under section 1983. In 1997 the Supreme Court held that private prison guards employed by a private firm are not entitled to qualified immunity from suit by prisoners charging a section 1983 violation (*Richardson v. McKnight*).

46. Clair A. Cripe, *Legal Aspects of Correctional Management,* p. 394.

47. Travis et al., "Private Enterprise and Institutional Corrections: A Call for Caution."

48. Each management firm was also asked to categorize the type of facility in operation (that is, state prison, jail, juvenile, detention, or community). This combined with information from secondary sources—such as Charles W. Thomas, *Private Adult Correctional Facility Census: Tenth Edition* (Gainesville, FL: Private Corrections Project, 1997), and George Camp and Camille Camp, *The Corrections Yearbook: 1997* (South Salem, NY: Criminal Justice Institute, 1997)—allowed us to distinguish state prisons from other types.

49. The Bureau of Justice Statistics is a branch of the U.S. Department of Justice. For comparative purposes, data from the BJS 1995 *Census* are presented together with NCCD's 1997 figures.

50. One private operator did not participate because of pending litigation. The other two did not respond to our requests.

51. Both maximum-security institutions are operated by Wackenhut Corporation. However, a number of other institutions do house maximum-custody inmates but identify themselves at a lower security level.

52. Three privately operated state facilities located in Puerto Rico were filtered to eliminate their potential bias effects. The three prisons consisted of 877 Hispanic staff members and 2,267 Hispanic inmates. The results again indicate a higher staff-to-inmate ratio in private state prisons.

53. George Camp and Camille Camp, *The Corrections Yearbook: 1997* (South Salem, NY: Criminal Justice Institute, 1997).

54. John L. Clark, *Inspection and Review of the Northeast Ohio Correctional Center.*

55. Ibid.

56. Gerald G. Gaes, Scott D. Camp, and William G. Saylor, "Appendix 2: Comparing the Quality of Publicly and Privately Operated Prisons: A Review," in D. McDonald, E. Fournier, M. Russell-Einhorn, and S. Crawford (eds.), *Private Prisons in the United States: An Assessment of Current Practice* (Boston: Abt Associates, 1998), pp. 1–38.

5

■

Doing Time

WAREHOUSING PRISONERS

Convicted primarily of property and drug crimes, 1.3 million prisoners and another 600,000 jailed inmates are being crowded into human (or inhuman) warehouses where they are increasingly deprived, restricted, isolated, and consequently embittered and alienated from conventional worlds and where less and less is being done to prepare them for their eventual release. As a result, most of them are rendered incapable of returning to even a meager conventional life after prison. Because most will be released within two years, we should be deeply concerned about what happens to them during their incarceration. As will be noted in Chapter 7, approximately 500,000 prisoners will be released from prison each year after having completed some portion of their sentence. The question to be answered is: what has been the nature of their prison experience?

Prisons have been called warehouses for decades, but in earlier periods the label was misleading. In most prisons in the first half of the twentieth century, prisoners were involved in complex prison societies where they performed all the essential tasks to operate the prison.[1] They cooked and served the meals; washed the clothing; fixed the plumbing, electrical wiring, and appliances; painted the buildings; tended the boiler; landscaped the grounds; delivered most of the medical services; and kept all the records. They worked in prison industries, making "jute" clothes, furniture, license plates, or other commodities consumed by the state. Prison staff oversaw all these activities and kept track of the convicts, but convicts supplied most of the labor.[2]

In addition, convicts played all the sports possible within limits imposed by the physical plant: baseball, football, basketball (when there was a court), handball (there was always a wall for this), boxing, tennis (occasionally there was a court), and even marbles. They carried on the favorite convict pastime, "shucking and jiving"—that is, telling stories about their and others' exploits, mostly in crime, drugs, and sex. They "wheeled and dealed"; they smuggled food from the kitchen and ran sandwich and other food businesses; made prison brew—pruno—which required sugar, yeast, fruit, and some place to stash it during fermentation (a stash was easy to locate, because prunes were such smelly stuff); or bought or sold any contraband that they could steal, smuggle in, or manufacture: food, coffee, stingers (to heat water with), special clothing items, radios, phonographs, typewriters, paper, illegal drugs, and even nutmeg (which gives one a cheap high when several spoonfuls are swallowed). Some participated in the special prison sexual life with its "punks," "queens," and "jockers."

Collectively, prisoners developed their own self-contained society, with a pronounced stratification system, a strong convict value system, unique patterns of speech and bodily gestures, and an array of social roles: "right guys," "politicians," "crazies," "regulars," "punks," "queens," "stool pigeons," and "hoosiers." Importantly, their participation in this world with its own powerful value system, the convict code, gave them a sense of pride and dignity. It was them against what they perceived as a cruel prison system and corrupt society.

The prison administration tolerated, even encouraged, most of the convict activities and their social organization because these features promoted a high degree of order within the prison. Rarely did the administration have to intervene to maintain control over the inmates. The convicts ran the prison and kept the peace. There was not much emphasis on reformation or "rehabilitation," and most inmates left prison without having improved or acquired skills for living a conventional life. However, society was more accepting of the ex-convict than it is now, and apparently most did not return to prison.[3]

THE DEVELOPMENT
OF THE CONTEMPORARY PRISON

Immediately after World War II, many state prison systems adopted the rehabilitative ideal and attempted to change their "big house" prisons into "correctional institutions."[4] In the "big houses" like Stateville, Illinois, and Jackson, Michigan, tough authoritarian wardens watched over populations of prisoners who, for the most part, did their time immersed in the prison society just described. In correctional institutions (which became the new name for prisons), offenders were imprisoned not for punishment but for rehabilitation. During the 1950s and 1960s, prisoners were sentenced under "indeterminate" sentence systems, which granted prison and parole board officials considerable discretion over when an inmate was to be released. Inmates were expected to be involved in a variety of treatment programs and were released when parole boards decided the inmate had responded to treatment. However, a variety of factors, particularly the lack of sufficient funds, undermined the delivery of rehabilitation, and consequently the rehabilitation model never was implemented as designed.

The Demise of Rehabilitation

The whole concept of treatment presumed that inmates had deficiencies that could be treated within a prison environment. By the late 1960s and early 1970s, many observers of the rehabilitative penal system began to question this assumption. Specifically, a number of questionable, discriminatory, and even illegal practices were being carried on in the name of rehabilitation and through the margins of discretion given prison administrators within the indeterminate sentence system.[5] Adding to the growing criticism of the rehabilitation model, criminologists who had conducted or reviewed studies found that prison-based rehabilitative efforts in prison did not work as well as they had hoped.[6] In general, they found that prisoners who participated in a wide range of rehabilitative programs were rearrested at the same rate as those who did not. Even when programs were found to be "effective," they only reduced the recidivism rate by 5 to 10 percent from that of inmates who did not participate in such programs.

Consequently, in the early 1970s, "liberal" reformers sought to abolish indeterminate sentence systems and replace them with the short and uniform sentences known as "determinate" sentencing. In the mid-1970s, as these efforts were beginning to produce some changes in sentencing statutes and policies across the country, conservatives took up the issue of criminal justice and also called for an end to not only the indeterminate sentence systems but all prison rehabilitation. Unlike the liberal-minded reformers, however, conservatives objected to rehabilitation and indeterminate sentencing because inmates were being released too quickly, only to prey again on the public, they insisted.

As the divergent efforts of liberals and conservative critics both sought to eliminate indeterminate sentencing for different reasons during the late 1970s, public fear of crime rose significantly, and conservatives had their way. Most states instituted sentencing and parole policies that made sentences more uniform and considerably longer (mandatory minimum prison laws) for many crimes (for example, residential burglaries, crimes involving the use of guns or violence, drunk driving, sex crimes, and/or criminals with prior convictions—habitual offenders).[7] In addition, most of the states that shifted their emphasis from rehabilitation to punishment reduced funding for rehabilitative programs, including education and vocational training.

Reduction in prison programs has been fueled by politicians who create an artificial view for the public of prisons being akin to luxury hotels. Former Massachusetts Governor William Weld, a moderate Republican, stated at then Attorney General William Barr's *Summit on Corrections,* that life in prison should be "akin to a walk through the fires of hell."[8] Michigan State Representative Mike Goshka stated, during a debate on prison conditions, "Prisoners have it too easy now. They got color TVs, weight-lifting equipment, libraries. . . . We need to return to the concept that prison is not fun."[9] In 1998, then-governor of California Pete Wilson ordered his Department of Corrections to revoke numerous privileges, including weight-lifting equipment. Wilson explained that "prisoners are there to be punished, and hopefully rehabilitated. . . . They're not there to be entertained and catered to."[10]

Prison Crowding

As the conservative sentencing agenda took hold, prison populations began to escalate. Though prison construction has proceeded rapidly, it still has not kept up with the prisoner population explosion discussed in Chapter 1. In 1998, only twelve states were operating their prisons below their rated bed capacities, and of these dozen states, six were at 97 to 99 percent of their rated bed capacities. Prisons nationwide were overcrowded by a factor of 22 percent. Ten states reported populations exceeding 150 percent of capacity. And as of 1998, nearly 25,000 prisoners were being held in local jails because of prison crowding.[11]

These statistics mean that to accommodate the excessive inmate population, cells built to hold one inmate had to be converted to double cells. Similarly, classrooms, gymnasiums, and recreation rooms have been converted to dormitories, thus increasing inmate idleness and reducing the level of security and safety for staff and inmates. Many prisoners are being held in new, quickly constructed prisons that have only the bare facilities and infrastructure required to house and maintain prisoners on a long-term basis.

But these short-term efforts to expand the capacity of existing prisons have not been sufficient to meet the growing need for more prisons. Consequently, most states have embarked on record-level prison construction programs. Between 1990 and 1998, the bed capacity of the country's prison system increased by approximately 350,000 prison beds from 580,362 to 933,478.[12] As of 1998, there were 83,500 beds under construction, with another 86,500 in the planning stages.[13] The projected costs of this new construction is at least $10 billion and does not include site development and financing costs, which can serve to double or triple these direct construction costs. Large states like California, New York, and Texas have already spent billions of dollars on prison construction and will require even more billions of dollars to keep pace with the exploding prison population.

In attempting to meet the never-ending demand for more prison capacity, states have adopted three strategies. With respect to prison construction, states have adopted two strategies for siting new prisons. One approach has focused on expanding the capacity of existing prisons by appending new prisons to existing sites. This strategy is popular because it bypasses the problem of siting prisons in communities where they are not welcomed. The only requirements are open space adjacent to the current prison and water and sewage systems sufficient to handle the additional prison and staff populations. This strategy has resulted in the emergence of megaprisons where 5,000 to 10,000 prisoners can be accommodated at a single site.

The second strategy has prompted many states to return to an old tradition by placing most new prisons in remote areas, far from urban centers.[14] There are three main reasons to do this: land is cheaper and more available in remote areas; most urban and suburban populations do not want prisons in their midst; and many rural communities that are experiencing financial difficulties welcome the economic benefits of a prison, which will provide employment and tax revenues. Building prisons in remote areas leads to other consequences, however. Since the vast majority of prisoners come from cities, this means that relatives and friends visit prisoners at much greater expense and much less frequently (if at all). Also, many fewer organizations—such as schools, churches, unions, businesses, and voluntary support groups—are available to offer services to prisoners. These circumstances have greatly increased the isolation and deprivation of prisoners.

The third and relatively new approach is to contract out inmates to other states or to "speculative" prisons constructed and operated by private prison companies. As of 1998, there were nearly 80,000 inmates housed in so-called "contract" prisons. Most of these inmates (47,000) were sent out of state to private prisons in remote areas far away from their home states. The other category, as referenced earlier, is the use of local jails to house sentenced inmates (25,500).[15] This latter option is quite undesirable given that jails are ill-equipped to hold long-term inmates. They frequently do not have the level of programming, recreational space, and medical or mental health services required by the inmates.

The bottom line is that crowding is now an accepted way of operating a prison system. There are few lawsuits being filed that challenge the crowding situation. Legislators and other policy makers are reluctant to spend even more money to alleviate the crowding condition unless it becomes intolerable or a major disturbance occurs. With crowding, there is an associated decline in access to programs and increased tension that can often result in increasing levels of violence and death.

Racial Skewing

As noted in Chapter 1, the number of black and Hispanic prisoners continues to grow. In 1923, the first year that the racial makeup of the nation's prison system was counted, 31 percent of the inmates were black. By 1997, that figure had reached 49 percent black, with another 18 percent of Hispanic origin.[16]

A major reason for the continual increase in racial skewing of the prison population stems from the fact that most convicts come from inner-city, lower-class populations. Increasingly, the urban lower class is made up of blacks and Hispanics as the middle and upper classes (of all races) flee the urban centers to seek a better way of life in America's suburbs. The young males in these lower-class ethnic groups have extremely high rates of unemployment, in some cases close to 50 percent. While idle, they often become involved in social worlds of deviance and crime (such as using and dealing crack cocaine) that offend and threaten the classes above them, and they are arrested and incarcerated at an astounding rate. As noted in Chapter 1, black and Hispanic males have from three to eight times the rate of incarceration as whites.

Before the 1950s, black and white prisoners were segregated into separate prisons in the South and into separate sections of prisons in other parts of the country. The convict societies in the East, Midwest, and West were dominated by white prisoners, who were a majority, were racially prejudiced, and enforced "Jim Crow" segregation patterns. Formal segregation was ended by the 1960s, and the growing numbers of nonwhite prisoners began asserting themselves, sometimes violently, in prison social affairs. The solidarity of prisoner society was shattered, and prisoners divided into hostile factions, mostly based on race and location of residence before prison.[17] A small but significant faction of the current inmate population consists of murderous racial gangs that have dramatically altered the traditional prison world.

Court Intervention

In the early 1960s, Black Muslim prisoners in Illinois won a case on their right to follow practices related to their religion. Their successful litigation and a few subsequent cases expanded the remedies available to prisoners under a writ of habeas corpus and removed procedural obstacles to filing such writs in federal courts, thereby ending the court's "hands-off" policy toward prisoners grieving their treatment in prison.[18] More and more prisoners, inspired and aided by the protest movements of the late 1960s and early 1970s, sought remedy for their treatment, and increasingly the courts intervened into the management of prisons. In the late 1970s, the Prison Law Project of the ACLU filed a case in Alabama arguing that the "totality" of conditions in the state's prison system constituted cruel and unusual punishment. The federal court heard the case, held for the complainants, and oversaw the correction of the unconstitutional conditions. Other "in-total" cases have followed.[19]

As of 1998, thirty-five states plus the District of Columbia, Puerto Rico, and the Virgin Islands were under court order or consent decree to either limit prison crowding and/or improve conditions in either the entire prison system or a specific facility.[20] However, the passage of the Prison Litigation Reform Act (PLRA) by Congress in 1996 greatly altered the direction and scope of prison litigation. In effect, the PLRA requires there be a burden of proof by the litigants that the contested conditions of confinement violate the inmate's constitutional rights. Essentially, the PLRA makes it far more difficult to use litigation as a means for correcting deficient prisons conditions. In effect, the courts have moved from "hands off" to active intervention in the management of prisons.

Breakdown of Administrative Solidarity

As mentioned earlier, the big houses before World War II were traditionally run by an authoritarian warden. White rural males, often raised in the small towns near the prison, filled the ranks below this figure of authority. A formal, militarylike hierarchy and an informal, "good ol' boy" social organization with its special guard culture produced a great deal of solidarity among administration and staff.[21]

As states embraced the rehabilitation concept, along with the need to hire more staff for the rapidly expanding prison population, many treatment-oriented administrators and staff were hired or advanced in prison agencies. As noted earlier, during this time, prisons tried the rehabilitation model. The terms *penitentiary* and *prison* were replaced with *correctional center* or *correctional facility*. Guards became "correctional officers," and "departments of prisons" were renamed "departments of rehabilitation and corrections." Staff with college degrees in the social sciences and a "treatment" orientation were hired to work in "program services" or "clinical services." These new staff were also expected to participate in all major operational decision making and were assigned to classification, program, and disciplinary committees at each prison. The influx of college-educated personnel with a nonsecurity orientation drove a wedge between the new staff and the old guard, who believed in punishment and maintenance of order. Furthermore, several court rulings on employment hiring practices that had excluded minorities and women resulted in the hiring of more and more nonwhite and female guards.

For example, the U.S. Department of Justice, Civil Rights Division, sued both the Florida Department of Corrections and the Parish of Orleans (New Orleans) because both agencies were restricting women from applying for many guard positions, arguing that these jobs posed a unique threat to the safety of women employees if assigned to these positions (*United States v. State of Florida: Florida Department of Corrections,* No. TCA 86-7330, N.D. Fla.; and *United States v. The Parish of Orleans Criminal Sheriff's Office*). In Seattle, minority officers sued their employer, claiming that they were being harassed by white officers who were attempting to drive them out of the workforce (*Hammer v. King County*).

As the size of the correctional system workforce increased, it was organized into increasingly powerful labor unions and professional organizations (such as the American Correctional Association and the American Probation and Parole Association), which have become very active in pursuing the interests of their rank and file. Consequently, the top administration has lost a considerable amount of control over its employees, who are now divided along many lines: race, gender, union versus management, and rural versus urban. The prison administration has belatedly followed the path of other government organizations in moving from a more homogeneous, informal social organization to a formal and professionalized bureaucracy.[22]

Administrative Confusion

Presently, prison administrators lack a vision to give their task purpose and direction. Rehabilitation, the guiding principle of penology for at least twenty years, has fallen into disrepute. For administrators, its replacement—punishment—converts simply to maintaining order in the prisons. Given the rapidly expanding prison populations, the new problems of keeping prisoners under control, and a more politically active labor force, prison administrators have their hands full dealing with the day-to-day exigencies of running a crowded, unstable, conflict-ridden prison system. In effect, they have evolved from captains of ships to bureaucrats. To cope, they increasingly turn to formal procedures, rules, standards, and use of force to manage the inmate population.[23]

Guards have taken the new emphasis on imprisonment for punishment as a mandate to employ excessively firm, even extreme, force to keep prisoners in line. The term *excessive use of force* refers to situations where correctional staff resort to the use of chemical agents such as tear gas, taser guns, and pepper spray to temporarily "neutralize" an inmate. Once controlled, inmates can be placed in "mechanical restraints" such as a restraint chair, leg irons, handcuffs, and other devices.

These situations often occur in the high-security or super-max units that are discussed in greater detail in the following chapter. Typically, an inmate, for any number of reasons, may be refusing to leave his or her cell. In such a situation, a "cell extraction" will occur, where a team of officers with special training in cell extraction forces its way into the cell and uses all of the methods and techniques discussed previously to remove the inmate. These events are often videotaped to ensure the extraction is done according to the department's standards. The following is an example of a cell extraction.

> On Monday July 2, 1990, at approximately 1710 hours, Inmate Smith refused to relinquish his tray following the evening meal. After numerous unsuccessful attempts were made by the Unit officers and sergeants to retrieve the tray, permission was given by the Administrative Officer of the Day to extract Smith from his cell. At approximately 1730 hours Sergeant Wilson incapacitated Smith with taser round and he was placed in mechanical restraints [handcuffs and leg irons] by an extraction team. Smith was treated by medical staff for minor abrasions and rehoused. There were no injuries to staff. Smith was written up on a 115 and charged with violation of D.R. 300(c), Force and Violence.[24]

The "news" of such actions spread quickly in the prisons. If viewed as "unfair" or "excessive" by the prisoners, these actions will serve to further widen the gap of hostility, hate, and violence between guards and prisoners.

THE BUREAUCRATIC PRISON

The trends noted here have forced states to move from what James Jacobs calls a "patriarchal organization based on traditional authority to a rational-legal bureaucracy."[25] This new management style requires a more centralized approach for managing prisons that takes authority and discretion away from the wardens and individual prisons. Directors of corrections now oversee a vast, corporatelike conglomerate of prisons, work release centers, and parole units supported by increasingly sophisticated accounting and computerized information systems. Many of the senior staff who work in the corporate headquarters have no experience in running prisons but have expertise in budgeting, report writing, public relations, information systems, and planning. It is not uncommon to have a director of corrections who has no experience in the field but has served in other areas of state government. The primary mission of the new corrections agency is not to question the status quo but to manage these huge agencies with minimal negative press that could embarrass the current governor.

In order for the agency to function effectively, the lines of authority, as well as the procedures, prescriptions, or guidelines for all practices, are formalized in the written rules and regulations appearing in elaborate manuals. An extensive and professionalized training program is needed to keep staff abreast of the most recent changes in an increasingly complex array of administrative regulations and procedures imposed by the central office. Routine audits are conducted by central office staff to ensure compliance. In effect, wardens and other key figures in the prison—unlike the formerly powerful captain—no longer have the autonomy and wide discretion they once possessed. They must now answer to the central command and do things according to the book.

As the workforce has become increasingly professionalized, with college-educated staff who claim to possess special expertise in the area of "corrections," salaries and status have increased correspondingly. Prison guards in a number of states, county jails, and the Federal Bureau of Prisons can earn $40,000 to $56,000 per year not including overtime, which can total tens of thousands of dollars more each year. However, most guards are poorly educated and poorly paid. The average starting salary for a guard is $21,246, with twenty-three states offering a starting salary of $15,000 to $18,000. Few of these guards have gone beyond a high school education, and about 15 percent of the workforce resigns or retires each year. Unlike the inmate population, the vast majority of guards are white (73 percent).[26] But despite the lack of formal education and training, by virtue of their work experience alone, they claim a specialized discipline of prison operations and have built a protective wall of esoteric knowledge to justify their actions.[27]

The procedures are based on ostensibly valid scientific methods and knowledge. For example, "classification" of prisoners for the purpose of assignment to particular prisons, to the custody levels they are to be held in, and to "programs," such as educational or vocational training programs, generally involves less discretion and individual judgment than was previously exercised by captains, lieutenants, and guards. Though the policy formation and decision-making procedures are now more centralized, they are also much more subject to outside influences. The intervention of the courts described earlier has meant that many procedures are either court-mandated or developed within court-mandated guidelines. In many states, for example, the courts have ordered that minimal due process procedures be followed in all disciplinary actions and that objective classification systems be implemented. And all states must conform to statutes or case law that guarantee certain prisoner rights.

Formerly, wardens and line staff relied mostly on informal and "subjective" systems of control. In most states, prisoner leaders were given power through various informal arrangements, and these inmates maintained order in the prison. In many states, these prisoners were "right guys" or "politicians" who were given special privileges in return for keeping other prisoners in line. In some southern states, such as Texas and Arkansas, convict "barn bosses" were given the right to control prisoners through intimidation and violence, including homicide. The informal prison social system effectively controlled by "right guys" and "politicians," who were almost always white, disappeared when prisoner populations became increasingly black, Hispanic, and militant. By 1980, most states were required by court intervention to eliminate these convict boss systems.[28]

Bureaucratic professional administrations now attempt to control prisoners through increasingly formal and rational systems. They have promulgated more extensive and restrictive formal procedures and rules governing prisoner behavior and have made greater use of classification and new formal incentives, such as time off for participation in work programs and compliance with prison regulations.

Administrators use three forms of classification. The first (external classification) is used to assign prisoners to a custody level that in turn is used to assign them to either a minimum-, medium-, or maximum-security prison. In many states, the committee or classification unit relies heavily on a quantified "objective" scoring system based on a prisoner's past criminal record, current conviction and sentence length, escape history, and social factors such as age, marital status, and employment history. After the inmate has been in custody for a certain period of time, he or she is reclassified on a different instrument that places greater emphasis on the inmate's record of institutional misconduct.

One of the positive results of using these new objective classification systems is learning that a large percentage of the prisoners are minimum custody. Minimum custody generally means that the inmates have no history of violence, have no prior or very few prior convictions, are not management problems, and pose little risk to public safety. In many states such as Illinois, Colorado, Idaho, North Carolina, Oklahoma, Texas, and Washington, approximately 50 percent of the average daily population now qualifies for minimum- or community-level security. The national average is 35 percent in minimum or lower custody.[29]

Once the inmate arrives at a facility, a second classification system (internal), often less objective and structured, determines which programs the inmate can participate in and assigns the inmate to a housing unit. Typically, the new bureaucratized prisons have several different sections, such as protective custody and honor cell blocks, to which a prisoner may be assigned. A prisoner's custody level also determines what range of jobs is available to him or her. For example, minimum-custody prisoners, even at a maximum-security prison, are usually allowed to leave the walled or fenced prison compound to attend to various work assignments: landscaping, working in staff houses on the prison grounds, assisting at the front gate, and the like.

Finally, prisoners who are seen as a threat to the prison social order or to other prisoners are frequently assigned, through another classification process, to highly secure units where—except for two or three two-hour exercise periods a week, restricted visits, and occasional official business (for example, talking to their lawyers)—they remain locked in their cells twenty-four hours a day. In most states, assignment to the "administrative segregation," "supermax," or "lockup" units (the common general names for these units) includes some limited due process mandated by state or federal courts. The next chapter discusses in greater detail these high-security units.

THE PRISONER EXPERIENCE

Inmates in state and federal prisons must presently cope with an extremely aggravating and threatening set of conditions brought on by crowding, racial conflict, new practices stemming from the punitive penological philosophy, and bureaucratic policies. The worst of these features is prisoner-to-prisoner violence.

Violence

As mentioned, prison populations have become much more racially heterogeneous and divided, and the old prison leaders have lost their control over other prisoners. Racial hatred, which often leads to violence, is endemic. Prison gangs attempt to control prison rackets, protect their members, pursue vendettas against their enemies, and earn prestige as "tough" convicts by menacing all other prisoners.

In general, most prisons and prisoners are not exposed to violence, as most inmates are minimum and medium custody. In 1998, there were only 79 homicides reported on a national level, which translates into a homicide rate of about 8 to 9 per 100,000 inmates.[30] This rate is about the same as the nation's homicide rate. But given that prison populations consist of a primarily young male population with a disproportionate number of known offenders, the overall rate is quite low. However, in the high-security units, where most of this violence occurs, the level of violence is quite common.

In the 1970s and 1980s, assaults and homicides in most high-security prisons became so common that the possibility of being attacked or killed has loomed as the major concern of offenders incarcerated in these prisons or anticipating going to one. Looking at California, where the new prison violence started, we see that prisoner homicides increased dramatically after 1970 (Table 5-1). The numbers stayed high until the late 1980s and then dropped, although there has been a recent upturn in the number of homicides and assaults.[31]

Table 5-1 Type of Incidents in CDC Institutions and Rate per 100 Average Daily Population (ADP) Calendar Year 1970 Through Calendar Year 1998

| | Number and Rate | | Type of Incident | | | | | | | |
Calendar Year	Total Incidents	Rate per 100 ADP	Assault with Weapon	Assault without Weapon	Possession of Weapon	Suspected Controlled Substances	Suicide	Attempted Suicide	Other	Homicides
1970	366	1.4	79	74	89	80	11	—	33	13
1971	445	2.0	124	56	103	105	14	—	43	24
1972	592	3.0	189	73	132	144	9	—	45	36
1973	777	3.7	197	94	200	230	18	—	38	20
1974	1,022	4.3	220	125	262	347	14	—	54	23
1975	1,089	4.7	212	113	249	430	9	—	76	16
1976	1,385	6.8	204	132	193	776	7	—	73	20
1977	1,815	8.8	241	182	302	951	12	—	127	18
1978	2,060	10.1	270	258	374	1,034	4	—	120	16
1979	2,427	10.9	309	407	420	1,099	8	—	184	16
1980	2,848	12.2	341	448	498	1,367	11	—	183	14
1981	3,084	11.7	397	541	539	1,352	12	38	205	18
1982	3,625	11.6	456	671	815	1,396	24	54	209	14
1983	3,904	10.9	573	800	861	1,370	19	93	188	10
1984	5,105	12.7	936	982	1,159	1,694	18	91	225	16
1985	5,225	11.5	914	903	1,289	1,763	17	131	208	16
1986	5,087	9.6	896	1,036	1,138	1,603	13	177	224	21
1987	5,317	8.5	1,008	1,195	1,053	1,642	16	150	253	20
1988	4,925	7.1	939	1,146	830	1,657	17	84	252	8

Continued on page 102

Table 5-1 continued

Calendar Year	Number and Rate		Type of Incident							
	Total Incidents	Rate per 100 ADP	Assault with Weapon	Assault without Weapon	Possession of Weapon	Suspected Controlled Substances	Suicide	Attempted Suicide	Other	Homicides
1989	5,178	6.5	952	1,705	763	1,384	16	94	264	9
1990	4,184	4.7	932	1,368	634	916	22	75	237	11
1991	4,120	4.3	1,040	1,386	711	624	16	125	218	4
1992	4,983	5.0	1,325	1,497	875	884	14	163	245	9
1993	6,243	5.7	1,786	1,796	1,028	1,141	32	199	281	11
1994	6,974	5.8	1,837	2,116	1,037	1,336	16	223	339	13
1995	6,610	5.3	1,562	2,455	792	1,106	22	188	485	5
1996	6,868	5.1	1,683	2,808	746	954	19	185	473	11
1997	9,574	6.6	2,123	4,102	824	1,059	19	243	1,204	16
1998	9,769	6.6	2,225	4,167	734	1,022	21	256	1,344	15

Note: These data are based on incident reports submitted by the institutions to the Offender Information Services Branch. Attempted suicides were added to the incident reporting system in 1981. Homicides are not computed in the rate per 100 ADP.

SOURCE: California Department of Corrections.

I've been on the yard watching people get shot, watching people die. You know how hard it is coming out with tears in your eyes knowing that you're going to get hit, knowing that someone is going to physically hurt you, or try to kill you. . . . Eighty-two, 83, 84, people were dropping like flies, people getting stuck. After two or three years of that, it's hard. People on the outside say, ah, that doesn't happen. You weren't there, man.[32]

Prisoners must constantly prepare themselves to cope with this possibility. What they actually do will be discussed later.

Restricted Freedom

Because of prisoner rights statutes and court rulings over the last twenty years, inmates may now receive any publication that may be legally sent through the mail (except those likely to incite violence); correspond and receive visits from many more persons than in earlier eras; enter into contracts, including marriage; receive conjugal visits (when eligible); have a partial due process hearing when they receive punishment within the prison; and are protected from systematic physical brutality delivered by the administration (or their agents, such as the convict bosses). However, only the last of these has substantially improved the prisoner's situation.

Much more important to prisoners is that they have lost much of their physical mobility and access to prison facilities and resources. In earlier years, when prisoners were not working, they were usually allowed to wander relatively freely around the prison facilities: in and out of their cell block to the yard, gym, library, canteen, and other sections of the prison, such as the school facilities. Now, most maximum- and medium-security prisoners may only make use of these areas and facilities during short designated periods. Most of the time during the day and night, prisoners are either at their work or school assignments or are restricted to their cell blocks or cells.

Reduced Resources and Contacts

As a consequence of the redefinition of prisons as locations for punishment (instead of rehabilitation), overcrowding, and the new quickly constructed, remote prisons, the resources prisoners may use to accomplish a variety of goals—education, vocational training, and recreation—have dramatically decreased. The states that have expanded their prison populations are driven by punitive sentiments and are usually fiscally conservative. Consequently, the proportion of money for programs and features other than those promoting security has been reduced. Moreover, the remote location of the new prisons has meant that most of the services and support voluntarily offered to prisoners from churches, prisoner support organizations, family, and other individuals have diminished greatly.

In preceding decades, particularly during the rehabilitative era (1950 to 1965), prison administrators greatly encouraged betterment activities, and

TABLE 5-2 Summary Attributes of Prison Programs

Key Prison Indicators	
Total Prison Population	1,300,000
Mental Health/Counseling Indicators	
Percent of inmates with mental health problems	16%
Percent in mental health programs	5%
Percent in some form of drug treatment	14%
Alternatives to Incarceration	
Percent classified as minimum or lower custody	35%
Percent of inmates granted furloughs	1%
Percent of inmates in boot camps	1%
Percent of inmates in halfway houses	1%
Work Programs	
Percent of inmates idle	24%
Percent in prison industries	7%
Percent in prison farms	5%
Percent in full-time vocational training or education programs	9%
Wages per day of work in public agency	Zero to $7.06
Health and Violence	
Percent with full-blown aids	6%
Percent with TB	4%
Inmate death rate per 1,000 inmates	2.44
Percent of deaths defined as "natural causes"	67%
Other Indicators	
Percent with 20 years to life sentences	23%
Percent in administrative/disciplinary segregation	6%
Percent in protective custody	2%

they supplied the resources and programs for accomplishing them. Educational opportunities, for example, expanded during this period; by the early 1970s, prisoners could receive a high school education in most prisons and some college credit in many. In addition, most prisons offered a wide variety of vocational training programs. Many forms of counseling were also available.

That is not the case today. Table 5-2 indicates that only a small percentage of the inmate population is involved in meaningful prison activities. About a quarter of them are idle. Those few who have prison work jobs often do low-skill maintenance jobs requiring them to only push a broom occasionally or pick up trash. Very few are in low-paying prison industry programs, vocational training, or education programs. Although an estimated 16 percent have some documented mental health problem, only 5 percent are in a treatment program.[33] What emerges is a picture of prison life that has minimal program opportunities and considerable idleness.

Lack of Access to Higher Education:
The Case of New York State Prison System

One of the major problems facing inmates is the lack of access to decent educational services. New York provides a recent example of this trend. New York's prison system is one of the nation's largest systems, with an inmate population of nearly 70,000 offenders. With respect to academic opportunities, the state standards proclaim:

> [The] objective of correctional education in its broadest sense should be the socialization of the inmates. . . . The objective of this program shall be the return of these inmates to society with a more wholesome attitude toward living, with a desire to conduct themselves as good citizens and with the skills and knowledge which will give them a reasonable chance to maintain themselves and their dependents through honest labor. (Corrections Law, Section 136)

To meet that standard, the department has concentrated its academic resources on assisting inmates who have limited basic education skills. According to the department, most of the inmates are functioning below the eighth-grade level. Consequently, most of the department's educational services are limited to Adult Basic Education (ABE), pre-GED, and GED curricula. In 1995, over 46,000 inmates received some form of educational services, with the vast majority involved in ABE (83 percent), pre-GED (75 percent), and GED (35 percent).

In 1991, over 1,000 inmates received college-level degrees and certificates. Since then, however, the numbers have steadily decreased so that by 1995, only 588 inmates had completed a college degree. The decline in college education within the department of corrections is directly due to funding cutbacks at both the federal and state levels. Presently, there is virtually no opportunity for inmates to participate in college-level coursework while incarcerated. This is especially troubling given the recent passage of numerous sentencing laws that have greatly extended the length of incarceration for many inmates who could benefit from such an advanced curriculum.

Beginning in FY1995/96, inmates were excluded from access to New York State Tuition Assistance Program (TAP) grants for college. At the same time, Congress also excluded inmates from receiving federal Pell grants. Collectively, these two actions have resulted in what the department of corrections calls "the virtual elimination of college programming for inmates." Consequently, 23 colleges that had provided college-level programming to 3,300 inmates at 45 facilities have ceased their operations.

Today, only a handful of academic institutions remain. The Consortium of Niagara Frontier has 205 male inmates from Attica, Collins, and Wyoming enrolled at no cost. Syracuse University offers programming to 20 inmates at Auburn. Bronx Community College provides programming to 27 inmates at Sing-Sing, and the New York Theological School has 15 students also at Sing-Sing. There are no programs available for women in the entire system.

The demise of college programming has occurred despite research findings suggesting that completion of a college-level program has a very positive impact on the probability of an inmate recidivating. In a study of 986 males who participated in the department of corrections's now defunct Inmate College Program completed by the department of corrections in 1991, it was found that inmates who had earned a college degree while incarcerated had a significantly lower twelve-month recidivism rate (26.4 percent) as compared to those who had enrolled but failed to complete the Inmate College Program (44.6 percent). Although the study did not control for other factors that might be associated with a lower recidivism rate among the college graduates, the study did provide preliminary evidence that participation in college-level programming can reduce the probability an inmate will return to prison.

Arbitrary Disciplinary Punishment

As mentioned, prison staff must follow a partial due process system in disciplining prisoners. However, prisoners view the due process disciplinary procedure as a sham and much more arbitrary than it was in preceding decades. The "judge" or "judges" in these hearings are prison officials who are far from impartial. In fact, they are often close associates of the persons who bring the charges against the prisoner. Moreover, their primary goal is maintaining order in the prison, not delivering fair, legal, and impartial decisions. In addition, much of the evidence used against the prisoner is hearsay and anonymous, often a "note dropped"—that is, an anonymous letter from a prisoner, sent to the administration through special mechanisms for this purpose. For example, a prisoner at San Quentin was placed in the "hole" (solitary confinement) for participating in a cell burning:

> When I was in the honor block, someone "dropped a note" on me and accused me of being the "point" for a cell burning. I had nothing to do with it, but I couldn't convince 'em in the hearing. I offered to take a lie detector test. They put me in Max B, and I wrote an appeal. After a few weeks, a guy came from Sacramento. Eventually, he arranged for a lie detector test and I passed it. They still left me in the hole for the rest of my sentence.[34]

"Chickenshit Rules"

In earlier eras, prisoners enjoyed considerable freedom to embellish their drab and monotonous prison life. For example, they decorated the walls of their cells, altered their prison clothing, acquired various pieces of furniture—such as rugs, chairs, and bookshelves—and kept birds and other small pets in their cells. These special touches enriched their lives with considerable comfort and individuality, which is very important in a world so marked by monotony.

The centralization of authority and the formulation of rules and regulations have resulted in a much more stringent and uniform prison routine that has mostly eliminated these special features and privileges. Dannie Martin, an ex-prisoner at Lompoc, a federal maximum-security prison, writes about the "gulag mentality" of Lompoc's recent wardens:

As the saying goes, it's the little things that make a house a home. To those of us who face the mind-killing boredom of long prison sentences, small changes take on large significance in this our home-away-from-home. Among the small things that matter most to us here are our routines and perks and possessions. They help to personalize this cold world.

A few years ago—in what convicts now call the good old days—there were said to be two kinds of wardens: those who lean toward punishment and those who believe in rehabilitation. These days, it seems there is only one kind. But the different ways they choose to do their punishing make a great difference to us, the punished.

The warden here at Lompoc from 1982 until 1987 was Robert Christiansen. We who lived here during his tenure called him "Defoliating Bob." He earned that nickname upon his arrival by chain sawing a row of stately and beautiful old eucalyptus trees in our "backyard," trees that for 50 years or more had served as a windbreak about 150 yards from the prison perimeter. Our cell-block view apartments had lost another amenity.

Not long after cutting down the trees, the warden poisoned all the squirrels that convicts enjoyed feeding near the prison fences, then mounted a genocidal war against the cats and raccoons that roamed the prison grounds. He also managed to curtail most of the small liberties enjoyed by the convict population. Before his arrival, we had been permitted to wear our own clothes. Now we were to wear strictly tucked-in and buttoned-up government issue. And our recreational opportunities and food went from bad to worse.

He did away with little niceties like Christmas packages from home and unrestricted telephone access. As he made these changes, he was busy installing electronic grill gates in the hallway so that the prison could be sectioned off in case of emergency. Sheet-metal plates went up over windows with an outside view.

Defoliating Bob retired last year. One of the first official acts of our new warden, R. H. Rison, was to close down our recreation yard until noon every weekday. Those of us who work on night jobs and ran and exercised in the mornings now sit in gloomy cell blocks watching the sun shine through the window bars.

No sooner did the warden close the yard than we lost our chairs, and that hurt. For as long as most of us can remember, we've had our own chairs in the TV rooms as well as in our cells. There's little enough in here for man to call his own, and over the years these chairs have been modified and customized to an amazing degree—legs bent to suit the occupant, arm rests glued on, pads knitted for comfort. And the final personal touch is always the printing of a name on the back.

A couple months ago, the guards came one day with no warning and confiscated all our chairs. Each of us was issued a gray-metal folding chair, along with a memorandum from the new warden stating that anyone writing on or otherwise defacing these chairs would be subject to disciplinary action.[35]

COPING WITH VIOLENCE

Because racial and gang violence has become increasingly prevalent in some prisons, prisoners in such situations must follow a strategy of doing time that reduces the stress of being robbed, raped, assaulted, or killed by other prisoners.

Gang Banging

Since the 1970s, many prisoners, if they are eligible, affiliate with a gang or clique for protection. Younger prisoners who were members of gangs on the outside or who graduated from youth prisons where they were members of gangs are automatically eligible. Other potential recruits have to prove themselves.[36] Gang affiliates are either core members or associates. The core members hang around fellow gang members and are very active in the gang's pursuits: robbing other prisoners, dealing drugs, controlling some of the prison homosexuals, and carrying on murderous feuds with other gangs, particularly those of other races. The associates, though they do not participate in the day-to-day activities, remain ready to be called on when some large display of force or some other form of assistance, such as smuggling drugs from one location to another or hiding weapons, is needed. In return, they have the gang's protection and may circulate much more freely in the prison public places and enjoy some of the fruits of the gang's illegal economic activities.

Prison administrators have responded to the gangs by attempting to identify the leaders and core members and place them in the administrative segregation or "super-max" units. In many prisons, those suspected gang members remain in lockup units for many years. For example, the official policy for inmates identified as being active gang members in Texas is to place them in the administrative segregation unit until they complete their sentences. This strategy, however, has not completely stopped gang activities, and assaults and murders of other prisoners and guards continue to occur in the special segregation units.[37] Moreover, unidentified and new gang members carry on the activities in the "mainline" (the general prison population). In addition, new prisoners from the same neighborhoods or towns, perhaps members of outside gangs, establish new prison gangs or cliques and continue to racketeer and do violence in the mainline.

Locking Up

Those who are being pressured to join a gang for protection but who want no part of it often have only one remaining option—requesting to be locked up in protective custody (PC). As noted earlier, about 2 to 3 percent of the prison population is classified as PC. These inmates are physically separated from the mainline population and are viewed as weak or "punks" because they cannot "make it." Often, inmates who are overtly homosexual, convicted of child molestation, or are snitches find their way to PC. But there are also inmates who just want to do their time, but the gangs, who are in such control, will not allow it to happen.

Such was the case in the Pontiac Correctional Center in Illinois a few years ago. The major gangs had gained control of the housing units by not allowing inmates of different gangs to be housed in certain cells. Since work and program assignments were associated with housing units, the gangs had gained control of them as well. Only after a lawsuit was filed did the department agree to take certain corrective actions to reassert its authority in determining where inmates were housed and which programs they would participate in. As these reforms occurred, the number of inmates in PC declined.[38]

Retired Convicts

A few older prisoners who have spent many years in prisons and have earned good reputations as being tough—usually through their affiliation with one of the gangs—can retire from gang banging and circulate freely in the prison with immunity from gang attack. Edward Bunker, in his novel about San Quentin in the 1970s, has accurately depicted this prison pattern:

> So, although Earl was at home, it was in the way that the jungle animal is at home—cautiously. He had no enemies here who posed a threat, at least none that he knew, though some might have been threats if he didn't have the affection of the most influential members of the most powerful white gang and friendship with the leaders of the most powerful Chicano gang.[39]

Withdrawal

The vast majority, particularly prisoners who are serving their first prison sentences and have not been involved in gangs on the outside, shy away from most prisoners and settings where masses of prisoners congregate and withdraw into small orbits or virtual isolation. Although they need not go to PC and they may occasionally buy from the racketeers, place bets, or trade commodities on a small scale with other unaffiliated prisoners, they stay out of the large-scale economic activities and dissociate themselves from the violent cliques and gangs. They stick to a few friends whom they have met in the cell blocks, at work, on the outside (homeboys), in other prisons, or through shared interests. Either alone or with their few trusted friends, they go to work and/or attend school or meetings of various clubs and formal organizations that the prison administration allows to exist in the prison. Otherwise, they stay in their cells.[40]

CRIPPLED

The fragmenting of prisoner society, the general physical and social isolation of prisoners, the increased use of segregation, and the elevated level of deprivation, fear, and distress act as socially and psychologically impairing forces on most prisoners.[41] For decades, students of the prison have recognized that the combined factors of being isolated from outside society, subjected to a reduced and deprived routine, and acculturated into a unique "convict" belief and value system work to "prisonize" men and women—that is, convert them into persons equipped to live in prison and ill-equipped to live outside.[42] It was this insidious process of prisonization that innovative penologists tried to avoid when they planned the "community corrections" approach in the late 1960s.[43]

Now prisoner administrators and other policy makers have completely abandoned the goal of reducing prisoners' isolation from outside society. They build prisons in the remotest regions of the state with only security in mind and further reduce contacts with outside organizations and individuals through their custody-oriented policies. These practices, along with greatly diminished rehabilitative resources, are producing prisoners who have deteriorated in prison and return to the outside much less well-equipped to live a conventional life than they were when they entered prison.

Inmates enter prison poorly educated, vocationally unskilled, and often suffering from serious physical and psychological problems. Most, particularly at the beginning of their sentences, are desirous of bettering themselves while in prison and improving their chances of living some form of rewarding, viable conventional life when they are released:

> I want to go to school and get a trade. Then when I get out I want to have my kids with me, have a good job so I can support them. I want to get the drugs out of my life. [Black drug addict, 28, convicted of armed robbery and episodically involved in crime]

> I think I will pass up getting involved in the gangs in prison. I'm going to go to school and get me a trade. I want a nice job, paying pretty good, something to keep me busy instead of running the streets. [Black ex-gang banger, 29, episodically involved in crime and convicted of armed robbery]

> I'm going to go to school and get a job. I'm going to try to get into electronics. I want a job I won't get laid off on. As long as I have a job, I don't get into trouble. When I get laid off, I get into trouble. [Eighteen-year-old corner boy who was "around crime" and convicted of possession of cocaine with the intent to deliver]

> When I get out I'm going to try to find a job. If I can't find a job, I'll do what I have to do to survive. But I won't do anything violent. I might get a license to sell something. That way you keep some change in your pocket. [Black petty drug dealer, 26, who was "into crime" and convicted of possession of cocaine]

As these statements indicate, many prisoners intended to take care of serious health problems, participate in drug or alcohol programs to deal with their addictions, and in general take advantage of whatever resources exist to better themselves. But as indicated earlier, these resources for change are less available in today's prisons.

ALIENATED

The general society has always held convicts in some contempt, but in earlier decades there was a greater willingness to forget their past and, once they had served their time, "give them another chance." In the 1960s, a large outpouring of sympathy was expressed for convicts, and substantial progress was made in reducing the barriers blocking ex-convicts' re-emersion into conventional society.[44] For a short period, ex-prisoners were folk heroes; many strutted around, loudly proclaiming and capitalizing on their ex-convict status. This period ended by the late 1970s, and once again the convict and ex-convict became a widely hated and feared pariah. In recent years, whenever an ex-convict is in the news, the media usually focuses negatively on that status. Politicians harp on criminal acts committed by released prisoners. Legislators and policy makers, usually with dramatic public display, have passed laws or established policies against hiring ex-convicts for a growing number of jobs. Consequently, most prisoners are acutely aware that they are among society's leading pariahs, and this awareness has greatly increased their alienation from conventional society.

Finally, in earlier decades most prisoners were somewhat psychologically buttressed by the convict identity. The prisoner society, with its solidarity underpinned by a special worldview and code of ethics, not only promoted peace but also greatly bolstered prisoners' self-esteem. Though they were society's outcasts and "losers," they took pride in being "right guys," "regulars," or "real convicts." They endured the deprivation of imprisonment, itself a matter for pride, and responded to their degradation by turning the conventional status system upside down. They viewed average citizens as "squares" whose behavior was petty, corrupt, weak, and hypocritical; and they felt particular contempt for society's representatives to whom they were closest—the guards and prison administrators. Most convicts sincerely believed that they were more honorable than squares.

Now most prisoners not only shy away from other prisoners, they feel contempt for their counterparts as well. A former politically active prisoner, about to be released after serving twenty years, addressed a prerelease class: "If I catch any convict coming around my neighborhood after I'm released, I'm calling the cops, because I know he is up to no good."

Partly as a reaction to their negative image, some prisoners become outlaws: "These are mainly persons who present themselves as 'convicts' in the prison and participate in the rapacious, violent activities of gangs. The outlaw scorns the disapproval of society, reveals no mercy or compassion for others, and remains ready to use violence to protect himself or achieve his ends." An archetypical outlaw, Jack Abbott, describes the type:

> The model we emulate is a fanatically defiant and alienated individual who cannot imagine what forgiveness is, or mercy or tolerance, because he has no *experience* of such values. His emotions do not know what such values are, but *imagines* them as so many "weaknesses" precisely because

the unprincipled offender appears to escape punishment through such "weaknesses" on the part of society.[45]

Most prisoners, however, just as they have withdrawn from most prison public activities, attempt to disassociate themselves from the convict identity. But their experience of being held in contempt and having no supporting countervalues is profoundly detrimental. Mainly, it completes their full alienation. This social malady has several separate components: a sense of *powerlessness*, the expectation that one's behavior will not succeed in bringing about the outcomes one seeks; *meaninglessness*, the lack of a sense of what one ought to believe; *normlessness*, the expectation that socially unapproved behaviors are required to achieve given goals; *detachment*, the disassociation from the central beliefs and values of the society; and *self-estrangement*, the experience of oneself as alien and unworthy.[46] All these aspects of alienation are cultivated in the contemporary prison milieu, making fully alienated convicts incapable of normal participation in conventional activities. They skulk in and around the edges and crannies of society (like the homeless), unexpectedly lash out at others, escape into drug addiction, or succumb to psychosis or suicide.

The disturbing truth is that growing numbers of prisoners are leaving our prisons socially crippled and profoundly alienated. Moreover, they understand that they will be returning to a society that views them as despicable pariahs. They are also aware that they will have more difficulty finding employment than formerly, and consequently their expectations are low. We will examine how these persons fare on the outside in Chapter 7.

NOTES

1. Starting with Donald Clemmer's *The Prison Community* (New York: Holt, Rinehart, 1958), social scientists produced an extensive literature on prisoner society as it existed from the 1930s through the 1960s. A few of the studies are Graham Sykes, *The Society of Captives* (Princeton, NJ: Princeton University Press, 1958); Rose Giallombardo, *The Society of Women* (New York: Wiley, 1966); David Ward and Gene Kassebaum, *Women's Prison* (Chicago: Aldine, 1965); John Irwin, *The Felon* (Upper Saddle River, NJ: Prentice-Hall, 1970); and James Jacobs, *Stateville* (Chicago: University of Chicago Press, 1977).

2. The increase of staff supervision is evidenced by the inmate-to-staff ratios, which ranged from one officer per nine to eleven inmates from 1926 through 1940. After 1945, however, the ratio continued to shrink until it reached its lowest level of 2:92 by 1979. See Margaret Werner Cahalan, *Historical Corrections Statistics in the United States, 1850–1984* (Washington, DC: Bureau of Justice Statistics, 1986).

3. See Daniel Glaser, *The Effectiveness of a Prison and Parole System* (Indianapolis, IN: Bobbs-Merrill, 1964), Chapter 1, for a summary of failure rates of released prisoners. The author estimates that in the 1950s and earlier, the rate was about 40 percent.

4. See John Irwin, *Prisons in Turmoil* (Boston: Little, Brown, 1980), for a more complete analysis of this shift.

5. The recognition of potential and actual abuses under the rehabilitative ideal began with Francis Allen's *The Borderland of Criminal Justice: Essays in Law and Criminology* (Chicago: University of Chicago Press, 1964). The criticism of rehabilitative routines culminated in *The Struggle for Justice,* written by a "working party" for the American Friends Service Committee, 1971. This book was followed by a series of works in which the "justice model" was offered as an alternative to the rehabilitative judicial and penological systems. See Norval Morris, *The Future of Imprisonment* (Chicago: University of Chicago Press, 1974); Andrew von Hirsch, *Doing Justice: The Choice of Punishments* (New York: Hill & Wang, 1976); and David Fogel, *We Are the Living Proof: The Justice Model for Corrections* (Cincinnati, OH: Anderson, 1975).

6. As mentioned earlier, a consensus that rehabilitation did not work was reached in the early 1970s. Since then, many persons have reexamined the reports on treatment attempts, particularly those that were planned and implemented after the late 1960s, and have argued many programs do work. Even Robert Martinson, the author of the article "What Works? Questions and Answers About Prison Reform," *Public Interest* 35 (April 1974): 22–54, and coauthor with Douglas Lipton and Judith Wilks of *The Effectiveness of Correctional Treatment: A Survey of Treatment Evaluation Studies* (New York: Praeger, 1975), which were the culminating criticisms of treatment effectiveness, retracted his hard position in a later review of the literature: "New Findings, New Views: A Note of Caution Regarding Sentencing Reform," *Hofstra Law Review* 7 (1979): 243–258. See also Francis T. Cullen and Paul Gendreau, "The Effectiveness of Correctional Rehabilitation: Reconsidering the 'Nothing Works' Debate," in Lynn Goodstein and Doris McKenzie (eds.), *The American Prison: Issues in Research and Policy* (New York: Plenum, 1989). In general, what Martinson,

Cullen, Gendreau, and others have found in reexamining the treatment literature is that programs that emphasize learning and "cognitive" rather than medical or emotional disturbance models can reduce recidivism. As noted in Chapter 9, there are a number of criticisms one can make regarding the potential of a treatment approach to reduce crime. First, the vast majority of crimes are not committed by persons released from prison; consequently, the success or lack of success of prison-based treatment programs and/or punishment will have little impact on crime rates in general. Second, most correctional treatment programs are not well administered, target the wrong clientele, and are too small to have any impact on crime rates or public safety. Third, factors that will undoubtedly serve to reduce the likelihood of maintaining a criminal lifestyle are age, absence of a juvenile career, no history of violence, no evidence of drug use or abuse, the ability to secure employment, and entering into a meaningful relationship or marriage. Treatment and punishment will have only moderate effects on crime rates.

7. For a discussion of this "cooptation," see David Greenberg and Drew Humphries, "The Cooptation of Fixed Sentencing Reform," *Crime and Delinquency* 26 (1980): 206–225.

8. Cited in Ken McGinnis, "Make 'Em Break Rocks," in John P. May and Khalid R. Pitts (eds.), *Building Violence: How America's Rush to Incarcerate Creates More Violence* (Thousand Oaks, CA: Sage Publications, 1999).

9. Ibid.

10. Ibid.

11. See U.S. Department of Justice, Bureau of Justice Statistics, *Prisoners in 1998* (Washington, DC: U.S. Government Printing Office, August 1999).

12. U.S. Department of Justice, Bureau of Justice Statistics, *Prisoners in 1998* (Washington, DC: U.S. Government Printing Office, August 1999); and

U.S. Department of Justice, Bureau of Justice Statistics, *Census of State and Federal Correctional Facilities, 1990* (Washington, DC: U.S. Government Printing Office, 1992).

13. Criminal Justice Institute, *The Corrections Yearbook, 1998* (Middletown, CT: Criminal Justice Institute, 1998).

14. This was the practice from about 1850 to 1950, when prisons were seen as places for banishment. However, during the rehabilitative era, during which more general sympathy existed for prisoners, there was some tendency to build new prisons closer to cities. In the late 1960s, progressive penologists recommended that all prisoners should be held close to urban centers. The idea of "community correctional centers" was advanced, though never actually realized (see Irwin, *Prisons in Turmoil,* Chapter 6).

15. Criminal Justice Institute, *The Corrections Yearbook, 1998* (Middletown, CT: Criminal Justice Institute, 1998).

16. For a number of years, Marc Mauer has been documenting the growing number of incarcerated blacks and Hispanics. His most recent book, *The Race to Incarcerate* (New York: The New Press, 1999), provides comprehensive documentation of this tragic trend. Also see Margaret Werner Cahalan, *Historical Corrections Statistics in the United States, 1850–1984* (Washington, DC: U.S. Department of Justice, Bureau of Justice Statistics, December 1986); and U.S. Department of Justice, Bureau of Justice Statistics, *Prisoners in 1998* (Washington, DC: U.S. Government Printing Office, August 1999).

17. See Leo Carrol, *Hacks, Blacks, and Others* (Lexington, MA: Lexington Books, 1974); Jacobs, *Stateville;* and Irwin, *Prisons in Turmoil,* for discussions of the conflict between racial groups in prison.

18. See Irwin, *Prisons in Turmoil,* pp. 100–106; Jacobs, *Stateville,* Chapter 5; and Ben Crouch and James Marquart, *An Appeal to Justice* (Austin, TX:

University of Texas Press, 1989), Chapters 1 and 8, for discussions of these changes.

19. Darlene Grant and Steve Martin, *Should Prison Reform Litigation Be Curtailed?* (San Francisco: National Council on Crime and Delinquency, 1996).

20. Criminal Justice Institute, 1998.

21. See Jacobs, *Stateville;* John DiIulio, *Governing Prisons* (New York: Free Press, 1987); and Crouch and Marquart, *Appeal to Justice,* for full discussions of the authoritarian prison regimes.

22. Jacobs *(Stateville)* and Crouch and Marquart *(Appeal to Justice)* trace these shifts in their books on Stateville and the Texas prison systems.

23. The recent study by John DiIulio, *Governing Prisons,* has this confusion as its underlying theme.

24. Reported in Robert Schultz, *"Life in SHU": An Ethnographic Study of Pelican Bay State Prison,* M.A. thesis, Humboldt State University, April 1991, p. 90.

25. Jacobs, *Stateville,* p. 73.

26. Criminal Justice Institute, *The Corrections Yearbook, 1998.*

27. See Jacobs, *Stateville,* and Crouch and Marquart, *Appeal to Justice,* for descriptions of the emergence of bureaucratic regimens.

28. See Crouch and Marquart, *Appeal to Justice,* for a description of the court's elimination of the convict boss system in Texas. Also see Thomas Murton and J. Hyams, *Accomplices to the Crime: The Arkansas Prison System* (New York: Grove, 1969), for a description of Thomas Murton's confrontation with the convict boss system in Arkansas.

29. Criminal Justice Institute, *The Corrections Yearbook, 1998.*

30. Ibid.

31. Data on prisoner fatalities were obtained from Offender Information Services Branch, California Department of Corrections, *Inmate*

Incidents in Institutions: Calendar Year 1998 (Sacramento, CA: May 1999).

32. Quoted in Schultz, "Life in SHU," p. 95.

33. U.S. Department of Justice, Bureau of Justice Statistics, *Mental Health and Treatment of Inmates and Probationers* (Washington, DC: U.S. Government Printing Office, July 1999).

34. Interview, San Francisco, 1981.

35. Dannie Martin, "The Gulag Mentality," *San Francisco Chronicle,* Sunday Punch Section, June 19, 1989, p. 5.

36. To be eligible, prospective gang members must be of the same race and sometimes come from the same city, town, or neighborhood. They must also have the respect of the other members. To gain this, they must present the persona of a tough convict who is willing to use violence to protect himself and his associates. The prospects may already have earned this reputation outside or in other prisons. If not, they must earn respect, perhaps by assaulting someone of another race or gang.

37. For example, in 1983 two guards were murdered by members of a white prisoner gang in the lockup sections of Marion, the federal maximum-security prison, and one guard was killed by several members of a black gang in a lockup unit in San Quentin.

38. See James Austin and Jim Aiken, "Final Report on Pontiac Classification System," *Inmates A, B, C and D v. Illinois Department of Corrections* Consent Decree, 1996.

39. Edward Bunker, *No Beast So Fierce* (New York: Norton, 1973).

40. In a study of prisons in Ontario, Canada, Edward Zamble and Frank J. Porporino found that more than 40 percent of the prisoners interviewed "stay on their own," and another almost 40 percent confine their socialization to a "few friends." The percentage who stay on their own increased to more than 50 percent by the time they had served 16 months. Over the span of this study, the percentage who spent the majority of their optional time in their cell increased from 19.8 to 28.6. We must note that these are Canadian prisons, and the violence and other pressures are probably not as acute as they are in the United States. See *Coping, Behavior, and Adaptation in Prison Inmates* (New York: Springer, 1988), p. 117.

41. In their study of Ontario prisoners, Zamble and Porporino did not find that prisoners reported either increases in depression, anger, anxiety, guilt feelings, boredom, and loneliness or increases in depression or anxiety, as measured by standard tests of these variables. The same absence of increases in psychological "symptoms" or indicators of emotional problems have been found in many other studies (see Zamble and Porporino, *Coping,* for a summary of these findings). However, they were measuring different aspects of the "personality" than those addressed here. We are not suggesting that prisoners are becoming emotionally ill but that they are being converted into a distinct personality type—a prisoner—who may not be anxiety-ridden, depressed, guilt-ridden, or even extremely angry. Rather, the prisoner becomes withdrawn, suspicious, untrusting, and socially unskilled. Zamble and Porporino did find that prisoners withdraw more as they serve their sentence.

42. Donald Clemmer introduced the concept in his seminal study of the prison, *The Prison Community.* Dozens of studies since his have further examined this class of detrimental aspects of imprisonment.

43. See the President's Commission on Law Enforcement and Administration of Justice, *Task Force Report: Corrections* (Washington, DC: U.S. Government Printing Office, 1967); and Irwin, *Prisons in Turmoil,* Chapter 6.

44. One of the authors, John Irwin, an ex-convict, took great advantage of these changes, finished college, and became a college professor.

45. Jack Abbott, *In the Belly of the Beast* (New York: Random House, 1981), p. 13.

46. See Melvin Seeman, "On the Meaning of Alienation," *American Journal of Sociology* 24 (1944): 783–891.

6

■

Super Max

WHAT IS SUPER MAX?

Within a prison system, inmates are housed according to a classification system that seeks to separate inmates by their risk to escape, assault staff and inmates, and commit other serious prison infractions (for example, possession of weapon, contraband, and so on). The vast majority of inmates are placed in the so-called "general population." These inmates are allowed to "program," meaning that they can participate in most inmate programs and inmate work assignments. However, a small but highly visible proportion are viewed as so dangerous and disruptive that they must be assigned to a special control unit usually referred to as "administrative segregation," "the hole," "maximum-security," "control," or "lockup" housing units, that is, "Super Max."[1]

Although the numbers of inmates assigned to these high-security units is growing, only a small percentage of the prison population ever experiences administrative segregation. Table 6-1 shows the most recent national estimates for inmates housed in the administrative segregation units as well those in disciplinary segregation and protective custody. The two latter categories have different meanings. Inmates in disciplinary segregation have been found guilty of a serious rule violation and have been sentenced to segregation for a specific time period (usually no more than fourteen days). There are also inmates in disciplinary segregation who are awaiting the outcome of an investigation. Protective custody (PC) inmates have been admitted to a segregated unit for

TABLE 6-1   United States Administrative Segregation
and Protective Custody Populations, January 1, 1997

Special Inmate Population	Number	% of All Inmates
Administration segregation	28,128	3.1%
Disciplinary segregation	18,503	2.1%
Protective custody	7,297	1.7%
Total segregated population	53,928	6.9%

SOURCE: *1998 Corrections Yearbook,* p. 26.

their own protection from other inmates. They cannot "make it" in general population because they are labeled as "snitches" or are simply too weak to survive without protection. They will remain there until they feel they can make it in the general population or until they complete their sentences.

The PC units are designed to be less punitive than administrative segregation or disciplinary segregation units. In these units, inmates are granted a considerable amount of freedom in respect to being out of their cells, recreation time, participating in self-help programs, and even holding paid work assignments. They are allowed to have reading materials, radios, and perhaps even televisions (all paid for by the inmates) in their cells. In many units, these inmates will have cell-mates rather than being single celled.

The conditions inmates experience in administrative segregation units are very different. In these units prison administrators have total physical control over all aspects of the inmate's behavior for extended periods of time (often two to five years). Inmates assigned to such housing areas spend twenty-two to twenty-three hours a day in their single, 60- by 80-square-foot, high-security barren cells with minimal (if any) access to educational, religious, or other self-help programs. The amount of reading material is extremely limited and controlled as well as basic amenities (toothpaste, shaving cream, plastic razor). The front of the cell is often closed with a solid-steel-plate door with a slot to send food, mail, and other items provided by the prison. When an inmate is removed for a shower, visit, or recreation, he or she must kneel down with his or her back to the door and place both hands through the cell door slot so they can be handcuffed.

When allowed out for "recreation," inmates are escorted to small and self-contained razor-wired recreation and exercise "cages" with no more than two to three inmates at a time allowed out on the yard. In general, these facilities and units represent the bottom end of a state's prison system. This trend should concern us greatly because it has many undesirable consequences for prison systems, for prisoners who experience long periods of lockup, and for the society that must receive most of these prisoners back when they are released.

Both PC and administrative segregation inmates have no set date for release from their segregated status. But unlike the "PC" units, "ad seg" units are designed to be extremely controlling and punitive. The prisoners will remain in these units until prison officials feel it is safe to release them once again. For these inmates, there is no known release date from these extremely punitive units. Inmates can remain assigned to "ad seg" for many years until they finish their entire sentence without ever returning to the general population.

HISTORY OF
ADMINISTRATIVE SEGREGATION

The concept of administrative segregation grew out of the practice of solitary confinement, which prison administrators began using in the nineteenth century along with many other methods (such as flogging, water torture, shackling of prisoners to cell walls) to punish particularly troublesome prisoners. By the beginning of the twentieth century, prison authorities had eliminated most of the other crueler forms of punishment but continued to confine prisoners in "solitary," or the "hole," as the major form of punishment for rule breaking. In his 1940 study of a "prison community," Donald Clemmer describes solitary confinement:

> The 24 solitary cells are in a small building known as the yard office. It is set off by itself and is heavily barred and isolated. The cells themselves contain no furniture. The one window is small, and the iron bars of the door have another wooden door which keeps the light from entering. The cells are cold in winter and hot in summer. The inmate is given one blanket and must sleep on a wooden slab raised about two inches from the cement flooring. One piece of bread and a necessary amount of water is allowed each day.[2]

During the first half of the twentieth century, all walled prisons had solitaries or "holes." Some, such as the tin sweat boxes in southern work camps or the "dungeon" in San Quentin, were extremely cruel places. The cells studied by Clemmer at the Illinois Menard maximum-security prison were about average. During this time, many prisons also had cells set aside for segregation of prisoners—such as persons who persistently broke the rules, open homosexuals, and persons who needed protection from others—who the administration believed could not be allowed to circulate freely among other prisoners (protective custody). Unlike solitary confinement, inmates could be held in segregation for long periods of time, sometimes years. When one of the authors of this book—James Austin—was first employed by the Illinois Department of Corrections in 1990, one inmate at the Joliet prison had been in administrative segregation ("the hole") for ten years.

By the 1950s, the old system of social order based on a convict code and a few prisoner leaders was breaking down, and new problems of disorder among prisoners developed. Consequently, states began developing new forms of administrative segregation to control an increasingly disruptive inmate population. Many states that had adopted the rehabilitative philosophy of penology—such as California, Illinois, New York, New Jersey, Wisconsin, Washington, and

Minnesota—were able to gain conformity for a few years (1950 to 1955) through the indeterminate sentencing system. Using the margins of sentencing discretion contained in the indeterminate sentencing system along with systems of good-time credits inmates could earn to reduce their prison terms, prison officials and parole boards threatened prisoners with longer lengths of stay if they did not conform in prison. However, a small percentage of the prisoners were responsive neither to these sentencing incentives nor to the threat of being placed in the hole. In particular, youthful leaders of well-organized street gangs who had received lengthy prison terms for violent crimes began to assume a greater presence in maximum-security prisons. Prison administrators then expanded the use of administrative segregation to manage this growing and difficult-to-manage population.

By 1970, California had established so-called high-security "adjustment centers" (ACs) at its major maximum-security prisons of San Quentin, Folsom, and Soledad.[3] In Illinois, special program units (SPUs) were established at Joliet, Stateville, and Pontiac prisons in 1972. Other states soon followed these states in their efforts to isolate and control the most disruptive or potentially disruptive segments of the inmate population. When these first adjustment centers failed to reduce the turmoil and violence, more sections of several prisons were converted into new segregation units (for example, "segregated housing units" and "management control units").

THE OFFICIAL PROGRAM

As indicated earlier, prisoners are "assigned" (not sentenced) to "administrative segregation" for their perceived status—such as being an ongoing threat to prison stability, staff, and other prisoners. This means that they are not necessarily charged with any specific rule violations. Although there are administrative procedures regulating the transfer of inmates to such units, these regulations are often not followed, and the assignments are based on subjective criteria. Administrators, therefore, can exercise almost unrestricted discretion in assigning prisoners to a lockup unit.

Additionally, because the official purpose of segregation units is not punishment, the prison administrators initially planned the units' physical structure and routines so that they would not have any special punitive aspects. When segregation first began, the cells in segregation units were different than those in solitary units. They usually had the same furnishings as mainline cells—a bunk, mattress, toilet, washbowl, and sometimes a small desk. Moreover, the prisoners were not intentionally denied other privileges beyond those that were impractical to deliver because the prisoners were restricted to their cells. Lockup prisoners could receive and keep about the same range of material and commodities as mainline prisoners. They either were allowed TV sets in their cells or could watch a TV mounted in the unit. Their mail was not restricted. They received and kept books (although their access to the prison library was and is greatly restricted because of their lockup status).

THE REALITY OF LOCKUP

Lockup status was inherently highly punitive from the outset. In the typical routine of a lockup unit, prisoners were confined to their cell almost twenty-four hours a day. Officially, they were supposed to spend one or two hours twice a week in a small exercise yard adjacent to their unit, which had limited recreational facilities. In actual practice, these periods were frequently denied prisoners. The prisoners were occasionally escorted, sometimes by two to four guards, to other parts of the prison to go to the hospital, for a visit, or for other special functions (for example, disciplinary hearings). Otherwise they stayed in their cells.

Most important, being locked up in segregation meant prisoners lost access to most programs and activities, which in most prisons are extensive: schooling, vocational training, movies, libraries, and recreational activities. They were cut off from socializing with other prisoners during work, dining, on the yard, and in the day rooms and from engaging in literally dozens or hundreds of games, hustles, rackets, and other cooperative enterprises that prisoners undertake. They did talk to each other through the barred fronts of their cells and even played games, such as chess, on the walkway directly in front of their cells. For all intents and purposes, however, prisoners in lockup units were cut off from the general, relatively full social life of the prison world.

Inmates in lockup or administrative segregation were often ineligible to receive good-time credits either because of disciplinary violations or because they could not participate in programs that rewarded inmates with additional good-time credits. Since most inmates in the general population served about 50 percent of their sentences, being placed in administrative segregation also served to greatly extend an inmate's time in prison. As will be noted later in this chapter and in Chapter 7, it is now common for some inmates to spend virtually all of their time in administrative segregation and to be released directly to the streets from "ad seg."

It is true that this situation also meant these prisoners were somewhat protected from hostilities and assaults that were increasingly occurring among mainline prisoners. What they sacrificed for this increase in safety, however, was tremendous. Moreover, hostility and violence eventually became more intense in the lockup units than in the "mainline" general population.

TURMOIL IN LOCKUP

During the 1970s and early 1980s, the segregation units became extremely tumultuous and violent. This atmosphere was partly a result of the administrative practice of concentrating the most recalcitrant prisoners in the prison system in a situation of relatively severe deprivation. Many of them had not conformed to the rules in the much less restrictive mainline and were even less willing to do so in segregation.

Prison administrators began locking up suspected members of organizations believed to be a threat to prison order. Suspected leaders of the Black Muslims were the first to be segregated, followed by members of other black religious and political organizations, such as the Black Panther Party. When organizations of other prisoners—Chicanos, whites, and Puerto Ricans—appeared, the suspected leaders were assigned to segregation. In the 1970s, gangs of prisoners of the same race involved in rackets and violence toward other gangs and individual prisoners became the main concern of prison administrations, and all suspected leaders and many suspected members were isolated in the lockup units.

Making matters worse, several prisoners believed that they had been unfairly placed and held in the segregation units. As we have seen, placement was an administrative decision by a "classification committee" that involved minimal due process and at best a pro forma appearance by the inmate at the classification hearing. When Illinois began using its SPUs in 1972, for example, hundreds of inmates were "reclassified" for the Joliet SPU during a single weekend. Inmates were "heard" in hearings that lasted less than a minute.

Once assigned to these segregation units, prisoners' "cases" were reviewed again in a cursory manner. Frequently, the classification committee based its decision on hearsay information, such as that supplied by informers, sometimes anonymously, or on suspicions, such as those expressed in memos from staff who reported that they had witnessed prisoners engaging in acts that suggested the prisoners had been involved in some prohibited behavior. Even if an inmate had not been involved in any disciplinary actions, he or she could remain in the units simply because of staff suspicions.

For these reasons, lockup units became centers of turmoil. Prisoners engaged each other and guards in constant verbal attacks. A prisoner describes his experiences on entering one of the first adjustment centers in California:

> [We] were transferred to Soledad Correctional Facility from "X" Prison. We were placed in the Max Row section, O wing. Immediately entering the sallyport area of this section I could hear inmates shouting and making remarks such as, "Nigger is a scum low-down dog," etc. I couldn't believe my ears at first because I know that if I could hear these things the officers beside me could too, and I started wondering what was going on. Then I fixed my eyes on the wing sergeant and I began to see the clear picture of why those inmates didn't care if the officials heard them instigating racial conflict. The sergeant was, and still is, Mr. M., a known prejudiced character towards blacks. I was placed in a cell, and since that moment up 'till now, I have had no peace of mind. The white inmates make it a 24-hour job of cursing black inmates just for kicks, and the officials harass us with consistency also.[4]

Racial hostilities ran high in these units, since they were filled with inmates representing most of the prison gangs. In Illinois, the dominant prison gangs—such as the Black P. Stone Rangers, Black Disciples, Vice Lords, and Latin Kings—were constantly warring with one another for control. In California, the Aryan Brotherhood, Black Guerrilla Family, the Mexican Mafia, and La Nuestra Familia were strongly committed to attacking members of rival groups. When the opportunity presented itself—such as when members of opposing groups were released together to the exercise yard—prisoners fought, knifed, and killed each other. In 1970, a fight between several white and black prisoners housed in Soledad's O Wing broke out as soon as the blacks and whites in the section were released together to the exercise yard. A gun tower guard fired at the prisoners and killed three black prisoners.

Prisoners often broke up their cell furnishings—the beds, cabinets, and toilets. On these occasions, water ran out of the cells down the tiers onto the floors. Often the floors in the cells were littered with trash thrown from cells and water running out of cells. To regain order, staff would shoot tear gas into the units and use "stun guns" or "tasers" to subdue inmates. In return, prisoners in lockup units constantly taunted and vilified their guards. They regularly threw any liquid material, sometimes urine and feces, on passing guards and occasionally assaulted and murdered them.

Not surprisingly, as these conditions worsened in adjustment centers, guards grew more hostile toward the prisoners. They were deeply offended and angered by the revolutionary rhetoric delivered by some of the more politically oriented prisoners, in which guards ("pigs" or "the police") were excoriated. For example, George Jackson, who was held in adjustment centers for most of his twenty years in California prisons, wrote in 1970:

> The great majority of Soledad pigs are southern migrants who do not want to work in the fields and farms of the area, who can't sell cars or insurance, and who couldn't tolerate the discipline of the army. And, of course, prisons attract sadists. Pigs come here to feed on the garbage heap for two reasons really, the first half because they can do no other work, frustrated men soon to develop sadistic mannerisms; and the second half, sadists out front, suffering under the restraints placed upon them by an equally sadistic, vindictive society. The sadist knows that to practice his religion upon the society at large will bring down upon his head their sadistic reaction.[5]

The guards' hate deepened when lockup prisoners increased their verbal taunts, began throwing objects and liquid on them, and occasionally succeeded in murdering them. Guards occasionally responded by punishing and harassing prisoners in every way they could. They delivered their own taunts and vilification, occasionally beat prisoners, and frequently shortened, disrupted, or denied privileges, such as correspondence, exercise, and visits, that lockup prisoners were supposed to receive. Evidence of these practices was obtained in 1975 by the federal district court investigating the conditions in lockup units:

> Two guards who used to work in the AC testified in support of plaintiffs' allegations that guards have beaten, threatened, and harassed plaintiffs and other first tier AC prisoners, that prisoner reports are at times altered, and that AC guards have a stereotyped view of plaintiffs and treat them in a dehumanizing fashion.[6]

Some guards entered into the conflicts between prisoner factions by aiding one group of prisoners against others or "setting up" individual prisoners. Occasionally, this was done in a routine fashion. For example, a white prisoner who was identified as being affiliated with the Aryan Brotherhood describes his setup by a black guard:

> This black guard was escorting me back to my cell in Max B [a section of the Adjustment Center] and he stopped and handcuffed me to the rail on the row housing black prisoners and said he would be right back. Then he went and unlocked the row to let all the black dudes out to exercise. As they passed by me, they kicked me, spit on me and punched me. Then he came back and put me in my cell.[7]

Sometimes guards set prisoners up to be killed or even participated in the homicides. In the fight and killings in the Soledad adjustment center yard, in which three black prisoners were shot to death, a Salinas, California, jury found that eight Soledad staff members had willfully and unjustifiably conspired to kill the three prisoners. The staff had released prisoners who were expected to begin fighting. The gun tower guard, who some prisoners report was leaning out of his tower aiming at the prisoners when the fight began, fired five shots and hit the three black prisoners in the middle of their torsos. Afterward, the guards took over 30 minutes to carry one mortally wounded prisoner to the hospital even though it was adjacent to the adjustment center.[8]

More recently, the "staging" of fights with inmates in high-security prisons has again surfaced in the California prison system. At the notorious Corcoran facility, a federal investigation has been launched by the FBI and the U.S. Department of Justice into allegations that guards would purposely put inmates from rival gangs in the same recreation yard and place bets on who would survive. In one such incident, an inmate was shot to death by a guard who claims he fired to break off the staged fight.

Guards and the administration steadily reduced the old privileges of the adjustment centers until the distinction between the former punitive solitary units and the nonpunitive adjustment centers had all but disappeared. A psychiatrist, appointed by the Northern California federal district court to examine the Adjustment Center unit in San Quentin in 1980, comments on the conditions:

> When I walked through Security Housing Unit 2 at San Quentin and heard constant angry screaming and saw garbage flung angrily from so many cells, I felt like I was in a pre-1793 mental asylum, and the excessive security itself was creating the madness. While the mainline playing fields at San Quentin are large and grassy, the various security units are small and paved. Prisoners are not allowed any furniture (desks, chairs, etc.) and are prevented by regulations from even draping their cells with blankets to improve insulation against cold winds. Deprived of most acceptable human means of expressing self, prisoners are left with a meager token of wall decorations.[9]

Instead of being locations where prisoners were incapacitated and pacified in a controlled but humane setting, the lockup units became the most dangerous (for both prisoners and staff), punitive, and deleterious settings in American prisons. Robert Slater, who worked at San Quentin as a psychiatrist between 1982 and 1984, describes the violence in that prison's adjustment center:

> Periodically, bursts of gunfire serve as unpleasant reminders of where we are. Occasionally, a prisoner is killed, maimed, or blinded by gunshot. Crude but effective spears, bombs, hot or corrosive liquids can, and are, hurled through the bars in either direction. In the summer of 1984, during a particularly violent period, the authorities in one of the lockup units brought together a Mexican leader and a Black leader, asking them to walk the tiers together to help cool things down. They agreed to do this. While walking the tiers, a Mexican inmate threw a knife through the bars to the Mexican leader, who proceeded to kill the Black leader.[10]

NEW MAXIMUM-SECURITY PRISONS

The apparent failure of administrative segregation units to pacify prisoners and restore order to the prisons during the 1970s and early 1980s did not cause penologists to abandon the policy of concentrating troublesome prisoners in permanent lockup units. What they have done instead is to construct new "maxi-maxi" prisons in which they have attempted to eliminate the features believed to have caused the breakdown of order.

In fact, the Federal Bureau of Prisons (FBP) first attempted this goal when it took over Alcatraz Island, the site of an old army prison, and opened a small, maximum-security federal prison in 1934. Alcatraz was intended to house the most "desperate criminals" (for example, "Machine Gun" Kelly, Al Capone) and the bureau's most troublesome prisoners. By the early 1960s, the feds, particularly the attorney general Robert Kennedy, considered the "Rock," which housed only 275 prisoners, an expensive failure and closed it in 1963. Its prisoners were dispersed among the other federal prisons, mostly Atlanta and Leavenworth, the two securest prisons next to Alcatraz.

At this time, the FBP was constructing a new small prison at Marion, Illinois, as an experiment in behavior modification. The prison had a range of units with varying degrees of security. About 350 prisoners were supposed to work their way through the levels, increasing their privileges by demonstrating good conduct.

In 1973, however, the FBP returned to the policy of concentrating its troublesome prisoners in one place and began transferring them to Marion's "control unit."[11] The feds continued to send more troublesome prisoners to Marion and reclassified it in 1979 as their only "Level 6" (highest-security) penitentiary, designated for prisoners who (1) threatened or injured other inmates or staff; (2) possessed deadly weapons or dangerous drugs; (3) disrupted "the orderly operation of a prison"; or (4) escaped or attempted to escape in those instances in which the escape involved injury, threat of life, or use of deadly weapons. Since its complete conversion to a prison for problem inmates, Marion has experienced difficulties very similar to those in California's lockup units. Through the 1970s, tensions, hostilities, violence, and disruptions increased. In the early 1980s, the unrest reached new heights. From February 1980 to June 1983, there were fifty-four serious prisoner-on-prisoner assaults, eight prisoners killed, and twenty-eight serious assaults on staff.

The turmoil escalated further in the summer and autumn of 1983. In July, two prisoners took two officers hostage in the disciplinary segregation unit; one officer was stabbed. In the following week, two inmates attacked two officers escorting prisoners from the dining hall. Prisoner-to-prisoner violence increased in this period, and most of the time the prison was placed on complete "lockdown" status. On September 5, a prisoner assaulted an officer with a mop wringer and a chair. On October 10, an officer was assaulted when he tried to break up an attack by prisoners on another prisoner. On October 22, when three officers were moving a prisoner housed in the control unit, the prisoner stopped to talk to another inmate in a cell, then turned to face the officers, his handcuffs unlocked and a knife in his hands. He succeeded in murdering one officer.

That evening another prisoner was being escorted by three officers from one section of the prison to the recreation cage. He too stopped in front of another prisoner's cell and turned around with his handcuffs removed and a knife in his hands. He succeeded in stabbing all three officers, one fatally. The turmoil in the prison continued for another month. Prisoners started fires, threw trash out of their cells, and continued to assault other prisoners and staff. Repeated searches produced weapons, handcuff keys, lock picks, hacksaw blades, heroin, and drug paraphernalia.

The FBP finally instituted new severe control procedures. David Ward and Allen Breed, who conducted a study of Marion for the U.S. House of Representatives, describe the clampdown:

> New custodial procedures were implemented. All correctional officers were issued riot batons and instructed to carry them at all times. A special operations squad, known as "The A Team," arrived from Leavenworth and groups of Marion officers began to receive training in techniques of conducting forced cell moves and controlling resistant inmates. These officers were outfitted with helmets, riot control equipment and special uniforms. A new directive ordered that before any inmate left his cell he was to place his hands behind his back near the food tray slot in the cell door so that handcuffs could be placed on his wrists and leg irons on his ankles. No inmate was to be moved from his cell for any reason without a supervisor and three officers acting as an escort. Digital rectal searches were ordered for all inmates entering and leaving the Control Unit along with strip searches of inmates before and after visits with the attorneys.[12]

As was the case in California, strategies to control troublesome prisoners greatly increased control problems. Because Marion had not been designed to hold the most troublesome prisoners, many of its features, such as open cell fronts, turned out to present problems to the staff in their attempts to maintain complete control over recalcitrant prisoners. Many states are building new maxi-maxi prisons that are designed specifically to hold recalcitrants. In general, these prisons are built to hold prisoners in small, secure, self-contained units. Ward and Breed, in commenting on the inadequacy of Marion's design, describe this type of prison:

> New generation prisons are generally comprised of six to eight physically separated units within a secure perimeter. Each unit of some 40–50 inmates, all in individual cells, contains dining and laundry areas, counseling offices, indoor game rooms, a wire enclosed outdoor recreation yard and a work area. The physical design of inmate rooms calls for only one or two levels on the outdoor side(s) of the unit to facilitate, from secure control "bubbles," easy and continuous staff surveillance of all areas in which inmates interact with each other and with staff.[13]

In addition, the cells in new maxi-maxi prisons usually have solid doors with a shatterproof glass window and an opening through which prisoners can be fed or handcuffed without opening the door. The basic idea is that prisoners, while being held in small secure units and unable to congregate or communicate with each other, can be delivered all essential services (for example, food and medical services). This would avoid the problems administrators encounter when they "lock down" an older prison, which greatly disrupts the delivery of essential services to prisoners. In addition, when prisoners in the new maxi-maxi prisons are kept in their cells, they cannot throw things, yell to each other, or assault guards, as is the case in the older prisons, even in the segregation units.

California has become the leader in the construction of super-maximum prisons. It has built four new maxi-maxi prisons with a total capacity of 12,000. Other such prisons have been constructed in Illinois, Nevada, New Mexico, Texas, and Minnesota, with many more planned for other states and cities with major jails (including Los Angeles, New York, and Philadelphia).

The four California maxi-maxi facilities have some common design features. All have "units" or "pods" that cluster around a central control center from which heavily armed guards look down on the units twenty-four hours a day. The cells have fully sealed front doors to restrict the throwing of objects by inmates at staff. Each unit typically has a small day room and adjacent exercise yard.

Pelican Bay facility, the last of the four to open, is located in an extremely remote area of northern California. Built in 1990 at a cost of $278 million, it was designed to hold 2,080 maximum-security inmates, but soon became overcrowded with an inmate population of 3,250. Within the prison itself, the segregated housing unit has the capacity for 1,056 prisoners.

Pelican Bay is entirely automated and designed so that inmates have virtually no face-to-face contact with guards or other inmates. For twenty-two and one-half hours a day, inmates are confined to their windowless cells, built of solid blocks of concrete and stainless steel, so that they will not have access to materials they could fashion into weapons. They do not work in prison industries; they do not have access to recreation; they do not mingle with other inmates. They are not even allowed to smoke because matches are considered a security risk. Inmates eat all meals in their cells and leave only for brief showers and ninety minutes of daily exercise. They shower alone and exercise alone in miniature yards of barren patches of cement enclosed by twenty-foot-high cement walls covered with metal screens. The doors to their cells are opened and closed electronically by a guard in a control booth.

There are virtually no bars in the facility; the cell doors are made of perforated sheets of stainless steel with slots for food trays. Nor are there guards with keys on their belts walking the tiers. Instead, the guards are locked away in glass-enclosed control booths and communicate with prisoners through a speaker system.

The segregated housing unit has its own infirmary, its own law library (where prisoners are kept in secure rooms and slipped law books through slots), and its own room for parole hearings. Inmates can spend years without stepping outside the unit.

California's former Governor George Deukmejian, dedicating the new prison in June 14, 1990, stated, "California now possesses a state-of-the-art prison that will serve as a model for the rest of the nation. . . . Pelican Bay symbolizes our philosophy that the best way to reduce crime is to put convicted criminals behind bars." The governor also noted that the annual cost of keeping a convicted felon in prison is $20,000, compared with the $430,000 that it costs society when a career criminal is at work on the street.[14] This unit is the most completely isolated prison since the early penitentiaries in Pennsylvania. Since 60 percent of the inmates housed at Pelican Bay are from the Los Angeles area, which is 900 miles away with no available air transportation, the prospect for regular visits from inmates' families is extremely remote.[15]

But California is not the only state constructing such units. Oklahoma's new "high-max" unit is described in this way:

> Inmates housed in the "high-max" security unit will live 23 hours a day in their cells, with the other hour spent in a small concrete recreation area with 20-foot walls. The space is topped by a metal grate. Theoretically, an inmate could move into the new cellhouse and never again set foot outdoors. The unit's first residents will be the 114 men on death row. The cellhouse also contains a new execution chamber.
>
> That's how the staff designed it. For about 45 days, workers representing a cross-section of the penitentiary's staff developed plans for the new unit with architects. Guards in the control room of each squad can eavesdrop on or talk to inmates in any cell at the touch of a button. Fields said the monitoring device should reduce the number of attacks on prisoners, nip conspiracies in the bud and protect officers. A corridor behind each cell run will allow officials to work on or shut off water and power to each individual cell.[16]

Finally, here is a description of New York's new super max, as reported in the *New York Times*:

The New York prison Southport Correctional Facility has the same mission: to take the worst prisoners. They will include those who have dealt drugs behind bars, attacked guards, even murdered inmates. At Southport, they are being kept isolated, shackled at the waist and wrists when allowed out of their 6 by 10 foot cells and made to spend their daily recreation hour in newly built cages.[17]

A CLOSER LOOK AT
A CONTEMPORARY LOCKUP UNIT:
THE TEXAS ADMINISTRATIVE
SEGREGATION POPULATION

In order to offer a more current view of administrative segregation units as they operate today, the following description of the Texas administrative segregation system is presented. These data are drawn from a recent study of the system conducted by one of the authors of this book at the request of the Texas Department of Criminal Justice and the National Institute of Corrections.[18]

The Texas prison system is one of the two largest prison systems in the world. As of July 1998, there were 129,893 inmates. During the early part of the 1980s, Texas experienced a rash of inmate murders and stabbings. This outburst of unprecedented violence led the agency to institute a policy where any inmate who was found to be associated with a known security threat group (STG) was placed in administrative segregation for an indefinite period of time. In Texas, an inmate is designated as a member of an STG if it can be confirmed that he or she is affiliated with one of ten gangs that the prison officials consider to be security threat groups. There are other gangs that exist in the inmate population, but they are not believed by prison officials to pose a threat to the security of the prison system. The segregation population is further separated into two groups: inmates in Group A are defined as assaultive inmates, while those in Group B are defined as nonassaultive. The latter group consists of inmates who have had no major (or even minor) disciplinary reports for many months and years. Yet, because they are viewed as a member of an STG, they will remain in administrative segregation status indefinitely.

As Table 6-2 shows, approximately 5.5 percent (7,813) of the prison population is assigned to administrative segregation. The largest number of inmates are classified as Group B, the "nonaggressive" administrative segregation status. Since 1994, the administrative segregation population has grown at a faster rate than the total inmate population—from 4,738 to 7,813, or an increase of 65%. During the same four-year time period, the total Texas Department of Criminal Justice (TDCJ) population increased from 97,490 to 142,941, or a net increase of 46%.

The basic demographics of this population is predominantly Hispanic (55 percent), male (99 percent), gang-affiliated (52 percent), and an average age of

TABLE 6-2 Trends in the Texas Administrative
Segregation Populations, 1994–1998

Population Category	May 31, 1994		May 18, 1998			
	N	%	N	%	Difference	% Change
Administrative segregation	4,738	4.9	7,813	5.5	3,075	64.9%
Protective custody	102	0.1	113	0.1	11	10.8%
Group A—Aggressive	2,674	2.8	2,936	2.1	262	9.8%
Group B—Nonaggressive	1,962	2.0	4,764	3.3	2,802	142.8%
Total inmate population	97,490	100.0	142,941	100.0	45,451	46.6%

SOURCE: *Texas Department of Criminal Justice Security Threat Group Management Report,* May 8, 1998.

31 years. Most significantly, the average years to the inmates' earliest release date is thirteen years. This means that unless the prison officials decide to alter their policy for keeping gang-affiliated inmates in administrative segregation status, many of these inmates can look forward to spending another thirteen years in what amounts to near total solitary confinement.

The majority of inmates assigned to Group A are Hispanic gang members who have had no recent disciplinary misconducts. Nearly 60 percent (2,810) of the Group A inmates have had no disciplinary incidents in the past year, and nearly 30 percent (1,374) have had no such reports in the past two years. Conversely, very few of the Group B inmates have been without disciplinary reports for the same time periods.

In Texas, there are two types of administrative segregation facilities. The System I units are old facilities that were never designed to hold such inmates. They have been retro-fitted to accommodate their "new inmates" and "new mission." By all accounts, these are ill-suited for this type of function. As noted in the report, the System I units are older, more traditional physical plants that were built prior to the development of modern correctional designs and are devoid of new technologies and hardware that enhance the security operations of the newer facilities. This becomes particularly important when facilities of this nature are housing high-security prisoners, such as by administrative seg-regation. By the nature of their design, visibility and lines of sight are restricted as compared to the modern System II units. Because access corridors, stair-wells, and the gangways in front of cells are narrower, movement is restricted. Movement in and out of cells is limited to a more confined area, and this impacts the responsiveness of staff to security emergencies. This also creates dif-ficulty when staff respond to emergencies and disturbances within a cell. The limitations of space restrict the number of staff who can directly respond and often limit the type of equipment that may be utilized.

The System II units are modern facilities and have been constructed to only hold the administrative segregation status inmates. One such unit is the Estelle Unit, which was constructed in 1996 with a capacity of 650 beds. This facility has several electronic security features including an extensive

TABLE 6-3 Current Trends in Admissions, Releases, and the ADP of the Administrative Segregation Population

Administrative Segregation Movements	7/1/97 to 6/30/98
Annual Admissions to Administrative Segregation Status	**2,441**
Protective custody	37
Gang admissions	631
Annual Releases from Administrative Segregation Status	**1,995**
Back to prison	1,542
From administrative segregation to society	453
Estimated Length of Stay in Administrative Segregation	**3.9 years**

SOURCE: Texas Department of Criminal Justice.

multipoint video system that provides enhanced observation capabilities from center control. The unit is very functional, secure, and efficient. Showers have been installed in each cell, thus controlling and reducing external cell movements. Remote control operations from center control further reduce the need for officer escorts and movements. Caged individual recreation areas provide the capacity for reduced officer involvement and interaction. There are no education programs. Inmates do have assigned caseworkers who visit the inmates in their cells. Inmates only come out of the cells for visits, recreation, and showers. When the inmates are brought out of the cell, they are fully restrained in handcuffs and leg irons. Three officers carry out the movement, with one officer videotaping the move.

The report recommended, among other things, that the TDCJ reverse its policy of holding inmates in administrative segregation for such long periods of time simply based on their affiliation with gang members. It was estimated that at least one-third of the current administrative segregation population could be released to the general inmate population. It was also recommended that the older System I facilities no longer be used for the ad seg inmate population.

Finally, the Texas study also found that a sizeable proportion of inmates who are released from administrative segregation is released directly from ad seg to the streets. As shown in Table 6-3, an estimated 450 inmates are released in such a manner each year. In other words, they go directly from lockup to the community with no parole supervision requirements, as they have "maxed out" their prison terms.

THE CONSEQUENCES OF LOCKUP

It is far from clear that the expanded use of lockup has made prisons easier to manage. However, lockup certainly has a very negative effect on the prisoners who experience long periods of isolation in the various lockup units.

The Self-Fulfilling Prophecy

When persons are treated as having certain characteristics, whether they actually have them or not, they are likely to develop such characteristics or have them magnified because of the treatment. This phenomenon frequently occurs when persons are classified as recalcitrant and placed in lockup units. Many persons who have been minor "troublemakers," or who are mistakenly believed to be intensely or intimately involved in prohibited activities (such as revolutionary or gang activities), have been placed in the lockup units and then have actually fulfilled the prophecy—that is, they have become serious troublemakers, committed revolutionaries, or gang members.

Several processes accomplish this transformation. In the first place, many persons are instilled with considerable frustration, anger, and a sense of injustice when they believe they have been unfairly placed in lockup. As mentioned earlier, the process of classifying persons to lockup is often based on hearsay information of dubious reliability. Administrators have always felt a great need to cultivate and rely on information supplied by informers, and they have regularly accepted anonymous information ("notes dropped") and often coerced many persons into supplying information on others. For example, administrators have usually required a prisoner who is seeking protection or is trying to drop out of a gang to name persons who were threatening him or were involved in prohibited activities, such as gang activities.

They also have offered such significant incentives to informers as transfers, letters to the parole board, and placement in protective custody. Though some of the information supplied by informers has been reliable, much has not.[19] What occurred simultaneously with the new forms of disruption that prison administrations have been trying to control through the use of informants was the loss of cohesion among prisoners and a weakening of the convict code, which dictated, above all, not to snitch. A new ethic has emerged and guides many prisoners based on the general principle of everyone for himself or herself, or "dog eat dog." Informing for self-gain is consistent with this new code and has become much more commonplace. Even falsely accusing persons for self-advantage is a practice approved of by many prisoners. For example, a prisoner who was transferred from Soledad to San Quentin's segregated housing unit claimed to have been the subject of false accusations by an informer:

> I had this good gig, disc-jockey on the prison radio, and this black dude wanted my job. So he told them that I was active in the AB [Aryan Brotherhood]. I wasn't. I got a lot of friends who were AB. But I've never been AB. I played a lot of Western music, and lot of people didn't like that and didn't like me. The rat who snitched me out of the job didn't like my music. But really he wanted to replace me. So he told the man I was an active AB.[20]

In making their decisions to segregate, the committees also regularly accept staff observations of questionable validity. The following is an example of many statements from memos in files of persons assigned to lockup because of gang affiliations:

> I observed inmate A talking to inmates B, C, and D on many occasions. They seem to have been involved in gang type activities together.[21]

The highly discretionary and arbitrary nature of the gang designation is revealed in the following California correctional officer's description of the process:

> There's three, four, five different ways that they can be designated as a gang member. They're either northern or southern Mexicans just by birth. If they're from south of Bakersfield, they're going to be southern unit. If they're from north of Bakersfield, they're going to be Nostra [Nuestra] Familia. And that's just something that doesn't change. Now after that, you get associations. If, for example, we're talking about Nostra Familia, and that's the northern gang, and there's an inmate you know associates, has been observed by staff who's seen writings in his letters, if you can use two of the five or six different methods of validation, then you can call him an associate. Letter writing, another inmate telling you, admission of the inmate himself, staff observation, there's several ways to observe and two of the five or six different ways, I believe, will validate him as an associate. Then to be validated member, then I think it's four out of five or six, you have to be observed by staff, have another inmate tell you, through incriminating himself, he can tell you. Now, you may never ever take any of these vows or do any of their footwork or anything, but just because you hang with people from where you come, you associate with them. Once you've been validated as an associate, or validated as a member, then they can give you indeterminate SHU term.[22]

Consequently, as was shown in the Texas study, many persons who have had minor behavior problems in prison or have had a weak or no affiliation with some of the organizations suspected of engaging in extremely rapacious, violent, and disruptive behavior have been placed in lockup units.

Once in the lockup units, the prisoners experience the ordinary deprivations inherent in lockup status and frequently witness or are subjected to the additional abuse that results from lockup guards expressing their extreme racism and general hostility toward lockup prisoners. This harassment further enrages many prisoners:

> One day when I got back from the visiting room, inmate M told me that the police had attacked W, a black inmate, while being handcuffed and taken to isolation. We protested according to their ways, and we threw some liquid on officer D, since he was the cause of W getting attacked. They came back and threw tear gas into our cells until we almost died— seriously—I had to wave a towel since I was choking from the gas. They told me that they wouldn't open the door until I got undressed, backed up to the door and stuck my arms out. I did just that. They handcuffed me and dragged me to the other side naked.[23]

In addition, the policy in many state prisons (such as Illinois, Texas, and California) throughout the 1970s and early 1980s was to locate suspected gang members in sections designated for a particular gang. This practice often forces persons with weak or no affiliation closer to the gang for two reasons. First, placing inmates in the unit with a particular gang results in their being viewed as a definite member of that gang and subjects them to the threats and attacks of other rival gangs. Second, if they are accepted by the other gang members, the dynamics of being held in close, exclusive interaction with these others strengthen the bonds between them. Consequently, weak or no affiliation is often converted to full membership by the lockup decision.

"Monsters"—"They Treat Me Like a Dog, I'll Be a Dog"[24] Many persons held for long periods in lockup, during which they have been subjected to extreme racial prejudice, harassment by the guards, and threats and attacks from other prisoners, are converted into extremely violent, relatively fearless individuals who profess and conduct themselves as if they do not care whether they live or die. They frequently attack staff as well as other prisoners. Examples of this extreme form of recalcitrance abound. George Jackson, held many years in lockup, writes:

> This monster—the monster they've engendered in me—will return to torment its maker, from the grave, the pit, the profoundest pit. Hurl me into the next existence, the descent into hell won't turn me. I'll crawl back to dog his trail forever. They won't defeat my revenge, never, never. I'm part of a righteous people who anger slowly, but rage undammed. We'll gather at this door in such a number that the rumbling of our feet will make the earth tremble. I'm going to charge them for this 28 years without gratification. I'm going to charge them like a maddened, wounded, rogue male elephant—ears flared, trunk raised, trumpet blaring. I'll do my dance on his chest, and the only thing he'll ever see in my eyes is a dagger to pierce his cruel heart. This is one nigger who is positively displeased. I'll never forgive, I'll never forget, and if I'm guilty of anything at all it's of not leaning on them enough. War without terms.[25]

Jackson, after he had succeeded in overpowering guards who had escorted him back to lockup in San Quentin and in releasing other prisoners in the unit, was shot and killed while running toward San Quentin's front gate. Some of the prisoners he had released proceeded to murder two prisoners and two guards in the lockup unit.

The two prisoners who each murdered a guard while being escorted by four guards at Marion in 1983 were fellow AB members who had been held in lockup for many years and who had vowed they would both kill a guard on that day. They murdered the guards even though they understood that they would suffer severe, immediate, and long-term consequences. They were beyond caring about consequences, or even their own lives.

In New York, Willie Bosket, who has served most of his life in prison and has been held in lockup for years, told the court that had just sentenced him to an additional twenty-five years to life for stabbing a prison guard:

The sentence this court can impose on me means nothing. I laugh at you, I laugh at this court, I laugh at Mr. Prosecutor, I laugh at this entire damn system. I'll haunt this damn system. I am what the system created but never expected.[26]

Psychological Impairment

Since the introduction of the first "penitentiaries," in which prisoners were placed in complete solitary confinement, observers have concluded that isolation from others and extreme reduction of activities produce considerable psychological damage. Charles Dickens, who visited Eastern Penitentiary, the first "solitary" prison, wrote:

> I am persuaded that those who devised this system [solitary confinement] . . . do not know what it is that they are doing. . . . I hold that this slow and daily tampering with the mysteries of the brain, to be immeasurably worse than any torture of the body.
>
> My firm conviction is that, independent of the mental anguish it occasions—an anguish so acute and so tremendous, that all imagination of it must fall far short of the reality—it wears the mind into a morbid state, which renders it unfit for the rough contact and busy action of the world. It is my fixed opinion that those who have undergone this punishment, must pass into society again morally unhealthy and diseased.[27]

Regrettably only a few systematic studies of the effects of confinement in lockup situations have been conducted. In one, Richard McCleery found that prisoners held in lockup settings for long periods were very prone to developing paranoid delusion belief systems. Terry A. Kupers, a psychiatrist with long experience with prisons who was assigned to give expert testimony in a suit involving California lockup units, wrote to the court:

> Certainly, patients I see in the community who have spent any length of time in Security Housing, Management Control or Adjustment Center units at San Quentin have continued to display irrational fears of violence against themselves, and have demonstrated little ability to control their own rage. I know from many psychotherapies I have conducted and histories I have taken, that even when a patient entered prison angry, the largest part of the fear and rage was bred by the prison experience itself.[28]
>
> Some of these men [prisoners held in lockup for long periods] suffer mental "breakdowns," be they schizophrenic, depressive, hysterical or other. A much larger number suffer less visible but very deep psychological scars. They do not "break down," but they remain anxious, angry, depressed, insecure or confused, and then likely cover over these feelings with superficial bravado. They might later commit suicide, or merely fail to adjust when released, and become another statistic of recidivism.[29]

Kupers summarized the psychiatric literature on the effects of lockup in the following statement to the court:

There is general agreement today in the scientific community that the stress of life in segregation is the larger cause of high incidence rates of mental disorders amongst prisoners.[30]

A Pelican Bay SHU prisoner puts it well:

If you have not been informed of this new SHU program here in Pelican Bay, well, I think hell is a better place than this as it is built to break people. Since I have been here [one month] a man has gone literally nutty in the mind. What can you expect when you're isolated from all human contact? You sleep, eat, go to a yard by yourself, go to classification just to be told that you'll stay in the hole until you parole, die, or debrief, rat![31]

The Northern California Federal District Court states:

Based on studies undertaken in this case, and the entirety of the record bearing on this claim, the court finds that many, if not most, inmates in the SHU experience some degree of psychological trauma in reaction to their extreme social isolation and the severely restricted environmental stimulation in the SHU.[32]

Social Impairment

Prisoners confront extreme difficulties in adjusting to outside life and achieving basic viability, and most of their problems stem from having been a prisoner. One of the reasons for this is that they have become profoundly habituated to the prison routine, which is quite different from outside patterns, and have been imbued with various forms and layers of the prisoner perspective. Prisoners who have been held in lockup encounter greater difficulties because the routine in lockup is more rigid and "abnormal." In addition, many or most lockup prisoners have been influenced by the more extreme and deviant viewpoints (for instance, that of the "outlaw") that prevail in lockup and suffer extreme anxiety and paranoia about living in a world of conspiracies, threats, and actual violence.

Most persons held in lockup settings are eventually released to the outside, often directly from lockup. An SHU prisoner makes this point well:

OK. I've been in jail now eight years. Let's say I was going home tomorrow, do you mean to tell me I sit here for eight years confined in a cell resentful of things, chained every minute of my time inside my cell. And they say I am just too dangerous for anything but tomorrow they will parole me to the streets. Is there logic there? There is no logic there. The guy is paroled from these units, straight from the cells, straight to the situation, straight to the streets. How in the hell are they suppose to function out there? Is it possible? It is not anywhere possible. There is no decompression time, there is no reorientation time or nothing. When I am paroled I will be paroled to the streets, the outside to where you're at, you know what I mean. But in the meantime every time I see you, I will be setting like this.[33]

We should be concerned by the fact that the prison systems are spewing out such damaged human material, most of whom will disappear into our social trash heap, politely labeled the "homeless" or the underclass, or, worse, will violently lash out, perhaps murdering or raping someone, and then be taken back to the dungeon.

NOTES

1. Prison authorities are placing more and more inmates in "administrative segregation," "maximum-security," "control," or "lockup" housing units.

2. Donald Clemmer, *The Prison Community* (New York: Holt, Rinehart, 1958).

3. When they first began this expansion, prison administrators usually presented the new policies as nonpunitive and planned new segregation units so they would not be as cruel as solitary confinement. In California, where segregation has been used more than in any other state, initial expansion of segregation units was justified with a therapeutic rationale. In 1956, California prison administrators requested and received funds from the state legislature to construct new housing units or convert existing units to sections called "adjustment centers," which were intended to hold prisoners who were not responding to their rehabilitative programs. According to the original plan, these prisoners would receive more intensive rehabilitative strategies, such as intensive counseling and therapy. The adjustment centers were built, but no special rehabilitative programs were introduced.

4. From a letter sent to the Prison Law Collective in San Francisco, California, and distributed by them in 1975 in an unpublished document titled "Descriptions of O Wing Soledad."

5. George Jackson, *Soledad Brother* (New York: Bantam Books, 1970), pp. 23, 164.

6. Ruling of Alfonso Zirpoli, federal district judge, Northern California District, in *Johnny L. Spain v. Raymond K. Procunier,* December 18, 1975, p. 5.

7. Interview, San Quentin prisoner, 1979.

8. See Min S. Yee, *The Melancholy History of Soledad Prison* (New York: Harper & Row, 1973), for a complete description of the events and the court decision.

9. Declaration for U.S. District Court for Northern California by Terry Kupers, M.D., *Wright v. Enomoto,* June 30, 1980, pp. 5, 7, 9.

10. Robert Slater, "Psychiatric Intervention in an Atmosphere of Terror," *American Journal of Forensic Psychiatry* 7, 1 (1986): 8, 9.

11. This description of Marion was taken from David A. Ward and Allen E. Breed, *The United States Penitentiary, Marion, Illinois: A Report to the Judiciary Committee, United States House of Representatives* (Washington, DC: U.S. Government Printing Office, October 1984).

12. Ibid., pp. 11–12.

13. Ibid., p. 32.

14. *Los Angeles Times,* May 1, 1990.

15. *Corrections Digest,* June 27, 1990, p. 9.

16. *Sunday Oklahoma,* February 24, 1991.

17. *New York Times,* February 20, 1991.

18. James Austin, Stan Repko, Robert Harris, Ken McGinnis, and Susan Plant, *Evaluation of the Texas Department of Criminal Justice Administrative Segregation Population* (Washington, DC: National Council on Crime and Delinquency, October 15, 1998).

19. One of the authors asked a former director of the California Department of Corrections, who had worked for several years overseeing the classification process, how reliable he thought information from informers was. He responded, "About 30 percent."

20. Interview, San Quentin, March 1983.

21. From prisoners' files read in March 1983.

22. Robert Schultz, *"Life in SHU": An Ethnographic Study of Pelican Bay State Prison,* M.S. thesis, Humboldt State University, April 1991, p. 104.

23. From a letter written to the Soledad Defense Committee in 1971 and circulated in an unpublished document labeled "Descriptions of O Wing Ciliated," p. 3.

24. A frequently repeated statement by prisoners who have adopted an extremely hostile and violent-prone identity.

25. Jackson, *Soledad Brother,* pp. 164–165.

26. *New York Times,* April 20, 1989.

27. Charles Dickens, *American Notes and Pictures from Italy* (London: Oxford University Press, 1957), pp. 99, 109.

28. Terry A. Kupers, "Authoritarianism and the Belief System of Incorri-gibles," in Donald R. Cressy (ed.), *The Prison* (New York: Holt, Rinehart, 1961).

29. Declaration to the U.S. District Court for the Northern District of California, *Wright v. Enomoto,* July 23, 1980, pp. 5, 15.

30. Declaration to the U.S. District Court for the Northern District of California, *Wright v. Enomoto,* July 23, 1980, p. 4. Kupers specifically cited the following articles in reaching his conclusions: W. Bromber et al., "The Relation of Psychosis, Mental Defect, and Personality Types to Crime," *Journal of Criminal Law and Criminology* 28 (1973): 70–89; S. B. Guze et al., "Criminality and Psychiatric Disorders," *Archives of General Psychiatry* 20 (1969): 583–591; J. Kloech, "Schizophrenia and Delinquency," in *The Mentally Abnormal Offender* (1968): 19–28; D. Wiersnian, "Crime and Schizophrenics," *Excerpta Criminologica* 6 (1966): 169–181.

31. Letter from Pelican Bay prisoner sent to Prisoners' Rights Union, Sacramento, California.

32. *Madrid v. Gomez,* 889 F. Supp. 1149 (N.D. Cal. 1995), p. 215.

33. Schultz, *"Life in SHU,"* p. 153.

7

■

Release

THE GROWING NUMBER
OF PRISON RELEASES

Eventually, the vast majority of prisoners leave prison and the numbers are escalating each year. The U.S. Department of Justice reported that in 1996, nearly 475,000 inmates were released from prison, the majority of these (nearly 370,000) to some form of parole or probation supervision (Table 7-1).[1] The Criminal Justice Institute reported that over 600,000 inmates were release from prison in 1998.[2] Compared to 1996, the 1998 data show that an increasing number of releases are not being paroled and are given minimal to no supervision, as some states abolish parole supervision or become increasingly reluctant to parole inmates. As will shown in this chapter, the numbers of inmates released with no supervision and services will increase as the full effects of "truth in sentencing" and more restrictive parole granting policies take hold.

In this chapter we examine what happens to inmates who are released after having spent several years in confinement and the obstacles they face in trying to make it on the streets without reverting to criminal behavior.

Time in Jail and Prison Before Parole

One of the objectives of this chapter is to estimate the total amount of supervision and incarceration convicts will experience before they are fully clear of their "legal obligations" to the state for the crime committed. For many years,

TABLE 7-1 Prison Releases—All States 1996

Prison Releases	Number	%
Total Releases	**473,243**	**100.0%**
Conditional/Parole Releases	**369,808**	**78.1%**
Parole releases	143,681	30.4%
Supervised mandatory releases	178,606	37.7%
Probation releases	28,788	6.1%
Other conditional releases	18,733	4.0%
Unconditional Releases	**103,435**	**21.9%**
Expiration of sentence	97,415	20.6%
Commutation of sentence	628	0.1%
Other	5,392	1.1%

SOURCE: U.S. Department of Justice, Bureau of Justice Statistics, *Sourcebook of Criminal Justice Statistics, 1996* (Washington, DC, 1998).

the U.S. Department of Justice only reported the amount of time inmates spent in prison until they were granted their "first release" either by the parole board or by virtue of the expiration of the sentence. The typical number often cited in these government reports was about two years. Currently, average length of stay (LOS) for first released prisoners has increased slightly to twenty-five months.[3]

However, this number greatly underestimates the total length of incarceration for most offenders for several reasons. First, it excludes the amount of time an inmate will spend in jail before going to prison. The first period of incarceration occurs when the defendant (at that time) is arrested and detained in the local (usually county) jail. Although many defendants arrested for minor crimes ranging from drunk driving, failure to pay parking tickets, and petty theft are quickly released within one to three days, those defendants who eventually are sentenced to prison will spend many months in jail awaiting the court's sentencing decision. According to the U.S. Department of Justice, the LOS in jail for inmates admitted to state prison is approximately five months. Thus, the total period of incarceration before being granted a "first" release averages thirty months (Table 7-2).[4]

Second, this figure only refers to persons who are making their first release to parole at their initial parole hearing, are being released on a subsequent parole hearing date, or are being discharged after being denied for parole or not being eligible for parole.[5] This category of releases excludes the large number of inmates who return to prison for parole violations and who spend many additional months in confinement before being rereleased to parole or being discharged after completing their entire sentence (that is, "maxing out"). Once released from prison, the inmate must deal with the rules and regulations associated with parole supervision for many more months. And, if an inmate fails to abide by these rules or is arrested for a new crime, he or she will be returned to prison for more incarceration. The latest national data show that about one-third of all prison releases return to prison after three years. There are no

TABLE 7-2 Prison Releases and Time Served—
Jail, Prison, and Parole 1996 Prison Releases

Time Served	Months	
	Average	Median
Incarceration		
Pretrial time in local jail awaiting sentence	5 mos	5 mos
Prison time until first release	25 mos	16 mos
Total incarceration time until first release	30 mos	21 mos
Parole Supervision		
Successful parole releases	21 mos	16 mos
Unsuccessful parole releases	19 mos	14 mos
Reincarceration for Parole Violation	**5 mos**	**3 mos**
Total Time Under Supervision	**54–56 mos**	**38–40 mos**

SOURCE: *Bureau of Justice Statistics, National Corrections Reporting Program, 1996* (1997).

national data on the amount of time parole violators remain in prison until they are rereleased. However, a recent study of California parole violators showed a length of stay of four or five months.[6] Using these figures, the total length of stay for many inmates is more like three years rather than the two years reported in government reports.

Although two versus three years might sound like a relatively small difference in periods of incarceration, changes of only a few months for a large number of inmates will have a direct impact on the size of the prison population. In this instance, unless there is a drop in prison admissions, an increase of only three months in the average LOS from twenty-five to twenty-eight months will produce a 12 percent increase in the national prison population. Based on the current national prison population of approximately 1.3 million, the prison population would increase by about 155,000 inmates.

Third, the current cohort of prison releases does not accurately reflect recent changes in sentencing laws that require greater numbers of inmates to serve extremely long periods of time.

It will take many years for the full effects of various sentencing laws designed to greatly increase the LOS to show up in release cohorts. However, the Bureau of Justice Statistics reports, in its report on felony sentences given in 1996, that the projected LOS for these offenders will increase from twenty-five to twenty-eight months.

In addition to jail, prison, and reincarceration for parole violations, inmates released to parole must spend the remainder of their original sentence either on parole or on some prescribed period of supervision (for example, twelve months, twenty-four months, and so forth). The average period of parole supervision for those who complete their parole period "successfully" is approximately twenty-one months, while those who fail parole do so within nineteen months. In total, offenders who are eventually committed to prison can look forward to spending three to five years either in jail, prison, or on parole. And these lengths of supervision and imprisonment are likely to increase.

Rates of Rearrest After Release

During this period of supervision, many released inmates experience tremendous difficulties in adjusting to the outside world without being rearrested and returning to prison and jail. In general, most inmates are rearrested at least once after being released from prison. The U.S. Department of Justice conducted a follow-up study of 108,580 inmates released from prison to parole in eleven states in 1983 and found that 63 percent were rearrested at least once for a felony or a serious misdemeanor within three years. However, the vast majority (85 percent) were for property, drugs, and public disorder crimes.[7] Studies by the Rand Corporation and the National Council on Crime and Delinquency (NCCD) of inmates released from Illinois and California prisons demonstrated that about 40 to 45 percent were rearrested within the first year, whereas 60 to 70 percent had been rearrested for felonies and serious misdemeanors within three years.[8]

These high arrest rates have led many to argue that more, not less, imprisonment is needed to reduce crime. Yet findings from several studies suggest that imprisonment, as compared to other penal dispositions, does not reduce convicted offenders' involvement in crime.

The often-neglected study by the Rand Corporation, sponsored by the U.S. Department of Justice, compared the two-year rearrest rates of a group of felons sent to California prisons with a group who were matched on crime seriousness, past record, and other relevant characteristics but who were granted probation instead of prison. The results revealed that the persons sentenced to prison were rearrested, reconvicted, and resentenced to jail or prison at significantly higher rates than the persons who were sentenced to probation (Figure 7-1).[9]

Even though prison has apparently increased the likelihood that they will commit future crimes, ex-prisoners are still less likely to commit crime than they were before being sent to prison. In other words, their rate of rearrest is declining compared to the rate that existed before they were sentenced to prison. Two studies of released felons in California and Illinois conducted by the NCCD showed that the arrest rates of released prisoners were about half of the rates before imprisonment. The California study found that the number of arrests for prisoners released to the streets over two years dropped by over 50 percent compared to the number that occurred two years before the inmates were sentenced to prison and that the severity of the crimes also declined by 50 percent during the two-year follow-up period.[10]

The Illinois study also found a 64 percent decline in the rate of arrest twelve months after release from prison as compared to the twelve months before imprisonment (0.8 arrests per year per released inmate versus 2.2 arrests per year before prison).[11] In addition, the study showed that significant proportions of those arrests were for minor property or drug use crimes that did not result in a conviction or resentencing to prison. Instead, the high arrest

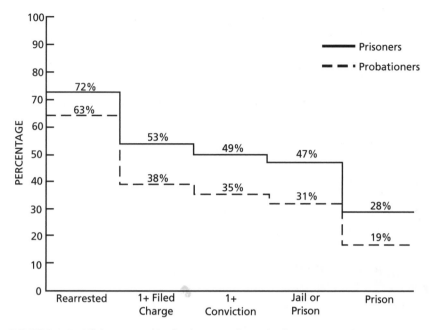

FIGURE 7-1 Recidivism Among Probationers and Matched Prisoners: Total Sample Combined

rates often reflected traditional police practices of "rounding up the usual suspects." The NCCD studies also demonstrated that although prison releases were frequently rearrested, their overall impact on crime rates in the two states was about 2 percent or less.

The reductions in arrest rates for released inmates are largely the result of maturation effects: as inmates get older, they burn out and are unable to maintain their previous criminal lifestyles. The highest crime rates are for males between the ages of 15 and 24, whereas the average age for released prisoners is over 30, well beyond their most productive crime-producing years. This point, in part, explains the limits of incarceration as a workable crime-reducing strategy. The ranks of released prisoners are replaced by the next generation of lower-class prison-bound males nurtured in inner-city communities riddled with poverty, drug abuse, and violence.

THE RISING TIDE OF PAROLE FAILURES

Although an arrest does not necessarily result in a conviction or a new sentence for the recently released inmate, an arrest or even behavior that is non-criminal can result in an inmate's return to prison for many months. As noted earlier in this chapter, about one-third of all parolees were returned to prison for new crimes or technical violations over a three-year follow-up period, and most of these arrests were for property and drug offenses. In an earlier report, the Justice Department estimated that, at that time, only 29 to 42 percent of all prison releases would be returned to prison in their lifetimes.[12]

Those earlier trends have changed considerably, however. Today most inmates do not get off of parole without some further legal difficulties. Since 1980, the number of parole violations has increased nationally from 28,817 to 175,305 in 1996, representing a 508 percent increase. Of the 1996 parole failures, approximately 120,000 were technical violators—meaning they were not convicted of a new felony crime.[13]

This trend is attributable in large part to dramatic changes in the nature of parole supervision and the imposition of increasingly more severe conditions of supervision on parolees. Instead of a system designed to help prisoners readjust to a rapidly changing and more competitive economic system, the current parole system has been designed to catch and punish inmates for petty and nuisance-type behaviors that do not in themselves draw a prison term.

Technical violations are by far the more frequent form of parole failure than being resentenced for a new crime, which occurs at a far lower rate. Technical violations represent a wide array of noncriminal behaviors (see Table 7-3). For example, an inmate may have failed to appear for scheduled office visits with the parole agent, failed to attend counseling sessions, failed to notify the parole agent of a change of address, or failed to maintain "gainful" employment. Technical violations can also include subsequent arrests without convictions or failure to pass drug tests—which suggests continued drug use—or may simply reflect unsubstantiated suspicions by parole authorities.

Unlike the criminal courts, parole revocation hearings do not require the same level of proof to trigger a return to prison. Although the *Morissey* decision by the U.S. Supreme Court grants parolees the right to a partial "due process" hearing, they still are not afforded such basic rights at these hearings as the right to counsel, the right to call witnesses, an impartial judge and jury, or most of the features of a full due process proceeding. More important, a parolee's parole status can be revoked if the board feels there is a preponderance of evidence that the parolee was not meeting parole obligations. This means that parolees who are arrested but not found guilty can have their parole status revoked, be returned to prison, and remain in prison until their original sentence expires.

Some parole board officials view these broad discretionary powers over parolees as a positive feature of parole, because it allows them to reimprison prisoners with greater speed and certainty than if the charges had been brought before the criminal courts. For example, revoking parole status and reincarcerating the prisoner is accomplished without involving the district attorney, public defender, law enforcement official, or judge. Parole revocation hearings often are pro forma ceremonies lasting less than five minutes before a parole board hearing officer, whose recommendation is forwarded to the full board for approval.

Texas reported in 1998 that 36 percent of its prison admissions were parole violations and another 40 percent were probation violators.[14] These kinds of

TABLE 7-3 Selected Conditions of Parole in Effect
in 51 Jurisdictions in 1988

Condition of Parole	Number of Jurisdictions	%
Obey all federal, state, and local laws	50	98.0
Report to the parole officer as directed and answer all reasonable inquiries by the parole officer	49	96.1
Refrain from possessing a firearm or other dangerous weapon unless granted permission	47	92.2
Remain within the jurisdiction of the court and notify the parole officer of any change in residence	46	90.2
Permit the parole officer to visit the parolee at home or elsewhere	42	82.4
Obey all rules and regulations of the parole supervision agency	40	78.4
Maintain gainful employment	40	78.4
Abstain from association with persons with criminal records	31	60.8
Pay all court-ordered fines, restitution, or other financial penalties	27	52.9
Meet family responsibilities and support dependents	24	47.1
Undergo medical or psychiatric treatment and/or enter and remain in a specified institution, if so ordered by the court	23	45.1
Pay supervision fees	19	37.3
Attend a prescribed secular course of study or vocational training	9	17.6
Perform community service	7	13.7

SOURCE: Edward E. Rhine, William R. Smith, and Donald W. Jackson, *Paroling Authorities: Recent History and Current Practice* (Laurel, MD: American Correctional Association, 1991).

high parole and probation failures mean that significant portions of the prison population consist of these violators. But what kinds of offenses have these offenders committed?

A 1993 study by NCCD for the Nevada legislature found that over 1,000 of the 6,200 inmate population consisted of either parole or probation technical violators.[15] A closer analysis of the behaviors surrounding these technical violations demonstrated that the vast majority were behaviors such as failing to maintain steady employment, not participating in drug treatment, failing to report changes in address, and getting arrested for misdemeanor or traffic violations. Some typical examples of the types of behaviors that triggered a parole violation in Nevada are as follows:

Case 1: This offender was originally received out of Clark County on 3/9/92, to serve a three-year term for attempted burglary under the influence of a controlled substance. He was paroled on 10/1/92 and returned to prison as a parole violator on 3/19/93. His parole was revoked to expiration for general rule violations (failure to maintain verifiable residence, failure to pay supervision fees). He was scheduled to be discharged from prison on 1/10/94; when he discharged, he would have served nine months in prison for his violation of parole.

Case 2: This prisoner was originally received on 2/22/90, from Clark County, to serve a five-year term for burglary. This subject paroled on 10/30/91 and returned as a parole violator on 10/8/92. This subject's parole was violated for failure to maintain verifiable residence and employment reports, failure to participate in drug testing and out-patient substance abuse counseling, and violating the house arrest program. He was scheduled to discharge this prison term on 5/24/93. This subject would have served over seven months in prison for violating these technical parole rules.

Case 3: She was originally received on 9/5/86, from Clark County, to serve a five-year sentence for attempted possession of a cheating device with a consecutive one-year sentence of attempted possession under the influence of a controlled substance. She was paroled on 3/25/88 and returned as a violator on 9/15/88 after being arrested by her parole officer for rules involving residence and employment reports, and failure to attend outpatient substance abuse counseling. At the time of the arrest, she was being treated for pneumonia at Washoe Medical Center, which was related to her deteriorating health problems from HIV infection. Her parole status was revoked, and she was eventually released on 4/4/89. This subject was completely incapacitated at the time of discharge and released to her parents. She died several days after discharge, and the medical bills accumulated by the Department of Prisons totaled $21,027.

OBSTACLES TO MAKING IT
AFTER RELEASE

Why is it that so many prisoners have such a difficult time making it on parole? Given their social and economic situation, one might better ask, why do so many actually make it? Their transition to the outside world is replete with hurdles, pitfalls, and traps that make it extremely difficult for all and that defeat many. These obstacles range from finding a job and staying off drugs to dealing with the parole agent. To probe the dimensions of this problem, we conducted interviews with fourteen parolees in April 1993. Their case studies illustrate some typical difficulties.[16]

The Shock of "Reentry"

Most ex-inmates pass suddenly from a highly routinized, controlled, reduced, and slow-paced prison life into the complex, fast-moving, impersonal world of the "streets." Because they are assimilated into prison routine and culture, the transition usually disorganizes, disturbs, and depresses them—especially those inmates who have spent many years incarcerated. Just imagine the problems that highly skilled and well-educated white males would have in getting a job, buying a car, and finding a place to live after two years of imprisonment. For the uneducated and unemployable who must face a rapidly changing and increasingly competitive and unforgiving society, the odds are almost insurmountable.

> The cars, buses, people, buildings, roads, stores, lights, noises, and animals are things [they have not] experienced at first hand for quite some time. The most ordinary transactions of the civilian have dropped from [their] repertoire of automatic maneuvers. Getting on a streetcar, ordering something at a hot dog stand, entering a theater are strange. Talking to people whose accent, style of speech, gestures, and vocabulary are slightly different is difficult. The entire stimulus world—the sights, sounds, and smells— is strange.[17]

Beyond overcoming the initial shock of "reentry," released prisoners must struggle to achieve some minimal level of economic viability. To do this in a conventional fashion, they must immediately locate some form of affordable housing, gather sufficient clothing and other basic accoutrements—tools and toiletries, and get a job. They have scant resources for accomplishing these meager goals. State prison systems usually provide a small amount of money ($200 or so), and a few provide transitional institutional supports, such as halfway houses or arrangements with social welfare agencies. In Nevada, inmates receive $21 to help them "transition" from prison to parole. These limited supports, however, are temporary and merely prolong the eventual problem of trying to make it without going back to prison.

Some prisoners have saved a little, even several hundred dollars, from money earned in prison "pay" jobs, which usually pay considerably less than $7 per day.[18] A minority have help from their families. However, most must make it on their own resources and capabilities, which are typically limited and damaged. As pointed out in Chapter 2, most prisoners enter prison poorly educated and vocationally unskilled, with limited work experience. And prison has done little to improve their preparation for the outside work world; in fact, it has often worsened it. As stated earlier, prisoners seldom receive any appropriate job training, and the habits they learn in prison are inconsistent with outside work routines.

Finding a Job

Despite research showing that providing employment or other forms of economic assistance significantly reduces the likelihood of recidivism, most prison systems are unable or unwilling to assist inmates.[19] Released inmates confront sizeable barriers to getting even the most demeaning forms of employment because they are stigmatized as ex-convicts. Most employers will not hire ex-convicts; and so, when applying for a job, the "ex" must either tell the employer that he has a record and likely be denied employment or take the chance that the employer will not run a record check and that a parole agent will not inform the employer. Also, many jobs require bonding, special licenses, or union membership, all of which are unavailable to most ex-convicts.

The ex-convict stands at the very end of society's growing line of job seekers. At the end of the 1960s, when the country had more employment opportunities for blue-collar workers than it does presently, there was some movement to reduce the employment barriers for ex-convicts when studies revealed an employment rate of around 50 percent (which seemed dismal at the time). At present, this rate is much lower. In California in 1991, only 21 percent of the state's parolees had full-time jobs. Seventy percent were not employed, and an additional 9 percent had "casual" employment.[20] The following two cases reveal the difficulties released prisoners have in trying to locate a job.

I've been looking for work for two weeks. I'm living with friends, 'cause my mother can't help me. I've been staying away from my old neighborhood and friends, 'cause I don't want to get back into that life. I've been pretty nervous 'cause I don't know how to live like this. If I was going back to selling drugs, I wouldn't be nervous, 'cause I would know what I was gonna do. But I made up my mind I wasn't gonna sell no drugs. I go to different places, fill out applications. I've been to San Leandro, Hayward, Oakland, Berkeley. I'm in the process of getting my California ID. I have to have that. Now every day I am going to different places and trying to get a job. I got a friend who got a job at the Oakland Airport. He says something might come up there. If I don't get a job through some agency or friends, I'm gonna do something I thought I would never do—work for McDonald's. [R.C., a 22-year-old black man]

I been meeting R.C. [above] and we been going up and down the streets applying everywhere. Wherever I tell him to meet me, he is there on time. I was supposed to get this light industrial job. They kept putting obstacles in front of me and I talked my way over them every time, till she brought up my being on parole and then she went sour on me. If they catch me lying on the application about being in prison or being on parole, they will violate me and give me four months. I was over to Hertz, applying for a job detailing cars. They pay $9 a hour. They told me they would give me a job if I had a driver's license. I gotta have $50 to get my license reissued. $35 for a ticket and $15 for the fee. The agent doesn't have a fund to loan me any. They used to have a fund, but the parolees didn't pay the money back. If I could get my license, I could work for Avis or Hertz. I had dry-cleaning training a long time ago, but this time I wasn't in long enough to go through the program. It takes several years. You have to have the paper to get a job. I could jump in and clean anything—silks, wools, remove any spot, use all the chemicals, but I don't got any paper. They won't let you start without the paper. And they don't have any programs where they are giving you the old training and certifying you. [K.B., a 38-year-old black man][21]

Trail 'Em, Nail 'Em, Jail 'Em

Being on parole means being under the supervision of parole agents, who have peace officer status. Parole officers are equipped with extraordinary police powers: they can enforce a set of "conditions of parole," which are much more restrictive than penal statutes, and they are not restrained by constitutional protections against invasion of privacy and illegal search and seizure. Parole agents can enter a parolee's residence at any time in the day or night, search the parolee at the agent's discretion, or place the parolee in jail any time they desire and charge the parolee with violation of parole, either for new crimes or for violation of the conditions of parole.

> I go to the parole agent and tell him I want to get a job. "Uh, come back and see me next week." I mean, it's not really his fault because he got 300 other guys. And he doesn't even know me. All he knows is my number is three seven such and such. All he knows—if he wants to keep his job, all he got to do is have me come in once a week, piss in the bottle. As long as the bottle don't show no drugs in it, I can stay on the street another week. First time the piss is not good, all he gotta do is send me to jail, that's it. He put my file over there in "inactive," and that's it. He's still got his job, he goes on—you know, they don't have to get personally involved with you. 'Cause they can't. You got 300 guys—how you get involved with 300 guys?[22]

Commensurate with the toughening of sentencing laws and the demise of the rehabilitation model, parole supervision has been transformed ideologically from a social service to a law enforcement system. During the rehabilitative era (the 1950s and 1960s), most states sought to combine policing and rehabilitative services in their parole administration. Parole agents were viewed as paternalistic figures who mixed authority and help. The punitive swing in corrections and the fiscal crisis experienced by most states have transformed parole more and more into a policing operation. Instead of developing individualized plans to help the prisoners locate a job, find a residence, or locate needed drug treatment services, the new parole system is bent on surveillance and detection. Parolees are routinely and randomly checked for illegal drug use, failure to locate or maintain a job, moving without permission, or any other number of petty and nuisance-type behaviors that do not conform to the rules of parole.

On detection of any of these acts or on the parolee's arrest for any crime, the parole officer holds the option of having the parolee arrested and placed in the local jail until the parole board can review the charges. In many states, parolees can wait weeks in the local jail until a representative from the parole board makes a determination on whether the behavior is sufficiently serious to warrant revocation and return to prison.

A parolee we interviewed ended up on general assistance, abusing drugs, and finally in a drug program after he lost a good job because of his agent's enforcement of the rules:

I looked for a place to stay in San Francisco, so I moved in with a friend across the bay in Hayward. I got a job as a bank courier. I wasn't carrying any money, and it was a good job. My agent told me to quit it and move back to the city. I hadn't been able to find a job in the city, so I told him, "Would you rather have me back on GA [general assistance welfare] and selling dope?" He said he couldn't tell me to do that. [D.H., a 51-year-old white man]

Drug Testing

As the system has been reoriented toward a law enforcement system, the methods of surveillance have been strengthened. The most powerful tool for the new parole agent is the urinalysis test. Nowhere is this tactic used more forcibly than in California, where almost all released inmates are subject to weekly urinalysis tests. The first thing a parolee is instructed to do on arrival at the parole officer's office is to urinate in a bottle and have a chemical test completed. Because most of these inmates have rather extensive histories of drug use, it is predictable that many will occasionally fail the drug test and subsequently have their paroles revoked.

Because of the widespread use of drug testing, California has led the country in parole violations. In 1993, two of every five parole violations that occurred nationally occurred in California. A more recent study in 1995 found that only 21 percent of all inmates released from parole had successfully completed their supervision requirements, as compared to the 54 percent rate for other state correctional systems. California also accounts for 40 percent of all parole violations that occur nationally. On any given day, over 26,000 prison beds were occupied by parole violators as of 1995.[23]

Intensive Supervision Programs

Intensive supervision programs (ISPs) also place additional obstacles in the path of parolees and result in more parole failures. Hailed by criminologists as the new wave of "intermediate sanctions," these programs were first created by the courts to divert offenders who otherwise would have been imprisoned had the program not existed. However, they have also been used by parole agencies to escalate levels of supervision for offenders paroled from prison. The ISPs for the "back end" of the correctional system are intended to encourage parole boards to release offenders who pose a somewhat higher risk to public safety and who would not have been released had the ISPs not existed. By releasing these marginal cases on ISP, the inmate's expected length of stay in prison can be shortened, thus reducing the prison population. For both probationers and parolees, specialized treatment programs were also to be part of the ISP regimen, although this rarely has been the case. The overall expectation was that these programs would also reduce these offenders' recidivism rates and therefore be more cost-effective as compared to traditional forms of incarceration.

Evaluations of these programs have shown just the opposite results. A number of experimental studies by the Rand Corporation have found that persons placed in these programs violate parole for technical reasons at a far greater rate than those receiving regular supervision, even though their rearrest rates are essentially equal. These programs also tend to be far more expensive than regular supervision and have had little if any impact on prison crowding. Because of the highly restrictive nature of the programs' eligibility criteria, these programs are quite small in size (50 to 150 offenders diverted or released on parole each year) and often cease to exist once federal funds used to start the programs dry up.[24]

The higher technical violation failure rates for ISP cases are simply the result of programs that provide more supervision but not many more services. Consequently, parole and probation officers are able to detect more petty behavior than before. But more important, the parole officer is able to use this information against the inmate to justify revocation and recommitment to prison.

Electronic Monitoring

Many ISP programs are also adding electronic monitoring technology to their monitoring capabilities. The last national estimate indicated that only 13,000 offenders were under electronic monitoring on any given day.[25] In such a situation, the inmate cannot, without calling his or her parole officer, leave his or her residence to do such normal things as purchasing groceries, picking up the mail, and running any number of regular errands associated with modern life.

As with the ISP evaluations, rigorous studies of electronic monitoring programs have found neither negative nor positive results relating to rearrest.[26] Offenders admitted to such programs respond the same as or worse than offenders placed under normal supervision. In fact, the study of the Oklahoma electronic monitoring program found that released inmates placed on electronic monitoring did worse, as a greater proportion were returned to prison for not abiding by the strict house arrest rules imposed by the electronic monitoring program.

THOSE WHO MAKE IT

Most prisoners we interviewed in our three-state study aspired to a relatively modest, stable, conventional life after prison. "I want a nice job, paying pretty good. Something to keep me busy instead of running the streets." "When I get out I want to have my kids with me, have a good job so I can support them." "I'm going to try to get into electronics. I want a job I won't get laid off on."[27] However, their chances of achieving these modest goals are slim. As already suggested, released prisoners are socially and economically damaged goods. Parolees are certainly no better equipped to make it in society after imprisonment than when they were admitted. They remain largely uneducated, unskilled, and without the necessary family support system to help them make a law-abiding transition from prison to the community.[28]

Despite these obstacles, most released prisoners eventually quit or scale down their criminal activities to a level that avoids arrest, or at least arrest for serious crimes. Because so many continue to have extreme difficulty finding and holding jobs, how, then, do they get by? What kind of life do they live?

Doing Good

A few released prisoners "do all right," that is, achieve more or less permanent viability in a relatively conventional manner. They usually do so only because of the random chance of securing a good job and a niche in some conventional social world by virtue of their own individual efforts to "straighten up," often with the help of their family, friends, or prisoner assistance organizations. But even members of this group are likely to face periodic obstacles in being accepted as full citizens. In applying for a job from which they are not excluded by virtue of their prior criminal record, they must publicly admit their ex-convict status. When crimes are committed in their neighborhoods, they are often arrested simply because they are known to the police. Their friendships and memories are forever tied to their past prison experiences. They will always be treated by others with suspicion, fear, and distrust.

A very few released prisoners—usually persons with better preparation when they leave prison; significant support from friends, family, or some program; and some luck—realize some of their higher aspirations. A 29-year-old white male who had a drug and alcohol problem since he was 15 and served two years for vehicular manslaughter was about to graduate from San Francisco State with a 3.7 grade point average and was applying for graduate school when we interviewed him. His progress demonstrates the difficulty experienced by persons who do make it.

> I had about $1,200 when I got out that I had saved when I was out on OR [release on own recognizance program]. I knew from my crime and record I was gonna get time, so I worked and saved my money. I first got a hotel room in downtown Burlingame, the only flea bag hotel there, and went to an AA meeting that night. The next day I went to see my parole officer, and he started right off reading all my arrests, saying you did this and that. But I finally struck a deal with him that if I didn't drink or drive a car without a license he would keep off my back. But if I did, he would violate me and charge me with everything he could. He lived up to the bargain for a year and then I got another parole agent.
>
> By then I was already in San Francisco State. I had signed up with the Rebound Project [a program that helps ex-prisoners enter San Francisco State University] while I was in CMC [a state prison near San Luis Obispo]. I had a small apartment in San Carlos for $400 a month. I was busing it to school three days a week. Two hours there and two hours back. I got a job at Walgreen's. I was selling liquor at night to guys who were just like me. But I was attending AA and had made up my mind that I was gonna change my life. And I never took a drink. Then I worked for a while selling cars. Then selling TVs at Mathews in

Daly City. I bought an old beat-up Buick that had a pretty good motor and got two years out of it. About 25,000 miles.

The next parole agent was a real tough guy. First thing he told me was, "It's obvious you've been pulling some scam for a year." So he put me back on maximum custody. The other agent, even though he put on the tough-guy act, he left me alone. This guy had me coming in once a week, had me pissing in the bottle, and he would show up at my house at six in the morning trying to catch me at something. But I had decided that if they were going to send me back, they were gonna have to fabricate something. I wasn't doing nothing. I didn't even have kitchen knives in my house. I made the decision, also, that I was gonna stay out of their face. I learned that in prison. If you stayed out of people's faces and stayed away from places where shit started, you wouldn't have any trouble. I never went in the day room or to the iron pile [the weight workout area]. That's where guys got stuck. So I did the same on the outside. I had to learn to keep out of people's faces outside, too. One time some guy in the library got in my face and I got back in his. I didn't have the little stamp on my ID card that you had to have to check out reference books and he wouldn't give me a book. They hadn't sent me the stamp yet. So we got into it. But I try now to keep out of everyone's face. Sometimes some of these PC [politically correct] students get on my nerves. The little assholes don't know shit, and they're telling me what's politically correct. But I still stay out of their face.

Then I got another agent. They didn't tell me and I went to the office and the old agent said he had sent me a letter telling me that I had been transferred to a new agent. He didn't send me no letter. It's lucky I had gone to see the old agent when I did, because I was supposed to report to the new agent the next day and I wouldn't have known it and they could have violated me. This guy was an asshole too, but then I got another agent and he was like the first one. By that time I had finished two years of college and had no arrests. So he left me alone. Now, I am gonna graduate with a 3.7. But I had a lot of luck, too. A lot of times I got behind in my rent, but I had good landlords. Really nice guys and they let me slide. They could have kicked me out and where would I have been? The parole agency wasn't gonna help me. They're too busy trying to bust guys.

Dependency

Many ex-prisoners refrain from further law violations but remain completely dependent on their families or social welfare. This is true for the following three parolees we interviewed.

I got out on Friday a year ago, and I got high right away. When I went to the parole agent on Monday, he asked me if I had been using and I told him I had. He said he liked my honesty, but he sent me right then to a 90-day detox at San Quentin. I didn't use no more. I been staying at home with my mother. She is just happy I'm clean. I haven't been able to find no job, but she thinks that's alright, just so I'm clean. You see, I got a younger brother and sister and an older sister, all on crack. I help them a little and protect the house. My mother is just glad I do that. She is proud of me. Shows me to her friends, says, "See how good he looks?" I go to meetings and just stay home. I got a lady and a seven-year-old daughter, too, who I see a lot. I'm on GA and get $340 a month. I couldn't live on that. It's lucky I got my mother. I got phlebitis in my leg and have to take medicine. It hurts when I stand or walk too much. But I'm still gonna take a job if I get one. I want the extra spending money. But I'm not going back on drugs. If I did, I'd just be back into buying some drugs, flipping them or burglarizing houses and factories like before. [K.W., a 30-year-old black man]

I get $620 a month through SSI [supplemental security income]. I got a room on Sixth Street [skid-row area] through Tenderloin Housing. It costs me $260 a month. I eat breakfasts at one of the restaurants around the hotel. For $2.50 I get eggs, bacon, and potatoes. Sometimes I eat at Glide for lunch, sometimes dinner, too. Once in a while I treat myself to steak dinner. I don't use drugs or alcohol. I mostly stay to myself, watch TV in the room. It's safer that way. Sometimes, I walk to Golden Gate Park. And I go to a movie once in a while. I can't read very much because I'm too nervous. I have a hyperactive thyroid. They found out I had it in prison. I kept losing weight. I went from around 190 to 130. The doctors there didn't know what it was and wouldn't give me any time. So I swallowed glass and told them I had. They sent me to the General Hospital and when I got there, I told them why I had done it. So they gave me all kinds of tests and found out I had the hyperactive thyroid. So I'm waiting to get some drugs for it. I've been on the list for seven months. I have an appointment in May. I'm not going back to prison. I can't live there. I don't know how they can treat a person like that. Least they could do is have some kind of program. There is no rehabilitation. They just shove you out the door with no support. It's scary as hell. What I want is a job. Any job. I don't give a fuck what it is. I'll clean shitters, or whatever. At least it is something to fill my time and make me feel better about myself, something constructive. [L.E., a 48-year-old white man]

I used drugs, speed, the first day. It scared the hell out of me. I've been clean ever since, since July, nine months. It's the first time I've been clean when I was out since I first went to the joint in the '60s. I feel kinda weird. I'm gonna stay clean and get off this parole. It's hard to do, but I'm not going back. I tried to get work, but there is this thing, you have to say you were in prison. If you don't, it's a violation. Who's gonna hire a 51-year-old that's been in prison most of his life? I'm getting GA. My room's $270. That leaves me 70 bucks. Not much. I'm trying to get SSI, drugs and having been in the system all these years. They tell me that you go once and they deny you. You go again and they deny you. Then the third time they give it to you. I eat in restaurants once in a while. But usually I buy food at the food bank. A friend of mine has a hot plate. Sometimes I eat at Glide or that gay church on Gough. I go there on Christmas, New Year, and Easter. I go up to the firehouse on Third Street where they collect toys for kids. They give hot soup in the afternoon. My sister sent me some clothes and every month I buy something, like these jeans. Most of the time I stay alone. I stay away from the TL [Tenderloin district, where there is a lot of drug dealing, prostitution, and crime]. I watch TV a lot. I go to the library and walk around a lot. I like to go to Golden Gate Park and the wharf. Last month I went back to Arkansas and visited my sister. The parole agent let me go. When I got back, he said he won a bet on me. The supervisor said I would never come back. I go to the shelters sometimes to talk to people. I try to tell the youngsters how it is. Maybe I can help them a little, so they can stay away from the shit I got into. [D.R., a 51-year-old Chicano]

Drift

Other parolees, even though their intentions before release and at the time we interviewed them were to avoid going back to prison, cross back and forth—outside and inside the law and the parole rules. For a while they hold menial jobs or live with their families, in halfway houses, or on welfare. Then they slip, start using drugs, lose their job, and begin selling drugs or stealing. Usually they are arrested or "violated" by their agent and sent back, often for short periods, perhaps a thirty-day detox, which in California can be done with no formal proceedings. Then they begin again to attempt to live within the law and parole rules. Two parolees we interviewed had been drifting for more than a year.

When I got out I moved in with my cousin in the Haight [the Haight-Ashbury district]. I wanted to stay away from the crime element, the prey-type environment. I met this guy at a club who said he thought I would be a good bouncer because I was big, so I worked at this place at Turk and Eddy [in the Tenderloin district] for 10 months. I lost that job because I was staying up so late and I started using some drugs. So then I started selling a little dope. I'd take $100 and buy some crack and make $300. But I was using and the agent sent me back to San Quentin for a 90-day violation. Then I got out and started scuffling to get by. I was cleaning the streets. A friend had a pickup and we'd go around and pick up anything. An old stove or refrigerator, sitting on the sidewalk. We picked up this old dirty Persian rug and we cleaned it up and sold it to some hippie. We were living from day to day. Then I got to using crack again and was busted in a car with a white guy, scoring. I got sent back for six months that time. Now I'm out, no job, and I don't want to go back; I'm not going back. My aspiration is to be a public relations man, but I haven't had any luck in finding anything like that. [A.R., a 30-year-old black man]

I stopped in Oakland on the way home and went to MacArthur and Telegraph, saw a couple of friends, and got high. I got a room in a little hotel there. After a few days I went to see my agent in San Francisco and told him I was high and needed some help. He put me in a detox program for 72 hours and then put me in Milestone. It's a halfway house for parolees. I stayed there for four months. I had a job in temporary service and had a bank account, $300. On a Friday I wanted to get high. I went back to Milestone, got my clothes, and went to the Tenderloin. I got busted on Turk Street. I had just bought some crack, had it in my mouth. I got sent back. When I got out, I went back to Milestone and I couldn't get no job, so I was hustling. I'm not gonna walk around begging, dirty, homeless when everyone else in America is eating. I was doing the smallest crimes so I'd do the less time. I passed a few $2 bills for 20s. Whenever I got a 20, I'd tear a couple of corners off and then I would get some $2 bills from the bank. Most people never see a $2 bill. So you glue the 20 on it and you just hand it to somebody and keep talking to them while they get your change. If they give you change for a 20, well, they gave it to you, you didn't tell them it was a 20. But I tried to pass one in this little store and this Chinese lady followed me out on to the street and started yelling. I got busted again. Now I been out since last month. I'm living in the FAD [Freedom Against Drugs] program out on 48th Avenue. I'm getting GA. I get $172 every two weeks. They help you get on welfare. I'm going to go to the Northern California Service League to see Nancy Lopez. She tries to get ex's a job. I'm gonna get a job, save me some money, become a functioning citizen of society. [R.R., a 30-year-old black man]

Dereliction

Most of those who do not find a rare niche in some conventional or marginal realm steadily gravitate to the world of the homeless street people who live from day to day, drinking, hanging out, and surviving (but not for too many years) by making the rounds of soup kitchens and homeless shelters. A recent study of homelessness by Martha Burt found that 80 percent of the homeless population has been in jail, prison, or a mental hospital.[29] We believe that a follow-up study (which has not been done) of prisoners after release would reveal that more than 25 percent eventually end up on the streets, where they live out a short life of dereliction, alcoholism, and drug abuse. A 43-year-old black man we interviewed appeared to have become a derelict.

I been violated three times. Twice for absconding, once for a dirty drug test. I've been to the county jail four times. I was in a substance abuse program for a little while. One time I had a little job for a while as a janitor in a machine shop. They fired me. Said I had a drinking problem. Now I'm living on the street. I just got out of an alcohol program. I stay at the shelters when I can. You sign up and they have a lottery. I'm getting welfare and am waiting for a room through the

Tenderloin Housing. As soon as I get a room, I can clean up and keep my clothes clean and get a little job. Been staying away from Safeway, stealing booze. I'm determined to stay out this time. I've been to the shelter on 5th and Bryant, a multiple service center for the homeless. They're gonna develop a job around my skills, fix my résumé.

Generally speaking, this is a very grave situation. Some ex-prisoners—with luck, resolve, and some help—do all right. But most of those who eventually stay out of prison do not live successful or gratifying lives by their or conventional society's standards. They remain dependent on others or the state; drift back and forth from petty crime to subsistence, menial, dependent living; or gravitate to the new permanent urban underclass—the "homeless." Many die relatively young: "I started getting real nervous. Most of the guys I ran with were dead from AIDS, shot, drugs, or whatever."[30]

Imprisonment is not the total cause of this depressing outcome, but its contribution is considerable. Any imprisonment reduces the opportunities of felons, most of whom had relatively few opportunities to begin with. Doing time in the new generation of warehouse prisons, in which routinization and isolation have increased and rehabilitative efforts have all but completely disappeared, only makes matters worse.

NOTES

1. The federal government uses the category "conditional release" to represent inmates released to parole supervision, either at the discretion of a parole board or as a requirement of the inmate's sentence, and releases to probation. The latter instance reflects sentences in which the court has the authority to place an inmate on probation after serving a brief period of incarceration at a state prison. Generally, this practice is referred to as "shock incarceration" and includes the recent interest in boot camps.

2. Criminal Justice Institute, Inc., *Corrections Yearbook 1998* (Middletown, CT: 1999), pp. 58–59.

3. U.S. Department of Justice, Bureau of Justice Statistics, *National Corrections Reporting Program, 1996.*

4. Ibid.

5. The rate at which parole boards grant parole at the first release varies dramatically by the type of crime the inmate was sentenced to prison for and from state to state. Parole boards in general, however, do not release the majority of inmates eligible for parole at the inmate's first hearing.

6. James Austin and Robert Lawson, *Assessment of California Parole Violators and Recommended Intermediate Programs and Policies* (Washington, DC: National Council on Crime and Delinquency, February 18, 1998).

7. U.S. Department of Justice, Bureau of Justice Statistics, *Recidivism of Prisoners Released in 1983* (Washington, DC: U.S. Government Printing Office, April 1989).

8. James Austin, "Using Early Release to Relieve Prison Crowding: A Dilemma in Public Policy," *Crime and Delinquency* 32, 4 (October 1986): 404–503; Joan Petersilia, Susan Turner, and Joyce Peterson, *Prison Versus Probation in California: The Implications for Crime and Offender Recidivism* (Santa Monica, CA: Rand Corporation, 1986).

9. Petersilia et al., *Prison versus Probation.*

10. James Austin, *Parole Outcome in California: The Consequences of Determinate Sentencing, Punishment, and Incapacitation on Parole Performance* (San Francisco: National Council on Crime and Delinquency, 1989).

11. James Austin, *The Effectiveness of Reduced Prison Terms on Public Safety and Costs: Evaluation of the Illinois Supplemental Meritorious Good-Time Program* (San Francisco: National Council on Crime and Delinquency, 1993).

12. U.S. Department of Justice, Bureau of Justice Statistics, *The Prevalence of Imprisonment* (Washington, DC: U.S. Government Printing Office, July 1985).

13. U.S. Department of Justice, Bureau of Justice Statistics, *Sourcebook of Criminal Justice Statistics 1998* (Washington, DC: U.S. Government Printing Office, 1999), Table 6.74.

14. Criminal Justice Policy Council. *Sourcebook of Texas Adult Justice Population Statistics 1988–1998* (Austin, TX: November 1999), p. 37.

15. James Austin, Aaron McVey, and Fred Richer, *Correctional Options for the State of Nevada to Constrain Prison Population Growth* (San Francisco: National Council on Crime and Delinquency, 1993).

16. This sample was not randomly determined. We had requested permission from the California Department of Corrections to conduct a far more systematic study that would have entailed a more rigorous design. However, the request to have access to lists of parolees was refused by the director. Faced with this obstacle, we decided to distribute ten fliers to persons waiting in line for a free lunch at the Glide Memorial Methodist Church in San Francisco. The fliers stated that we were seeking parolees to be interviewed and that we would pay $20 per interview. We were flooded with respondents and had to refuse to take any more after four days of interviewing. It should be noted that more than 112,000 parolees are on supervision in California as of 1999.

17. John Irwin, *The Felon* (Upper Saddle River, NJ: Prentice-Hall, 1970), pp. 113–114.

18. Criminal Justice Institute, Inc., *Corrections Yearbook 1998,* p. 111.

19. Richard Berk and David Rauma, "Remuneration and Recidivism: The Long-Term Impact of Unemployment Compensation on Ex-Offenders," *Journal of Quantitative Criminology* 3, 1 (1987): 3–27.

20. These figures were supplied by the California Department of Corrections Research Branch, 1993.

21. Interviews with authors.

22. From interviews conducted by staff at the Center on Juvenile and Criminal Justice, San Francisco, California, reported in its *Parole Violators in California: A Waste of Money, a Waste of Time* (September 1991), p. 8. Actually, the typical caseload of a California parole agent is 75 cases.

23. Austin and Lawson, *Assessment of California Parole Violators and Recommended Intermediate Programs and Policies,* p. i.

24. Joan Petersilia and Susan Turner, "An Evaluation of Intensive Probation in California," *Journal of Criminal Law and Criminology* 82, 3 (Fall 1991), 610–658.

25. Criminal Justice Institute, Inc., *Corrections Yearbook 1998,* wp. 124.

26. James Austin and Patricia Hardyman, *The Use of Early Parole with Electronic Monitoring to Control Prison Crowding* (San Francisco: National Council on Crime and Delinquency, 1992); Terry L. Baumer and Robert L. Mendelsohn, *Final Report: The Electronic Monitoring of Non-Violent Convicted Felons: An Experiment in Home Detention* (Indianapolis, IN: School of Public and Environmental Affairs, Indiana University, January 1990).

27. Excerpts from quotes included in Chapter 2.

28. According to the U.S. Department of Justice, 64 percent of all prison releases

to parole had less than a high school education, with a median education level at the eleventh grade. The eleventh-grade level is the same for prison admissions, which indicates the absence of any improvement in education level while imprisoned. See U.S. Department of Justice, Bureau of Justice Statistics, *National Corrections*

Reporting Program, 1996. Washington, DC: U.S. Government Printing Office.

29. Martha Burt, *Over the Edge* (New York: Urban Institute and Russell Sage Foundation, 1992).

30. Interview, 51-year-old parolee, San Francisco, April 1993.

8

■

The Correctional
Treatment Industrial
Complex

INTRODUCTION

Some believe that the key to turning around the imprisonment binge is the concept of rehabilitation. In other words, we must redirect our focus on treating inmates rather than punishing them. Inmates are seen as problematic but possibly salvageable if sufficient levels of treatment services can be delivered to them *while they are incarcerated*. This perspective has led to a resurgence of the rehabilitative ideal and with it an emerging offender treatment industrial complex.[1]

The rehabilitation movement is being led by drug treatment advocates who see much of the crime problem as linked to drug use. To them the best hope for reducing crime and incarceration is to greatly expand the availability of drug treatment services. This has lead to the rapid expansion of such innovative programs such as drug courts, boot camps, and residential substance abuse programs. All of these programs have been largely funded by the federal government over the past decade and promise to reduce recidivism and prison costs. The latter goal is achieved by either diverting prison-bound offenders to alternative programs or reducing the likelihood that inmates will be readmitted to prison as parole violators or with a new sentence. Very few, if any, programs are designed to reduce the inmate's length of stay.

This chapter examines two widely touted "alternatives to incarceration" (boot camps and prison-based drug treatment) that claim to be effective in reducing crime, reducing the use of imprisonment, and reducing costs. But first we present an overview of what is known regarding those factors that are known to be associated with criminal behavior. For a treatment program to be effective, it should incorporate factors known to suppress or influence criminal behavior.

In evaluating these two types of programs and any other program or policy, there are two fundamental criteria that such programs must meet. Obviously, there must be a reasonable expectation that the treatment being administered to the inmate will have a significant and long-lasting impact on the inmate. Programs that show short-term and/or minimal impact on the offender should not be viewed as effective. For example, a program that only demonstrates an initial 5 to 10 percent reduction in a recidivism rate of 40 percent (as compared to a control population) may be statistically significant (based on the number of cases analyzed) but will have little substantive significance, especially if the differences between the experimental and control populations narrow over time.

Second, there must be evidence that the treatment program can be successfully applied to a large proportion of the inmate population. In other words, what is the potential market share of the prison population for this program? Having a program that works successfully with only 1 percent of the inmate population is simply not impacting a significant share of the inmate population to produce real cost savings. Even a pilot program must hold the promise of being expanded so that a large proportion of the inmate population can be "exposed" to the treatment.

Lack of a significant "market share" can happen for a number of reasons. First, the eligibility criteria may be so restrictive that only a very small segment of the prison population can even be considered eligible for the program. Second, programs that seek to divert so called "prison-bound" inmates often end up selecting "probation-bound" inmates and thus widen rather than reduce the net of criminal justice control.[2] Third, programs that have a high drop-out or in-program failure rate result in too few inmates successfully completing the program. Although the "successful" graduates often have very low recidivism rates, by not including the program failures, which may be substantial, the impact results are unfairly skewed in favor of the "treatment" group.

Before we look closely at the boot camp and prison-based programs, we should note that the lack of market share is already apparent for boot camps and drug treatment programs. As shown in Table 8-1, the numbers of inmates in these programs are (1) relatively small and (2) are declining. As of 1998, there were 99,210 inmates in drug treatment programs and 6,857 in boot camps. Collectively this represents less than 10 percent of the 1.3 million prison population. Although there may be some level of reporting bias in these data, it is certainly clear that most inmates do not participate in these rehabilitative programs. This finding is consistent with the program participation data presented in Chapter 5 (Doing Time). Why so few inmates are in programs that have been touted as highly successful is the subject of this chapter.

TABLE 8-1 Numbers of Inmates in Prison, Boot Camps, and Drug Treatment, 1994–1998

Year	Prison Population	Boot Camps	Drug Treatment	Total in Treatment	% of Prison Population
1994	990,147	8,255	158,158	166,413	17%
1995	1,078,542	9,121	130,560	139,681	13%
1996	1,127,528	8,510	92,155	100,665	9%
1997	1,185,800	7,250	96,078	103,328	9%
1998	1,302,019	6,857	99,210	106,067	8%
% Change	31%	–20%	–59%	–57%	–52%

SOURCES: Criminal Justice Institute, *Corrections Yearbook, 1999*, pp. 117–119; Bureau on Justice Statistics, *Sourcebook of Criminal Justice Statistics, 1998*, Table 6-1.

FACTORS RELATED
TO CRIMINAL BEHAVIOR

Considerable research has been conducted by criminologists that shows that criminal careers for both adults and juveniles do not follow a predictable and stable pattern. For example, most youth (especially males) commit delinquent acts during their adolescent years but cease to continue their criminal activities as they pass into adulthood. Similarly, many adult offenders have *not* had extensive juvenile careers but become involved in serious criminal activity when they reach adulthood. However, they are highly unlikely to continue their criminal behaviors indefinitely. Rather, there are many factors that will collectively impinge upon the individual and will impact the likelihood of the initiation and duration of a criminal career.

Gender and Age

Of all the factors that impact criminal behavior, sex and age are by far the most important and powerful. The vast majority of crimes are committed by young males. Based on the Uniform Crime Reports (UCR) data, approximately 70 percent of all arrests are for persons under age 30.[3] Thereafter, the rate of offending for offenders declines dramatically—youthful offenders "burn out" and are no longer high-risk cases. There are, of course, exceptions to this generalization, but they tend to be adults with extensive juvenile and adult criminal histories who are unable or unwilling to pursue any form of legitimate lifestyles.

The fact that most active criminals are youthful is especially relevant to a significant number of adult prisoners, probationers, and parolees. As reported earlier in Chapter 7, the average age of released prisoners and parolees is in the 32- to 33-year range and will increase as inmates are required to serve longer sentences. Probationers are a couple of years younger but still well above the peak crime rate years of 15 to 24. The contrast between those who commit crimes and those who are incarcerated suggests that many offenders under correctional supervision are well above their peak years of criminal behavior and should be viewed as low risk due to what is known as maturation effects.

The aging phenomenon explains why several studies have found that only a small proportion of the crimes committed each year can be attributed to released prisoners or parolees. The Bureau of Justice Statistics estimated that approximately 3 percent of all arrests for serious crimes could be attributed to released prisoners. Other studies of early release have reached the same conclusions.[4] These data underscore that correctional treatment and punishment initiatives will have minimal if any impact on crime rates.

Married with Children

Another major life event that reduces offenders' probability of continuing their criminal behavior relates to their ability to maintain a stable and supportive marriage.[5] It must be emphasized that it is not marriage, per se, but the nature of that relationship as it serves to solidify the other key life events of job stability, drug abuse, drinking, and residency.[6] Clearly there are many examples where marriage has actually encouraged rather than diminished criminal behavior. But in general, offenders who are able to become involved in a common-law or legal relationship are less likely to continue criminal careers than those who do not.

Job Stability

Beginning with the pioneering work of Rushe and Kirchheimer in 1939, criminologists have long noted the relationship of employment to crime.[7] On a structural level, many studies have found that within capitalistic societies, incarceration rates increase as unemployment increases. On a more individual level, we know that prisoners have very high rates of unemployment, which is related to their criminal behavior—if nothing more than for basic economic needs. Consequently, the ability of an ex-offender to maintain any form of stable employment that generates sufficient income to economically survive coupled with marriage and the aging process will significantly reduce that person's criminal tendencies.[8] Having a job means one can get a credit card, phone service, a car, an apartment, go shopping, eat out, go the movies, and travel. These are the symbolic activities and attributes of the middle-class lifestyle that many Americans strive to realize. Even a little "dosage" of economic independence can have a significant impact for offenders released from prison. One important study by Berk and Rauma in California found that providing even a very modest level of economic assistance to released prisoners greatly reduced their rates of recidivism as compared to a control group that did not receive such assistance.[9]

Drugs

Research also shows a strong association between alcohol and illegal drug use and involvement in crime. Simply stated, people arrested or reporting to have committed serious crimes tend to have higher rates of recent alcohol and drug use than people who are not involved in such criminal activities. Between 50 to

80 percent of adults arrested test positive for drug use at the time of arrest. As will be reported later in this chapter, it has been estimated that approximately 70 percent of the inmate population has some type of drug use or abuse history.

However, it is also true, as is the case with other individual attributes of criminals and noncriminals, that a much larger number of people of who regularly use alcohol and illicit drugs do not become involved in criminal activities (other than possession, use, or the purchasing of illegal drugs).

According to the Office of National Drug Control Policy (ONDCP), approximately 77 million Americans have admitted to using illicit drugs since age 12. Most of that drug use is linked to marijuana. Over 11 percent (or approximately 28 million) of Americans have used illicit drugs in the past year, and 6.7 percent (or 15 million) have used these drugs in the past thirty days. Despite these large numbers of drug users (which, by the way, exclude people who are incarcerated), only 1.6 million of them are arrested each year, with the vast majority being arrests for possession (1.3 million).[10] Moreover, there has been virtually no change in the level of drug use by Americans since 1990, as shown in Table 8-2, even though the crime rate has dropped during this time period.

What these data suggest is that alcohol and/or drug use alone is not a necessary or sufficient condition for one to commit a crime. Rather, it can be argued that some of the other factors, in combination with drug use, can serve to greatly increase the probability of criminality.

Societal and Economic Structure

Related to these individual offender considerations are the more macro-level and structural influences on crime rates. This perspective focuses on social and economic forces that produce social stress, which in turn is associated with variations in crime rates. We have already alluded to the unemployment-high incarceration association first stipulated by Rushe and Kirchheimer. Linsky and Strauss have developed a more elaborate and comprehensive explanation designed to explain why similarly situated states had very dissimilar crime rates.[11] They found that the following social and economic factors are reflective of *social stress* and that states with higher rates of social stress have higher rates of violent crimes, mental illness, and suicide. The indicators they found to be predictive of these three forms of deviant behavior were:

1. Business failures
2. Unemployment claims
3. Workers on strike
4. Personal bankruptcies
5. Mortgage foreclosures
6. Divorces
7. Abortions
8. Illegitimate births

Table 8-2 National Estimates of Americans Age 12 and Above
Reporting Illicit Drug Use, 1979–1995

Type of Drug Use	1979	1990	1995
Ever used	31.3%	34.2%	34.2%
Past year	17.5%	11.1%	10.7%
Last 30 days	14.3%	6.7%	6.3%

SOURCE: Office of National Drug Control Policy.

9. Infant deaths

10. Fetal deaths

11. Disaster assistance

12. State residency of less than five years

13. New houses authorized

14. New welfare cases

15. High school dropout rates

The Negative Effects of Incarceration

There have been numerous studies of the relative effects of incarceration on individual offenders. Sampson and Laub, in their pioneering study of 880 juveniles from adolescence through adulthood, found that both the number of incarcerations and the length of incarceration had no direct impact on one's criminal career.[12] They went on to note that incarcerations actually have a deleterious effect on recidivism, as they severely disrupt all efforts to maintain one's relationship or bonds with the offender's family and to secure stable employment. On a more macro level, Linksy and Strauss in their study did not find an association between incarceration rates and crimes rates. In fact, there is a well-established positive correlation that states with high incarceration rates tend to have high crime rates.[13] Similar to Sampson and Laub, this study concludes that high rates of incarceration may contribute to high levels of social stress and thus increase crime rates in both the individuals experiencing incarceration and the society in general.

WHAT DOES WORK?

There has been a major debate among criminologists on whether treatment works for juvenile and adult offenders. It began with the now famous publication by the late Robert Martinson that left the unfortunate impression that "nothing works."[14] Martinson's publication was based on a review of existing evaluations of prison treatment programs—one of the first "meta-analyses" that attempt to summarize the findings of numerous experimental and quasi-experimental studies of rehabilitation programs. This pioneering work has been followed by several other major meta-analyses, all of which have concluded that under certain conditions, some treatment interventions can have a significant impact on recidivism rates.[15] Put differently, many treatment programs fail, but a sizeable number succeed.

Many have disagreed with these findings. Put simply, they argue that the meta-analyses methods are suspect and overstate the merits of rehabilitation. In particular, the studies cited by these meta-analyses have tended to use small sample sizes (under 250 cases for experimental and control groups), and the differences between control and experimental subjects in their recidivism rates have been minimal (5 to 10 percentage points) in many of the studies. Furthermore, the recommended conditions necessary for treatment to succeed have been difficult either to define or to replicate in other sites.

For example, Palmer's recent summary of these studies concluded that only 25 to 35 percent of all the programs he reviewed showed significant positive results, with about 10 percent of the studies reporting significant positive results for the controls (nontreatment offenders). For the remaining 55 to 65 percent of the studies, two-thirds showed some positive results for the experimental cases, as opposed to one-third for controls. These data provide both optimism for the protreatment advocates and affirmation for the critics.

Well-designed and -administered correctional treatment programs are more frequently the exception rather than the rule. The so-called "program integrity" factor is often weak and may well explain the absence of strong treatment effects for many treatment programs. Correctional agencies are often ill-equipped to design and implement effective treatment programs. Our belief is that most agencies do not themselves believe that effective treatment is possible or that it is part of their agency mission. For example, a survey of prisons wardens indicated that only 25 percent of their inmates were amenable to treatment. The wardens also stated that involving inmates in rehabilitation programs was not a high organizational priority. Conversely, they also believed that such programs have an important place in a prison setting.[16]

In summary, it is difficult to find alternatives to incarceration that have been implemented properly, have undergone a rigorous impact evaluation, have demonstrated significant effects on reducing recidivism, and have served to either divert offenders from prison or reduce their lengths of stay. One recent example of this pattern was a national evaluation of "correctional options" programs that were funded by the federal government and were intended to reduce prison populations. The evaluation found that of the more than forty programs funded, only a handful was implemented as designed, largely due to a lack of commitment by the implementing agency. Although there was no impact on recidivism, a few programs did demonstrate that they were successful in reducing the projected length of stay of inmates. Programs that attempted to divert offenders from prison were less successful in achieving that goal. This led the researchers to conclude that so-called "back-end" programs are more likely to at least show cost savings than "front-end," diversion-type programs.[17]

The most recent meta-analysis was conducted by the University of Maryland at the request of Congress to advise policy makers on which programs and policies should be implemented. Unfortunately, this assessment also found that most of the innovations in the corrections have been less than successful. This includes intensive supervision for parolees and probationers, drug testing, boot camps, home confinement, community residential programs, juvenile wilderness programs, and deterrence programs such as Scared Straight and shock probation.[18]

BOOT CAMPS

The Argument for Boot Camps

The first boot camps emerged in the early 1980s. They were advertised as a means for reducing the high rate of recidivism among offenders and for reducing prison crowding. Often categorized as an intermediate sanction, boot camps were designed to punish and treat juvenile and adult offenders convicted of less serious nonviolent crimes for relatively short periods of time. In confining offenders for shorter periods, it was hoped that boot camps would simultaneously reduce the length of stay for those incarcerated and reduce recidivism. In so doing, the costs of imprisonment would be reduced by inmates' spending a shorter period of time in custody and not returning to prison once released. Over the next decade, the boot camps phenomenon expanded from adult male prisons to include local jails, juveniles, and women.

The well-publicized images of a typical boot camp have generated a tremendous level of popular appeal. The sight of inmates being forced to rise early in the predawn night, to adhere to a rigorous regime of physical exercise led by a mean and dog-faced drill instructor, and to march up and down the prison yard in precisely choreographed drill ceremonies has much allure for the general public. These images not only reflect the desired infliction of pain upon criminal offenders—pain that is often found wanting in traditional prisons—but also have the utilitarian effect of developing character and discipline among the prisoners—characteristics associated with the good and law-abiding, and which are almost invariably lacking in the young men and women who find themselves confined in correctional facilities.

Research on Boot Camps

Impact While in the Boot Camp Program Some evaluations have examined the impact of boot camps on offender adjustments while institutionalized.[19] In general, these studies indicate that boot camps—as compared to traditional prisons—seem to result in the more positive adjustments of inmates to institutionalization. These studies are consistent in finding that boot camp offenders tend to develop more prosocial attitudes and more favorable reactions to the correctional environment than do offenders incarcerated in more traditional correctional facilities.

For instance, MacKenzie's multisite evaluation of eight state-level adult boot camps found that, across all sites, inmates who went through the boot camp programs developed more positive attitudes toward their prison experience over time and displayed more prosocial attitudes than did comparison samples of inmates incarcerated in conventional settings. Some studies also suggest that boot camp participants witness significant increases in a number of desirable short-term outcomes, such as improved self-esteem and improved scores on standardized measures of educational achievement.[20]

It remains unclear, however, whether these effects are attributable to anything unique about a military-style boot camp. For instance, these findings may be simply the result of the boot camp participants being directly and intensely supervised by professional staff, suggesting these effects may extend to a variety of treatment-oriented, and not just boot camp, programs.[21] Some of these findings may also be an artifact of initial surveys being conducted after boot camp inductions have taken place, which may result in decreased pretest scores on the measures of adjustment administered. But in general, it does appear that offenders do respond favorably to well-administered and intense counseling and educational services.

We cannot leave this topic without also noting some of the dangers and atrocities that have occurred in boot camps. In these programs, staff can easily take advantage of their authority over their inmates and use excessive force against them. A number of incidents have occurred in boot camps where staff have physically and verbally abused youthful offenders to the point that the programs had to be terminated. The most recent incident occurred in Maryland where guards were found to routinely punch, kick, and slam juveniles to the ground during their twenty weeks of boot camp programming. According to media reports, these physical abuses occurred when youth arrived at the camp shackled and in handcuffs. The abuses were so great that an FBI investigation was launched.[22]

Impact on Recidivism The area of greatest concern has been the effectiveness of boot camps in reducing offender recidivism. A number of studies of both adult and juvenile boot camps have been completed with very similar results.

MacKenzie's multisite evaluation of eight adult correctional boot camps has been the most important research in this area.[23] This multifaceted study of eight state-level adult boot camps generally found that boot camps do not appear to be reducing offender recidivism rates. It was found that the boot camp experience did not result in a reduction in recidivism in five states. In three states, boot camp participants who successfully completed the programs had lower recidivism rates than comparable inmates who served longer prison terms in conventional prisons on at least one measure of recidivism.

The three state boot camp programs that appeared somewhat successful in positively impacting offender recidivism rates had some common characteristics. First, postrelease intensive supervision of boot campers was a program component in all three states, while prison releasees in those states were not generally as intensively supervised upon release from prison. Second, the institutional phase of these programs tended to be longer, to contain a stronger rehabilitative focus, and to generate lower in-program drop-out rates than the other boot camp programs examined. Other apparently unsuccessful programs also shared some of these characteristics, so it is unclear how these program characteristics influenced failure rates. The analyses could not disentangle the effects of particular program features (for example, intensive supervision), although the authors do suggest that it is quite unlikely that the military boot camp atmosphere alone had much impact on program participants.

The negative results have been reported for those few evaluations that utilized experimental and control populations. These include the California Youth Authority's internal evaluation of its LEAD boot camp program and the Office of Juvenile Justice and Delinquency Prevention's sponsored evaluation of juvenile boot camps in Cleveland, Mobile, and Denver. These studies found that although youth improved while in the boot camp with respect to educational achievement and prosocial values, there were no statistical differences between experimental and control groups in terms of reoffending once they left the boot camp.[24]

In summary, both adult and juvenile boot camps have not succeeded in reducing recidivism or in reducing crowding and costs. The positive gains realized by offenders while assigned to a boot camp appear to diminish once the offender is released to the community. A major challenge for the "next generation" of boot camps will be developing effective aftercare components that will sustain the gains realized in the institutional phase of the program. Furthermore, most boot camps are relatively small in size and have problems operating at full capacity. Unless a larger pool of incarcerated offenders is made eligible for these programs, they cannot function as a viable means for controlling prison crowding or reducing the costs of the correctional system.

PRISON DRUG TREATMENT[25]

The Argument for Drug Treatment

The past few years have also witnessed a growing interest in the possible impact of drug treatment for inmates in jail and prison as an effective crime-control strategy. This interest has been fueled, in part, by the dramatic growth of inmates incarcerated for drug crimes and the high percentage of inmates who were using either alcohol or drugs at the time of the crime or have a history of drug abuse. This movement is much larger than the boot camp fad discussed. There is no question that drug treatment can be extremely successful and useful for specific individuals. What is new is the promise that most of the serious crime in the country could be virtually eliminated through a massive expansion of prison drug treatment. Because such a proposal would require a considerable initial investment by taxpayers (as shown in the following text, nearly $8 billion per year would be required), it demands close scrutiny.

Perhaps the leading organization in support of drug treatment for offenders is the National Center on Addiction and Substance Abuse (CASA). In a report released in 1998 to great fanfare, CASA estimated that approximately 1.2 million of the 1.7 million inmates now housed in the nation's jail and prison system have a substantial drug/alcohol problem that is directly related to their criminal behavior.[26] By placing these inmates in effective drug treatment programs while incarcerated, the likelihood of them continuing their criminal careers will be greatly reduced. Specifically, the report states that assuming that drug addicts commit an average of 100 crimes per year, for each inmate who successfully completes a treatment program at a cost of $6,500, a state will realize $36,700 in avoided criminal justice and health care expenditures. It is also argued that each successfully treated inmate will likely secure employment at an annual salary of $21,400, which will produce $32,100 in economic benefits (see Table 8-3). Given this enormous cost-benefit ratio, the CASA report claims that only 10 percent of the inmates entering drug treatment have to succeed for the programs to be justified.[27]

In addition to the CASA report, Congress appropriated a significant amount of funds to support treatment and sanctions of drug users and violent offenders (the Violent Crime Control and Law Enforcement Act of 1994). The Residential Substance Abuse Treatment program (RSAT) is part of this federal effort and provides funding for comprehensive strategies for the treatment of substance-abusing offenders who are incarcerated in state prisons and local jails. It is anticipated that over $260 million will be appropriated over the next five years to fund a large number of intensive residential drug treatment programs within state prison systems.

To test the merits and feasibility of the plan, three central components or assumptions of strategy need to be examined. First, there are the two interrelated assumptions that (1) most inmates are drug abusers, and (2) they commit a large number of crimes per year primarily because of their drug use. CASA reports that approximately 70 to 80 percent of all inmates (prisons and jail) have either committed a crime while under the influence of drugs, committed a drug crime, or used a drug on a regular basis. If these inmates are untreated while incarcerated, they will commit very large amounts of crime (100 per year) once they are released from prison or jail. However, if properly treated, both the drug use and criminal behavior will sharply diminish.

Putting aside the thorny issue that inmates' criminal behavior may well predate their drug use, how realistic is the claim that most inmates are substance abusers who, if not incarcerated, would be committing such a large proportion of the crime occurring in the United States? There is no question that the use of drugs (especially alcohol) is related either directly or indirectly to inmates' current legal problems. The questions are (1) how serious is this addiction? and (2) how much crime are these inmates engaged in?

Second, it is assumed that a sufficiently large market exists for expanding drug treatment within prisons. There is little disagreement that in many states the amount of drug treatment made available to inmates represents a small proportion of the inmate population. However, in order for cost savings to be

**TABLE 8-3 The Proposed Cost-Effectiveness
of Prison Drug Treatment**

Cost/Savings Factors	Estimated Cost/Savings
Drug Treatement Costs	
Residential prison drug treatment	$3,500
GED/vocational training	$3,000
Total costs	$6,500
Savings to Society	
Avoid 100 crimes per year at $50 per crime	$5,000
Avoid 2 arrests/prosecutions at $3,650 each	$7,300
Avoid 1 year of state prison at $19,600 per year	$19,600
Avoid $4,800 in health care and substance abuse treatment	$4,800
Total savings	$36,700
Economic Benefits (at $21,400 salary times 1.5 escalator)	$32,100

SOURCE: National Center on Addiction and Substance Abuse (CASA).

realized at levels that would result in significant reductions in recidivism and the associated averted costs for law enforcement, the courts, and corrections, large numbers of the inmates must successfully complete both the residential drug treatment and the aftercare components. Of particular concern are the number of inmates who, for a variety of reasons related to prison operations and security concerns, cannot be assigned to a treatment program and the number of inmates who will fail to complete the program (drop-out rates).

The third critical assumption is that treatment will have a dramatic effect on most participants in reducing their high rates of drug use and associated high rates of criminal behavior. In other words, a body of scientific evidence using experimental designs must exist showing that treatment works.

Directly related to this assumption is the requirement that inmates selected for treatment are high-rate drug users with high rates of criminal activity (100 crimes per year). If a drug treatment program selects inmates who are low-rate offenders, the cost benefits of the program collapse. If prisons and jails contain significant numbers of low-rate offenders who, upon release from prison, will either cease or reduce their criminal activities regardless of treatment, then treating these inmates will not be cost-beneficial. The questions remain: (1) how many inmates have a severe drug addiction problem and are career criminals? and (2) how many of these inmates can we reasonably expect to successfully treat?

The Drug Offender Crime Rate Assumption   One of the major assumptions underpinning the argument to greatly expand residential drug treatment in prisons is that most inmates (70 to 80 percent) are drug abusers who, if left untreated, will commit large amounts of crime (100 per year). These are large numbers that suggest that most of the crime being committed each year in the

TABLE 8-4 Projected Amount of Crime Being Committed by Released Prisoners with Drug Problems, 1997

Factor	Estimates
A. Number of prisoners released per year (DOJ)	465,942
B. Percent with drug problems (CASA)	365,555
C. Rate of crimes committed per year by drug offenders (CASA)	100 per year
D. Total crimes committed by released prisoners (B × C)	36.6 million
E. Total crimes reported to police (FBI)	14.0 million
F. Total crimes reported by victimization surveys (DOJ)	42.4 million

United States can be directly traced to untreated inmates who are released to the streets each year.

Using CASA's estimates of prevalence and frequency, one can evaluate the validity of this assumption. As shown in Table 8-4, there were approximately 470,000 prisoners released from state and federal prisons in 1997. Assuming that 80 percent of these prisoners have a drug problem, one can estimate that nearly 366,000 prisoners released to society are committing an average of 100 crimes per year. Multiplying the number of releases times the 100 crimes per year figure produces a total of 36.6 million crimes per year attributed to these inmates.

But there appears to be something wrong with these estimates. The 36.6 million number is more than two times the total amount of serious crimes reported to police and 86 percent of all crimes reported on the victimization surveys. Moreover, these numbers do not include the nearly 10 million inmates released from jail each year nor the nearly 4 million adults on probation or parole. What these data show is that most prisoners and jail inmates released each year cannot be committing 100 crimes per year. A significant number of inmates will either cease or reduce their rate of offending regardless of whether they have been exposed to drug treatment. This can be clearly seen in the studies reviewed in the following text that show that large proportions of the "control" groups (inmates who received no treatment) did not reoffend or resume their drug use behavior.

The argument that drug treatment can have a dramatic impact on crime rates was also put forth by the advocates of selective incapacitation who claimed that most inmates are committing large numbers of crime and need to be incarcerated for long periods of time.[28] But instead of advocating drug treatment as the best means for curbing high-rate offenders, selective incapacitation proponents claimed that greater use of imprisonment would have the same effect.

The Number of Inmates Who Can Be Treated Assumption The CASA estimate that approximately 1.2 million inmates would benefit from drug treatment is based upon data from several U.S. Department of Justice surveys in which inmates were interviewed regarding their drug use patterns. Offenders who self-reported to interviewers that they either were regular users of drugs, were under the influence of drugs at the time of their arrests, were convicted of drug crimes, or had prior criminal histories for drug offenses were identified as being in need of drug treatment. It is important to note that the type of treatment being advocated was the therapeutic community (TC) model in which inmates nearing the end of their prison terms are admitted to an intensive treatment program for six to twelve months.[29]

However, a closer analysis of the jail and inmate population suggests that the number of inmates who could be reasonably admitted to a TC is far smaller than 1.2 million. More directly, this estimate fails to take into account those aspects of prison operations and security that would preclude most inmates from participating in an intense drug treatment program regardless of their "need" for such treatment. Here are some of the major factors that would preclude participation in TC-type programs (see Table 8-5):

1. As indicated by CASA, approximately 500,000 inmates do not require drug treatment, as they have no drug/alcohol addiction problems.

2. Most of the 500,000 jail inmates are in pretrial status and will spend no more than a few days in custody on relatively minor charges before being released on bail or having their charges dropped. Those who stay in jail have very serious charges pending and cannot enter treatment until their cases are resolved by the court. Only a very small number are in jail long enough to even begin a treatment program that requires nine to twelve months to complete.

3. Approximately 225,000 are either high-security risks, have severe mental health and medical problems, or are serving short sentences and will be released before a nine- to twelve-month treatment program can begin.

4. Another 375,000 will not or cannot participate in treatment because they are working full-time and making money in a prison industries program, learning a vocational skill, getting a high school degree, or simply learning to read and write.

5. Finally, of the 200,000 left who might benefit from drug treatment, a significant number simply do not want to participate. Our research shows that 25 percent of all inmates screened for drug treatment do not enter a program because they are uninterested or unmotivated. Unless one is suggesting that drug treatment will be coercive, the numbers one is expecting simply will not materialize.

These data show that the true drug treatment eligibility pool for most state prison systems will be less than 15 percent, or no more than 150,000. And, as will be discussed later, these estimates do not include the fact that significant numbers of program participants will either fail to complete the program or will not benefit from the treatment. Using the results of published reports, one can assume that approximately 35 percent of the inmates admitted to treatment will fail to complete the program and that another 25 percent will recidivate. With these assumptions, the total number of inmates who will benefit from

TABLE 8-5 How Many Inmates Can Participate in Drug Treatment Programs?

Drug Treatment Eligibility Factors	Number	%
Inmate Population as of 1997		
Jails	518,492	30%
State prison	1,076,625	63%
Federal prison	105,544	6%
Total inmates	1,700,661	100%
Drug Treatment Exclusionary Factors		
Have no drug treatment needs	500,000	29%
Pretrial and short-term jail inmates	400,000	24%
Inmates in high-security or special management units	225,000	13%
Full-time participants in other programs/work assignments	375,000	22%
Unwilling to participate	50,000	3%
Total Pool Left for Drug Treatment	150,700	9%
Program failures at 35% of drug treatment pool	52,700	3%
Program recidivists at 25% of drug treatment pool	24,500	1%
Total Inmate Population Benefiting from Treatment	73,500	4%

drug treatment is approximately 73,500, or less than 5 percent of the total inmate population.

To further illustrate this point, a recent analysis was conducted by the Michigan Department of Corrections to determine how many of its current inmate population could be assigned to a TC-type treatment program (see Table 8-6). Using some of the same factors noted earlier, approximately 85 percent of the Michigan prison population would be ineligible for a TC-type program. The largest exclusionary factor is "time left to serve." A significant number of inmates are either "too short" or have too much time left to serve to participate in a TC program. It is noteworthy that of the 6,140 eligible for drug treatment, approximately 1,200 had no clinical recommendation for such treatment by the DOC mental health staff. And these numbers do not account for inmates who would volunteer for the program, could successfully complete the program, or are already participating in a drug treatment program.

Even if there were large numbers of inmates able to participate in drug treatment, there are real limitations on expanding the bed capacity of TC-type programs. These limitations were experienced by Texas when it proposed to fund 12,000 treatment beds—a number that, according to the research report, "has no scientific or empirical basis."[30] That number was reduced to less than half (5,200) as the state learned about the difficulties in trying to provide quality treatment to such a large segment of the Texas prison population. Even at 5,200, which reflects only 5 percent of the state's inmate population, the following implementation problems were noted:

TABLE 8-6 Estimates of the Michigan Prison Population Eligible for a Therapeutic Community-Type Drug Treatment Program

TC Drug Treatment Eligibility Factors	Number	%
Total inmate population	41,949	100%
High-security risks (Level V)	6,566	16%
Insufficient time left for treatment (less than 10 months)	710	2%
Too much time left for treatment (more than 2 years)	24,090	57%
No reported history of substance abuse	3,243	8%
Do not have a confirmed diagnosis for treatment	1,200	17%
RSAT initial eligibility pool	6,140	15%
No clinical recommendation for drug treatment	1,200	3%
Remaining pool	4,940	12%

SOURCE: Michigan Department of Corrections.

1. The programs did not have the requisite trained and experienced counseling staff to operate programs of this size.
2. There was a lack of a standardized screening, assessment, and selection processes for placing offenders in the treatment programs.
3. The postrelease programs were not fully developed.

For these and other reasons, Texas has stabilized its bed treatment program at the 5,200 level rather than expanding to 7,200. If expansion had continued, the state would have risked having a "very popular but ineffective and costly intervention."[31]

The Impact of Treatment Assumption There is a growing body of research on the effectiveness of drug treatment for incarcerated offenders. The most frequently cited summary of the research literature on the effectiveness of drug treatment programs is a report published by the National Institute of Justice (NIJ) entitled "The Effectiveness of Treatment for Drug Abusers Under Criminal Justice Supervision."[32] In the 1995 NIJ report, Lipton lists seven model drug treatment programs for inmates in prison and jail settings. Lipton's review focused on the TC model in which inmates must be within a year of their release date and the treatment should last from nine to twelve months and have a strong aftercare component. For all of the programs evaluated, the inmates had volunteered to participate. Table 8-7 summarizes the attributes and research findings associated with each program evaluated.[33] A complete listing of each study is contained in footnote 33.

In general, Lipton's report is quite favorable with respect to the ability of treatment to reduce recidivism and drug use. His summary of the research literature shows that inmates who have participated in the referenced programs and have completed all phases of treatment have very low rates of recidivism and continued drug use. Clearly, inmates who stay in treatment are far less

likely to continue their criminal careers. However, despite these positive findings, there are a number of issues that must be noted that can undermine a
drug treatment strategy in terms of being able to have a dramatic impact on
crime rates and criminal justice costs.

1. *TC-type programs are small in terms of the numbers of inmates in the programs.* The
   model programs cited by the drug treatment proponents tend to be relatively small, with bed capacities at 300 or less. For example, the Stay'n Out
   in New York State and Amity Right Turn in California programs have fewer
   than 300 inmates in the programs at any given time. The prison population
   in New York State is approximately 70,000, while California has an inmate
   population of more than 150,000. With the exception of California, the
   Federal Bureau of Prisons, and Texas programs, TC programs have been
   unable to significantly expand their treatment bed capacity.

2. *There is a considerable level of in-program failure in many programs.* Researchers
   have consistently found that the drop-out rate for TC programs ranges
   from 30 to 60 percent. For example, the Texas program reported that
   58 percent of its participants failed to complete all phases of treatment.[34]
   The Federal Bureau of Prisons (FBP) program reported in-program failure rates of 25 to 42 percent. In California's Amity Right Turn program,
   significant numbers had already been unsuccessfully terminated from the
   program, according to Lipton's 1995 report. In fact, only 23 percent of
   the cases used to evaluate the success of the program had successfully
   completed all phases of the program. More significantly, 23 percent failed
   to complete the first phase of in-prison treatment.[35]

3. *The evaluations have not used randomized experimental designs.* In order to
   truly measure the effects of any treatment program, the best methodology
   is to implement an experimental design in which inmates screened as eligible for the program are randomly assigned to the treatment and nontreatment conditions. To date no such evaluations have been completed.
   Only the Amity Right Turn program has implemented a true experimental design, but its results have not been formally published and reviewed
   by other researchers. Consequently, one cannot know if the positive
   results of the evaluations are due to the drug treatment or differences
   between the experimental and control groups.[36]

4. *Most of the studies show marginal differences between experimental and control
   groups when the recidivism rates are calculated properly.* The Stay'n Out Female
   evaluation showed a difference of only 6 percent between the treatment
   group and a matched control group. For Project New Vision in Texas, the
   difference between controls and program graduates (excluding failures)
   was only 4 percent. The FBP evaluation results (as released in an Executive Summary) showed a difference of less than 9 percent and did not
   include the program failures. Significantly, the overall recidivism rates for
   both the FBP controls and experimentals were very low (less than 15
   percent), suggesting that large numbers of inmates would not have been
   rearrested even without the benefit of treatment.[37]

TABLE 8-7 Summary of Major Studies of Prison Drug Treatment Programs

Programs	State	Prison Population	Program Capacity	Research Design	Year	Cases Studied	Outcomes	References
Amity Right Turn	California	153,000	200	Experimental with random assignment of inmates to treatment and no treatment	1994	425	23% drop-out rate for residential phase; 8% lower reincarceration rate for treatment group as compared to control cases	Wexler, 1995; Lipton, 1995; & CDC, 1997
Stay'n Out Males	New York	69,530	143	Nonequivalent control group design, with controls being program eligibles who did not participate for administrative reasons and milieu treatment program	1977–1984	1,626	No differences between controls and two forms of treatment; TC cases had 14% lower rearrest rate compared to the other groups	Lipton, 1995; Wexler et al., 1990
Stay'n Out Females	New York	69,530	40	Nonequivalent control group design, with controls being program eligibles who did not participate for administrative reasons	1977–1984	398	No difference between control and experimental cases	Lipton, 1995; Wexler et al., 1990
Cornerstone	Oregon	7,899	Closed	Nonequivalent control study	1984–1989	Unknown	Less than 8% difference between experimental and control cases	Field, 1989 & 1992

TABLE 8-7 continued

Programs	State	Prison Population	Program Capacity	Research Design	Year	Cases Studied	Outcomes	References
Wharton	New Jersey	27,766	Closed	Nonequivalent control study	1980	348	Treatment group had 12.2% lower recidivism rate—program failure not included	Lipton, 1995
IPTC	Texas	136,599	2,000	Nonequivalent control study, with controls being cases defined as eligible for program	1995	1,067	5% lower rearrest rate for experimental cases; 58% drop-out rate	Lipton, 1995; Fabelo, 1995
Key-Crest	Delaware	5,313	Unknown	Nonequivalent control study, with no nontreatment group	1995	Unknown	Various forms of treatment have different rates of success	Lipton, 1995; Inciardi, 1995; Lockwood et al., 1995
Federal Bureau of Prisons	Federal	110,160	6,000	Nonequivalent control study, with control cases matched with experimental cases	1995	1,569	25–41% drop-out rate; experimental group had 9% lower rearrest rate as compared to nontreatment group	FBP, 1998; Pellissier & McCarthy, 1992

Some studies inappropriately fail to include the program failures in calculating the program's success rate. By discounting these failures, the researchers are distorting the true effects of the program's impact. The success rate of most drug treatment programs with program failures included is considerably more modest than that of programs excluding the failures from the calculations.

SUMMARY

In light of the external factors related to criminal careers as noted in this chapter, it is clear that among various forms of rehabilitation programs, the interventions that better equip an individual to secure meaningful employment in today's increasingly competitive economy will be the most successful. Consequently, program interventions that are based simply on counseling, drug treatment, or cognitive learning and do not provide basic enhancements in the offender's ability to perform basic tasks essential for any form of employment will not be successful. Furthermore, the private and public sector must recognize the need to provide such employment opportunities for this segment of the population.

Based on many studies, the following conclusions can be made regarding the impact of treatment and punishment on crime rates and individual offenders:

1. The vast majority of crimes are not committed by persons released from prison. Consequently, the success or lack of success of prison-based treatment programs and/or punishment will have little impact on crime rates in general.

2. Under certain circumstances, treatment of offenders can have positive results. These positive results are strongest for programs that provide for long-term aftercare and serve to increase the offender's ability to secure employment and to develop a stable family situation. However, it is also true that under certain circumstances, treatment of offenders can have negative results. Furthermore, change (positive and negative) can also occur and often does occur based on other factors that have nothing to do with treatment (for example, maturation, random events, and so on).

3. Most correctional treatment programs are not well administered, target the wrong clientele, and are too small to have any impact on crime rates or public safety.

4. It is extremely rare to find a well-administered treatment program that has been properly evaluated and has demonstrated dramatic treatment effects.

We do not advocate the abolition of treatment within prisons. These programs can and do play a very important role in turning some lives around and, more importantly, humanizing the prison experience. For this reason alone, the use of rehabilitation and treatment programs that serve to make for a more humane and less costly correctional system is warranted and should be expanded. But in a strange and twisted way, the need for treatment has also served to justify the use of incarceration. No matter how well intentioned, imprisonment in the name of treatment should be strongly resisted.

NOTES

1. See D. A. Andrews, Ivan Zinger, Robert D. Hoge, James Bonta, Paul Gendreau, and Francis T. Cullen, "Does Correctional Treatment Work? A Clinically Relevant and Psychologically Informed Meta-Analysis," *Criminology* 28, 3 (1990): 369–404; and Don Gendreau and Peter Ross, "Revivification of Rehabilitation: Evidence from the 1980s," *Justice Quarterly* 4, 3 (1987): 349–407.

2. See James Austin and Barry Krisberg, "The Unmet Promise of Alternatives to Incarceration," *Crime and Delinquency* 28, 3 (1983): 374–409.

3. Federal Bureau of Investigation, *Age-Specific Arrest Rates and Race Specific Rates for Selected Offenses* (Washington, DC: U.S. Department of Justice, 1990); Travis Hirschi and Michael Gottfredson, "Age and the Explanation of Crime," *American Journal of Sociology* 89 (1983): 552–584; Robert J. Sampson and John H. Laub, *Crime in the Making: Pathways and Turning Points Through Life* (Cambridge, MA: Harvard University Press, 1993).

4. U.S. Department of Justice, Bureau of Justice Statistics, *Recidivism of Prisoners Released in 1983* (Washington, DC: April 1989); James Austin and Melissa Bolyard, *The Effectiveness of Shorter Prison Terms* (San Francisco: National Council on Crime and Delinquency, March 1993); James Austin, "Using Early Release to Relieve Prison Crowding: A Dilemma in Public Policy," *Crime and Delinquency* 32, 4 (1986): 404–502; James Austin and Patricia Hardyman, *The Use of Early Parole with Electronic Monitoring to Control Prison Crowding* (San Fran-

cisco: National Council on Crime and Delinquency, 1992); Michael R. Geerken and Hennessey D. Hayes, "Probation and Parole: Public Risk and the Future of Incarceration Alternatives," *Criminology* 31, 4 (1993): 549–564.

5. Sampson and Laub, *Crime in the Making: Pathways and Turning Points Through Life.*

6. T. C. N. Gibbens, "Borstal Boys After 25 Years," *British Journal of Criminology* 24 (1984): 49–62; B. J. Knight, S. G. Osborn, and D. West, "Early Marriage and Criminal Tendency in Males," *British Journal of Criminology* 17 (1977): 348–360; Alicia Rand, "Transitional Life Events and Desistance from Delinquency and Crime," in Marvin Wolfgang, Terrence Thornberry, and Robert M. Figlio (eds.), *From Boy to Man: From Delinquency to Crime* (Chicago: University of Chicago Press, 1987), pp. 134–162.

7. For an excellent review and current study of the Rushe/Kirchheimer unemployment-imprisonment relationship, see Raymond Michalowski and Susan M. Carlson, "Unemployment, Imprisonment, and Social Structures of Accumulation: Historical Contingency in the Rushe-Kirchheimer Hypothesis," *Criminology* 37, 2 (May 1999): 1–250.

8. John Braithwaite, *Crime, Shame, and Reintegration* (Cambridge: Cambridge University Press, 1989); Robert D. Crutchfield, "Labor Stratification and Violent Crime," *Social Forces* 68 (1989): 489–512; Sampson and Laub, *Crime in the Making: Pathways and Turning Points Through Life;* Neal Shover,

Aging Criminals (Beverly Hills, CA: Sage Publications, 1985).

9. Richard Berk and David Rauma, "Remuneration and Recidivism: The Long-Term Impact of Unemployment Compensation on Ex-Offenders," *Journal of Quantitative Criminology* 3, 1 (1987): 3–27.

10. Office of National Drug Control Policy, *Drug Data Summary* (Washington, DC: April 1999).

11. Arnold S. Linsky and Murray Strauss, *Social Stress in the United States* (Dover, MA: Auburn House, 1986).

12. Sampson and Laub, *Crime in the Making: Pathways and Turning Points Through Life.*

13. National Council on Crime and Delinquency, *Why Is Crime Going Down? A Congressional Briefing* (Washington, DC: National Council on Crime and Delinquency, 1996).

14. Robert Martinson, "What Works?—Questions and Answers About Prison Reform," *The Public Interest* 35 (1974): 22–54.

15. D. A. Andrews et al., "Does Correctional Treatment Work?"; William Davidson, L. Gottschalk, L. Gensheimer, and J. Mayer, *Interventions with Juvenile Delinquents: A Meta-Analysis of Treatment Efficacy* (Washington, DC: National Institute of Juvenile Justice and Delinquency Prevention, 1984); C. Garrett, "Effects of Residential Treatment on Adjudicated Delinquents: A Meta-Analysis," *Journal of Research in Crime and Delinquency* 22 (1985): 287–308; Don Gendreau and Peter Ross, "Revivification of Rehabilitation"; R. Gottschalk, William Davidson, L. Gensheimer, and J. Mayer, "Community-Based Interventions," in H. Quay (ed.)., *Handbook of Juvenile Delinquency* (New York: Wiley, 1987); Martin Lipsey, *The Efficacy of Intervention for Juvenile Delinquency,* paper presented at the American Society of Criminology (1989); and Ted Palmer, *The Re-Emergence of Correctional Intervention* (Newbury Park, CA: Sage Publications, 1992).

16. Francis T. Cullin, Edward J. Latessa, Velmer S. Burton, Jr., and Lucien X. Lombardo, "The Correctional Orientation of Prison Wardens: Is the Rehabilitative Ideal Supported?," *Criminology* 31, 1 (1993): 69–92.

17. James Austin, Dean Hoffman, and Claire Johnson, *National Evaluation of the Correctional Options Program* (Washington, DC: National Institute of Justice, 1996).

18. Larry Sherman, Denise Goffredson, Doris MacKenzie, John Eck, Peter Reuter, and Shawn Bushway, *Preventing Crime: What Works, What Doesn't, What's Promising* (Washington, DC: National Institute of Justice, 1998).

19. D. L. MacKenzie and J. W. Shaw, "Inmate Adjustment and Change During Shock Incarceration: The Impact of Correctional Boot Camp Programs," *Justice Quarterly* 7 (1990): 125–150; and D. L. MacKenzie and C. Souryal, *Inmate Attitude Change During Incarceration: A Comparison of Boot Camp and Traditional Prison* (University of Maryland: Part II, Final Report to National Institute of Justice, 1992).

20. James Austin, Michael Jones, and Melissa Bolyard, "The Growing Use of Jail Boot Camps: The Current State of the Art," in *Research in Brief* (National Institute of Justice, October 1993); James Austin, Michael Jones, and Melissa Bolyard, *Assessing the Impact of a County Operated Boot Camp: Evaluation of the Los Angeles County Regimented Inmate Diversion Program* (National Council on Crime and Delinquency, March 16, 1993); Little Hoover Commission, "Boot Camps: An Evolving Alternative to Traditional Prison" (Sacramento, CA: Little Hoover Commission, 1995).

21. R. C. McCorkle, "Correctional Boot Camps and Change in Attitude: Is All This Shouting Necessary?," *Justice Quarterly* 12, 2 (1995): 365–375.

22. "Juvenile Justice Chief, Aides Ousted Over Boot Camp Violence," *The Sun,* December 16, 1999, pp. 1, 18a.

23. MacKenzie and Souryal, *Inmate Attitude Change During Incarceration.*

24. See J. Bottcher, T. Isorena, and M. Belnas, *Lead: A Boot Camp and Intensive Parole Program: An Impact Evaluation: Second Year Findings* (State of California, Department of the Youth Authority, Research Division, 1996); M. Peters, *Evaluation of the Impact of Boot Camps for Juvenile Offenders: Denver Interim Report* (Washington, DC: U.S. Department of Justice, Office of Juvenile Justice and Delinquency Prevention, 1996); M. Peters, *Evaluation of the Impact of Boot Camps for Juvenile Offenders: Cleveland Interim Report* (Washington, DC: U.S. Department of Justice, Office of Juvenile Justice and Delinquency Prevention, 1996); M. Peters, *Evaluation of the Impact of Boot Camps for Juvenile Offenders: Mobile Interim Report* (Washington, DC: U.S. Department of Justice, Office of Juvenile Justice and Delinquency Prevention, 1996).

25. Much of this section is derived from an earlier article titled "The Limits of Prison Drug Treatment," published in *Corrections Management Quarterly* 2, 4 (Fall 1998): 66–74.

26. National Center on Addiction and Substance Abuse (CASA), *Behind Bars: Substance Abuse and America's Prison Population* (New York: Columbia University, 1998).

27. CASA, *Behind Bars: Substance Abuse and America's Prison Population,* pp. 18–19.

28. Peter W. Greenwood and Allan Abrahamse, *Selective Incapacitation: Report Prepared for the National Institute of Justice* (Santa Monica, CA: Rand Corporation, 1982); Edwin W. Zedlewski, *Making Confinement Decisions* (Washington, DC: National Institute of Justice, 1987).

29. Douglas S. Lipton, *The Effectiveness of Treatment for Drug Abusers Under Criminal Justice Supervision* (Washington, DC: U.S. Department of Justice, 1995).

30. Tony Fabelo, "Why It Is Prudent Not to Expand the Correctional Substance Abuse Treatment Initiative," *Bulletin from the Executive Director,* No. 16 (Austin, TX: Criminal Justice Policy Council, 1995).

31. Fabelo, "Why It Is Prudent Not to Expand the Correctional Substance Abuse Treatment Initiative."

32. Lipton, *The Effectiveness of Treatment for Drug Abusers Under Criminal Justice Supervision.*

33. The various studies referred to in this table are as follows:

California Department of Corrections (CDC) Office of Substance Abuse Programs, *Overview of Substance Abuse Programs* (Sacramento, CA: California Department of Corrections, 1997).

Fabelo, Tony, "Why It Is Prudent Not to Expand the Correctional Substance Abuse Treatment Initiative," *Bulletin from the Executive Director,* No. 16 (Austin, TX: Criminal Justice Policy Council, 1995).

Federal Bureau of Prisons (FBP), U.S. Department of Justice, *New Research Reveals Federal Inmate Drug Treatment Programs Reduce Recidivism and Future Drug Use* (Washington, DC: U.S. Department of Justice, TRIAD Press Release, 1998).

Field, G., "Oregon Prison Drug Treatment Programs," in Leukefeld, C. G., and Tims, F. M. (eds.), *Drug Abuse Treatment in Prisons and Jails* (Washington, DC: U.S. Government Printing Office, 1992), pp. 142–155.

Field, G., "A Study of the Effects of Intensive Treatment on Reducing the Criminal Recidivism of Addicted Offenders," *Federal Probation* 48 (1989), 50–55.

Inciardi, J. A., "The Therapeutic Community: An Effective Model for Corrections-Based Drug Abuse Treatment," in Haas, K. C., and Alpert, G. P. (eds.), *The Dilemmas of Punishment* (Prospect Heights, IL: Waveland Press, 1995), pp. 406–417.

Lipton, Douglas S., *The Effectiveness of Treatment for Drug Abusers Under Criminal Justice Supervision* (Washington, DC: U.S. Department of Justice, 1995).

Lockwood, D., Inciardi, J. A., and Surratt, H., "CREST Outreach Center: A Model for Blending Treatment and Corrections," in Inciardi, J. A., Fletcher, B., Delany, P., and Horton, A. (eds.), *The Effectiveness of Innovative Approaches in the Treatment of Drug Abuse* (Westport, CT: Greenwood Press, 1995).

Martin, S. S., Butzin, C. A., and Inciardi, J. A., "Assessment of a Multi-Stage Therapeutic Community for Drug Involved Offenders," *Journal of Psychoactive Drugs* 27, 1 (1995): 109–116.

Pellissier, B., and McCarthy, D., "Evaluation of the Federal Bureau of Prisons Drug Treatment Programs," in Leukefeld, C. G., and Tims, F. M. (eds.), *Drug Abuse Treatment in Prisons and Jails* (Washington, DC: U.S. Government Printing Office, 1992), pp. 261–278.

Pellissier, B., Rhodes, W., Gaes, G., Camp, S., O'Neill, J., Wallace, S., and Saylor, W., *Alternative Solutions to the Problem of Selection Bias in an Analysis of Federal Residential Drug Treatment Programs* (Washington, DC: Federal Bureau of Prisons, 1998).

Wexler, H. K., *Amity/Prison TC: One Year Outcome Results,* unpublished report to NDRI, from Lipton, D. S., *The Effectiveness of Treatment for Drug Abusers Under Criminal Justice Supervision* (Washington, DC: U.S. Department of Justice, 1995).

Wexler, H. K., Falkin, G. P., and Lipton, D. S., "Outcome Evaluation of a Prison Therapeutic Community for Substance Abuse Treatment," *Criminal Justice and Behavior* 17, 1 (1990): 71–92.

34. Fabelo, "Why It Is Prudent Not to Expand the Correctional Substance Abuse Treatment Initiative."

35. Lipton, *The Effectiveness of Treatment for Drug Abusers Under Criminal Justice Supervision.*

36. Ibid.

37. Federal Bureau of Prisons, U.S. Department of Justice, *New Research Reveals Federal Inmate Drug Treatment Programs Reduce Recidivism and Future Drug Use* (Washington, DC: U.S. Department of Justice, TRIAD Press Release, 1998).

9

■

The Three Strikes
and You're Out
Movement*

INTRODUCTION

The past decade has witnessed many efforts by policy makers to further increase the use of imprisonment. One of the most popular reforms has been "three strikes and you're out." It began in 1993 when an initiative was placed on the ballot in the state of Washington to require a term of life imprisonment without the possibility of parole for persons convicted for a third time of certain specified violent or serious felonies. This action was fueled by the tragic death of Diane Ballasiotes, who was murdered by a convicted rapist who had been released from prison. Shortly, thereafter, Polly Klass was kidnapped and murdered by a California-released inmate, who also had an extensive prior record of violence. The rallying cry of "three strikes and you're out" caught on, not only with Washington and California voters, who passed their ballot measures by wide margins, but with legislatures and the public throughout the country. By 1997, twenty-four other states and the federal government enacted laws using the "three strikes and you're out" phrase. In 1994, President Clinton received a long-standing ovation in his State of the Union speech when he endorsed three strikes as a federal sentencing policy.[1]

The three strikes movement is the most recent anticrime policy to sweep the United States. Such reforms have included the Scared Straight Shock Incarceration programs in the 1970s, boot camps, mandatory minimum sentencing for certain crimes (for example, "use a gun, go to prison"), and truth in sentencing.[2] These often short-lived campaigns have widespread appeal to a disenchanted public who, through the media, have perceived the criminal justice system as overly lenient and incapable of protecting them from violent offenders. Highly publicized cases where the courts or correctional officials have allowed violent and habitual offenders to be released from prison only to commit yet another violent crime has fueled the public's appetite for harsher sentencing policies to correct a criminal justice system run amok.

The theoretical justification for such policies in general, and for the "three strikes and you're out" policy in particular, is grounded in the punitive ideologies of deterrence, incapacitation, and/or just deserts. General deterrence is achieved by delivering swift, certain, and severe punishment (life imprisonment without parole) to habitual offenders in order to suppress the criminal tendencies of potential habitual criminals.[3] Knowing that the next conviction will result in life imprisonment, the offender would weigh the consequences of committing another offense or living a crime-free life to avoid such punishment. In order for this sequence of events to occur, however, two critical but highly questionable conditions must exist: (1) offenders must be well informed of the new sentencing policies; and (2) they must believe there is a high probability of arrest and conviction should their criminal activities persist.

Malcolm Klein has argued that three strike-type legislation is unlikely to significantly enhance deterrence effects with respect to gangs, as the laws do little to "increase the likelihood of detection, apprehension and court conviction, which precede punishment."[4] Nor is it likely that would-be three strikers keep fully abreast of the complex and foreign legislative activities conducted by politicians in remote state capitals. For these and other reasons, the justification of three strikes legislation as an effective crime-control strategy remains problematic.

Incapacitation effects may be realized by accurately targeting habitual or career offenders who are unamenable to deterrence and rehabilitation and must be permanently separated from society. This perspective was popularized by Rand's research on habitual offenders in the 1970s and 1980s. Peter Greenwood and Joan Petersilia were early advocates of sentencing reforms that would isolate and incapacitate habitual offenders.[5] This perspective assumed that (1) the courts could readily identify the so-called "career offender," and (2) the offender's career would continue unabated over time.

Both assumptions have been widely criticized. First, previous studies have documented that the courts and social scientists have not yet been able to accurately identify the so-called rate offender without also punishing an equal or higher number of "false positives." In fact, Greenwood's own, but less publicized, research discredited his claim that career offenders can be identified, or that they even exist. Second, reforms such as "three strikes" run counter to knowledge that criminals' careers are strongly impacted by age. As noted by the national panel on criminal careers:

> From the perspective of incapacitation, prison capacity is used inefficiently if offenders are imprisoned beyond the time their criminal activity would have terminated if they were free on the street. Therefore, it is

reasonable to ask whether "habitual-offender" laws, which mandate very long sentences, may result in incarceration of offenders well after they ceased to be serious risks.[6]

It should be added, here, that incapacitation effects of a three strikes law on crime rates must be viewed as long-term if the goal is simply to extend incarceration. Assuming a portion of the targeted offenders is already being incarcerated, the added benefits are not realized until the offenders' "normal" release dates have been extended. For example, if the targeted group already serves ten years, the crime reduction effects will not occur for ten years after the bill's passage.

The last possible justification for this policy is consistent with wide public and political appeal—punishment, or just deserts. As Shichor and Sechrest noted, three strikes and you're out, in its purest form, is "vengeance as public policy."[7] This ideology requires no empirical validation or justification. As Greenwood and his Rand colleagues (the same scholars who had advocated selective incapacitation as a viable sentencing policy) note in their analysis of the California three strikes law:

> It is the "right thing to do." Aside from the savings and other effects, justice demands that those who repeatedly cause injury and loss to others have their freedom revoked.[8]

DIVERSITY AMONG THE STATES

As of 1996, twenty-four states and Congress had adopted some form of three strikes legislation. Table 9-1 summarizes the key provisions of these laws based on a national assessment completed in 1996.[9] Although there are variations among the states in how they decided the rules of the three strikes game, there are some common themes.

First, in terms of what constitutes a strike, the vast majority of states include on their list of "strikeable" offenses violent felonies such as murder, rape, robbery, arson, and assaults, and some states also include nonviolent charges.[10] Some states have included other charges, such as:

- the sale of drugs in Indiana;
- any drug offense punishable by imprisonment for more than five years in Louisiana;
- the sale of drugs to minors, burglary, and weapons possession in California;
- escape in Florida;
- treason in Washington; and
- embezzlement and bribery in South Carolina.

There are also variations in the number of strikes needed to be out, with two strikes bringing about some sentence enhancement in eight states.[11]

TABLE 9-1 Variations in State Strike Laws

State	Strike Zone Defined	Strikes Needed To Be "Out"	Meaning of "Out"
Arkansas	Murder, kidnapping, robbery, rape, terrorist act.	Two	Not less than 40 years in prison; no parole.
	First-degree battery, firing a gun from a vehicle, use of a prohibited weapon, conspiracy to commit: murder; kidnapping; robbery; rape; first-degree battery; first-degree sexual abuse.	Three	Range of no-parole sentences, depending on the offense.
California	Any felony if one prior felony conviction from a list of strikeable offenses.	Two	Mandatory sentence of twice the term for the offense involved.
	Any felony if two prior felony convictions from list of strikeable offenses.	Three	Mandatory indeterminate life sentence, with no parole eligibility for 25 years.
Colorado	Any Class 1 or 2 felony, or any Class 3 felony that is violent.	Three	Mandatory life in prison with no parole eligibility for 40 years.
Connecticut	Murder, attempted murder, assault with intent to kill, manslaughter, arson, kidnapping, aggravated sexual assault, robbery, first-degree assault.	Three	Up to life in prison.
Florida	Any forcible felony, aggravated stalking, aggravated child abuse, lewd or indecent conduct, escape.	Three	Life if third strike involved first-degree felony, 30–40 years if second-degree felony, 10–15 years if third-degree felony.
Georgia	Murder, armed robbery, kidnapping, rape, aggravated child molesting, aggravated sodomy, aggravated sexual battery.	Two	Mandatory life without parole.
	Any felony.	Four	Mandatory maximum sentence for the charge.
Indiana	Murder, rape, sexual battery with a weapon, child molesting, arson, robbery, burglary with a weapon or resulting in serious injury, drug dealing.	Three	Mandatory life without the possibility of parole.

TABLE 9-1 continued

State	Strike Zone Defined	Strikes Needed To Be "Out"	Meaning of "Out"
Kansas	Any felony against a person.	Two	Court may double term specified in sentencing guidelines.
	Any felony against a person.	Three	Court may triple term specified in sentencing guidelines.
Louisiana	Murder, attempted murder, manslaughter, rape, armed robbery, kidnapping, any drug offense punishable by more than 5 years, any felony punishable by more than 12 years.	Three	Mandatory life in prison with no parole eligibility.
	Any four felony convictions if at least one was on the above list.	Four	Mandatory life in prison with no parole eligibility.
Maryland	Murder, rape, robbery, first- or second-degree sexual offense, arson, burglary, kidnapping, car jacking, manslaughter, use of a firearm in felony, assault with intent to murder, rape, rob, or commit sexual offense.	Four, with separate prison terms served for first three strikes	Mandatory life in prison with no parole eligibility.
Montana	Deliberate homicide, aggravated kidnapping, sexual intercourse without consent, ritual abuse of a minor.	Two	Mandatory life in prison with no parole eligibility.
	Mitigated deliberate homicide, aggravated assault, kidnapping, robbery.	Three	Mandatory life in prison with no parole eligibility.
Nevada	Murder, robbery, kidnapping, battery, abuse of children, arson, home invasion.	Three	Life without parole: with parole possible after 10 years; or 25 years with parole possible after 10 years.
New Jersey	Murder, robbery, car jacking.	Three	Mandatory life in prison with no parole eligibility.

TABLE 9-1 continued

State	Strike Zone Defined	Strikes Needed To Be "Out"	Meaning of "Out"
New Mexico	Murder, shooting at or from a vehicle and causing harm, kidnapping, criminal sexual penetration, armed robbery resulting in harm.	Three	Mandatory life in prison with parole eligibility after 30 years.
North Carolina	47 violent felonies; separate indictment required finding that offender is "violent habitual offender."	Three	Mandatory life in prison with no parole eligibility.
North Dakota	Any Class A, B, or C felony.	Two	If second strike was for Class A felony, court may impose an extended sentence of up to life; if Class B felony, up to 20 years; if Class C felony, up to 10 years.
Pennsylvania	Murder, voluntary manslaughter, rape, involuntary deviate sexual intercourse, arson, kidnapping, robbery, aggravated assault.	Two	Enhanced sentence of up to 10 years.
	Same offenses.	Three	Enhanced sentence of up to 25 years.
South Carolina	Murder, voluntary manslaughter, homicide by child abuse, rape, kidnapping, armed robbery, drug trafficking, embezzlement, bribery, certain accessory and attempt offenses.	Two	Mandatory life in prison with no parole eligibility.
Tennessee	Murder, especially aggravated kidnapping, especially aggravated robbery, aggravated rape, rape of a child, aggravated arson.	Two, if prison term served for first strike	Mandatory life in prison with no parole eligibility.
	Same as above, plus rape, and aggravated sexual battery.	Three, if separate prison terms served	Mandatory life in prison with no parole eligibility for first two strikes.
Utah	Any first- or second-degree felony.	Three	Court may sentence from 5 years up to life.

TABLE 9-1 continued

State	Strike Zone Defined	Strikes Needed To Be "Out"	Meaning of "Out"
Vermont	Murder, manslaughter, arson causing death, assault and robbery with weapon or causing bodily injury, aggravated assault, kidnapping, maiming, aggravated sexual assault, aggravated domestic assault, lewd conduct with child.	Three	Court may sentence up to life in prison.
Virginia	Murder, kidnapping, robbery, car jacking, sexual assault, conspiracy to commit any of above.	Three	Mandatory life in prison with no parole eligibility.
Washington	Murder, assault, child molestation, kidnapping, rape, robbery.	Three	Mandatory life in prison with no parole eligibility.
Wisconsin	Murder, manslaughter, vehicular homicide, aggravated battery, abuse of children, robbery, sexual assault, taking hostages, kidnapping, arson, burglary.	Three	Mandatory life in prison with no parole eligibility.

California's law is unique in that it allows for any felony conviction for any felony crime to be counted if the offender has a prior initial conviction for its list of strikeable crimes.

The laws also differ regarding the length of imprisonment that is imposed when the offender "strikes out," although most are designed to incapacitate the offender for extremely long periods of time.[12] For example, mandatory life sentences with no possibility of parole are imposed when offenders are "out" in Georgia, Indiana, Louisiana, Montana, New Jersey, North Carolina, South Carolina, Tennessee, Virginia, Washington, and Wisconsin.[13] In three states, parole is possible after an offender is "out," but only after a significant period of incarceration. In New Mexico, such offenders are not eligible for parole until after serving thirty years, while those in Colorado must serve forty years before parole can be considered. In California, a minimum of twenty-five years must be served before parole eligibility.

Arkansas, Connecticut, Kansas, and Nevada have recently enacted laws enhancing the possible penalties for multiple convictions for specified serious felonies but leave the actual sentence to the discretion of the court. Several states—Florida, North Dakota, Pennsylvania, Utah, and Vermont—provide ranges of sentences for repeat offenders that can extend up to life when certain violent offenses are involved.

COMPARISON OF THE NEW LAWS WITH PREEXISTING SENTENCING PROVISIONS

To understand the potential symbolic nature of these laws, one must consider how each state sentenced repeat violent offenders *prior to* the enactment of three strikes. In other words, did the new legislation successfully close a loophole in the state's criminal sanctioning authority as hoped, or was the new law in effect targeting a population already covered by existing laws?

In general, it was the latter condition that existed in all of the states. As shown in Table 9-2, provisions were already in place to enhance penalties for repeat offenders in all twenty-four of the three strike states before the passage of the latest three strike legislation. In four of these states—Louisiana, Maryland, South Carolina, and Tennessee—the mandatory penalty for a person found to be a repeat violent offender (life in prison without the possibility of parole) already existed and remained unchanged, but the definition of such an offender was expanded under the new legislation.

The definition of a repeat offender was expanded in two additional states, with the penalties remaining the same (Vermont and North Dakota). Virginia moved from providing no parole eligibility for those convicted of three separate violent felonies, no matter the sentence, to mandating life sentences with no parole eligibility for this group. In some states, the changes involved both expanding the definitions of repeat violent offenders and enhancing the

TABLE 9-2 Comparison of New Strike Laws with Preexisting Sentencing Provisions

State	Features of New Strike Legislation	Year Implemented	Features of Preexisting Sentencing Laws
Arkansas	Range of no-parole sentences starting at 40 years for second conviction for specified violent felonies; no-parole sentences for third conviction for other specified felonies.	1995	Extended prison terms for repeat offenders, broken down by seriousness of new conviction and number of prior convictions.
California	Mandatory doubling of sentence for any felony if one prior serious or violent felony conviction; mandatory life for any third felony if two prior serious or violent felony convictions.	1994	Life with no parole eligibility before 20 years for third violent felony conviction where separate prison terms were served for the first two convictions; life without parole for fourth violent felony conviction.
Colorado	Mandatory life in prison with no parole eligibility for 40 years for third conviction for Class 1 or 2 felony or Class 3 felony that is violent.	1994	Mandatory tripling of presumptive sentence for third conviction for any Class 1, 2, 3, 4, or 5 felony.
Connecticut	Up to life in prison for third conviction for many violent offenses.	1994	Upon second violent felony conviction in which period of imprisonment was served for the first, court could sentence as Class A felony.
Florida	Added new category of "violent career criminal" to existing habitual offender statute; for third conviction for specified violent offense, life if first-degree felony, 30–40 years if second-degree felony, 10–15 years for third-degree felony.	1995	Categories of habitual felony offender and habitual violent offender; range of enhanced sentences.
Georgia	Mandatory life without parole for second specified violent felony conviction.	1995	Upon fourth felony conviction, offender must serve maximum time imposed, and not be eligible for parole until maximum sentence served.
Indiana	Mandatory life without parole for third specified violent felony conviction.	1994	Habitual offender law requiring enhanced sentencing upon third felony conviction.
Kansas	Allows court to double sentencing guidelines for second and third convictions for many "person felonies."	1994	No provisions for enhancing sentences on guidelines for repeat offenders.

TABLE 9-2 continued

State	Features of New Strike Legislation	Year Implemented	Features of Preexisting Sentencing Laws
Louisiana	Mandatory life without parole for third specified felony conviction or for fourth conviction for specified felonies.	1994	Same law, except that for fourth felony conviction, at least two of the convictions must have been among listed violent or drug offenses.
Maryland	Life without parole for fourth violent felony conviction for which separate prison terms were served for the first three.	1994	Same law, except that car jacking and armed car jacking were not on the list of offenses receiving this sentence.
Montana	Mandatory life without parole for second conviction for certain offenses and third conviction for other offenses.	1995	Persistent offender statute allowing extended sentence of 5–100 years, to be served consecutively to any other sentence, for person convicted of any felony with one or more prior felony convictions.
Nevada	Range of options for enhancing sentence upon third conviction for violent felony.	1995	Same options, but upon conviction for violent felony if three prior felony convictions of any kind.
New Jersey	Mandatory life without parole for third conviction for certain violent felonies.	1995	Rarely invoked "persistent offender" provision allowing sentence of one degree higher than the conviction offense upon third felony conviction for first-, second-, or third-degree felony.
New Mexico	Mandatory life with parole eligibility after 30 years for third violent felony conviction.	1994	Mandatory increased sentence of 1 year upon second felony conviction, of 4 years upon third, and of 8 years upon fourth or more.
North Carolina	Mandatory life without parole for third conviction for violent offense.	1994	"Habitual criminal" statute mandating an additional consecutive term of 25 years upon third conviction for any felony, with the court specifying minimum number of years to be served before parole eligibility.
North Dakota	Enhanced sentences for second conviction for Class A, B, or C felony.	1995	Enhanced sentences for second conviction for only Class A or B felony.
Pennsylvania	Mandatory minimum enhanced sentence of 10 years for second conviction for violent crimes, and 25 years for third such conviction.	1995	Mandatory minimum enhanced sentence of 5 years for second or subsequent conviction for certain specified crimes of violence.

TABLE 9-2 continued

State	Features of New Strike Legislation	Year Implemented	Features of Preexisting Sentencing Laws
South Carolina	Mandatory life without parole for second conviction for specified felonies.	1995	Mandatory life without parole for third conviction for same specified felonies.
Tennessee	Mandatory life without parole for second conviction for designated violent felonies; same for third conviction for other violent felonies.	1995	Mandatory life without parole for third violent felony conviction.
Utah	Second- and third-degree felonies sentenced as first-degree felons, and first-degree felons not eligible for probation if have two prior convictions for any felonies and a present conviction for a violent felony.	1995	Second- and third-degree felonies receive enhanced sentence of 5 years to life if have two prior convictions at least as severe as second-degree felonies.
Vermont	Up to life with no probation eligibility or suspended sentence and no early release for third conviction for violent crimes; up to life for fourth felony conviction of any kind.	1995	Up to life for fourth felony conviction.
Virginia	Mandatory life without parole upon third conviction for specified violent felonies.	1994	No parole eligibility if convicted of three specified violent felonies, separate violent felonies, or drug distribution charges.
Washington	Mandatory life without parole upon third conviction for specified violent felonies.	1993	Number of prior convictions factored into offender score on state's sentencing guidelines.
Wisconsin	Mandatory life without parole upon third conviction for specified serious offenses.	1994	For repeat felony offenders, up to 10 years can be added to sentences of 10 years or more; 6 years can be added to sentences of 1–10 years.

sentences. For example, the habitual offender statute in effect in California prior to the enactment of the three strikes law mandated a sentence of life imprisonment with first parole eligibility after twenty years for persons convicted for the third time of a listed violent offense where separate prison terms were served for the first two convictions. It also provided that upon the fourth conviction for such a felony in which three separate prison terms had been served, the offender was to be sentenced to life without parole.

In summary, from a national perspective, the "three strikes and you're out" movement was largely symbolic. It was not designed to have a significant impact on the criminal justice system. The laws were crafted so that in order to be "struck out," an offender would have to be convicted two or more, and often three, times for very serious but rarely committed crimes. Most states knew that very few offenders have more than two prior convictions for these types of crimes. More significantly, all of the states had existing provisions that allowed the courts to sentence these types of offenders for very lengthy prison terms. Consequently, the vast majority of the targeted offender population was already serving long prison terms for these types of crimes. From this perspective, the three strikes law movement is much ado about nothing and is having virtually no impact on current sentencing practices. For example, in Washington, the state that started the three strikes movement, only 115 offenders were admitted to the Washington state prison system on their third strike after 1993.[14] The Federal Bureau of Prisons reported that no inmates had been sentenced under the three strikes law as of 1998. In Georgia, a two strikes state, Fulton County (Atlanta) has reported that less than ten cases are being prosecuted under the new law per year.[15] The only noted exception to the national trend is California, which has sentenced nearly 40,000 offenders to prison under its three strikes law.

DESCRIPTION AND LEGISLATIVE HISTORY
OF THE CALIFORNIA LAW

There are two, nearly identical versions of the California strike law. The first, found in the California Penal Code, section 667(b) to (j), was passed by the legislature and signed into law by the governor on March 7, 1994. The second, found in Penal Code section 1170.12, was enacted by voters as Proposition 184 on November 8, 1994.

The legislative history of this bill requires some elaboration. The legislative version of the law was initially introduced in the California legislature on March 1, 1993, but no action was taken on the bill during the 1993 session. Meanwhile, after adjournment of the 1993 legislative session, a petition began to circulate among voters to include a proposition on the November 1994 ballot that would, by voter initiative, enact the three strikes law. While the petition was circulating, a three strikes bill was reintroduced in the 1994 legislative session. This was done in an attempt to circumvent the voter initiative, which was seen as more difficult to amend if passed. Under California law, voter initiatives can be amended only by a vote of the electorate or by a two-thirds vote in each house of the legislature.

By the time the bill had passed, enough signatures had been collected to qualify Proposition 184 for the November ballot. The only difference between the two versions of the law was that the voter initiative did not state explicitly, as did the legislature's version, that juvenile adjudications and out-of-state prior convictions were to be counted as strikes. Two provisions in the California law[16] make it one of the most severe in the country. First, the law provides for a greatly expanded "strike zone," or charges that constitute a strike. The strike zone for the first two strikes is similar to that in other states—serious and violent felonies. The third strike in California, however, is any felony—a provision found in no other state's strike law. Persons with two or more convictions for qualifying offenses who are convicted of a third felony of any kind are to be sentenced to an indeterminate term of life in prison. The minimum term is calculated as the greater of: three times the term otherwise provided for the current conviction; twenty-five years; or the term provided by law for the current charge plus any applicable sentence enhancements.[17]

Second, the California law contains a two strike penalty in which a person convicted of any felony who has one prior conviction for a strikeable offense is to be sentenced to double the term provided for the offense, and must serve at least 80 percent of the sentence before being released from prison. Under California's criminal code, nonstrike inmates typically serve less than half their sentence. Only six other states have two strike provisions, all of which limit the offenses that trigger a strike penalty to those that are serious or violent.[18]

The intent of the legislature in enacting the law is stated explicitly in the statute as being "to ensure longer prison sentences and greater punishment for those who commit a felony and have been previously convicted of serious and/or violent felony offenses."[19] The law was designed to limit the discretion of system officials by prohibiting plea bargaining.[20] Also, if the offender is to be sentenced as a second or third striker, the law mandates that the court may not grant probation, suspend the sentence, place the offender on diversion, or commit the offender to any facility other than a state prison.[21]

Even with these explicitly stated limitations on discretion, the law conveys a great deal of authority to the prosecutor to determine the ultimate sentence that the offender will receive if convicted. While the law requires that the prosecution provide evidence of each prior conviction for a qualifying offense, it permits the prosecutor to discount a prior conviction for a qualifying offense if there is insufficient evidence to prove the prior conviction, or if the prosecutor believes that a two or three strike sentence would not be "in the furtherance of justice."[22] It is this latter clause that allows individual district attorneys throughout the state to establish their own policies on how the law should be applied.

Given the law's broad scope and the fact that it was so much more stringent than preexisting repeat offender sentencing provisions,[23] concerns were raised by officials in California that the new law would have a substantial impact on the criminal justice system at the local and state levels. Judges might tend to set higher bails on strike defendants because the longer potential sentences may create an incentive to flee to avoid prosecution, thus increasing the number of pretrial detainees being admitted to local jails. Defendants facing strike charges might demand jury trials (with nothing to gain by pleading guilty), resulting in the courts becoming backlogged with pending trials, causing long delays in case processing. These delays would increase the length of stay of pretrial detainees, exacerbating already serious overcrowding problems in local jails.[24]

At the state level, attention was focused on the potential impact of the new law on the prison system. The California Department of Corrections (CDC) projected that the prison inmate population would more than double in five years from its 1993 level of 115,534 to 245,554 by 1999—with 80,000 of these additional inmates being second or third strikers. The "stacking effect" of so many prisoners who would have to remain in prison by virtue of the law would result a prison population of approximately 500,000 inmates by the year 2035, of which half would be second and third strikers.[25] Rand projected that the prison population would quickly rise to over 350,000 by the year 2000 and eventually plateau at nearly 450,000.[26]

At first blush, it would appear that California's law has indeed had a major impact on the criminal justice system and the prison system. As of 1998, over 40,000 offenders had been sentenced to California's prisons under the two or three strike provision. However, as will be shown in the following text, the projected effects of the law have not been realized, as the state's local criminal justice system (the courts in particular) has found ways to circumvent the law and use it along local political and organizational interests.

IMPACT OF CALIFORNIA'S LAW
ON THE COURTS

The law has generated much publicity for the harsh sentences that have been imposed for offenses that are portrayed as minor,[27] and a great deal of litigation in the California appellate courts.[28] Among the many constitutional issues the courts have had to address are: whether the law is unconstitutionally vague,[29] whether the sentences required by the law constitute cruel and unusual punishment,[30] whether requiring strike offenders to serve 80 percent of their sentences through limitation on good-time credits that do not extend to nonstrike offenders is a violation of equal protection,[31] and whether counting as a strike a prior conviction that occurred before the enactment of the law violates ex post facto constitutional provisions.[32] On each of these issues, the courts have been ruling that the law meets state and federal constitutional requirements.

Several legal issues have arisen that ultimately were resolved by the California Supreme Court. The state's highest court ruled in *People v. Hazleton* that out-of-state prior convictions for offenses with comparable elements to offenses that are strikes in California should count as prior strikes,[33] as should prior juvenile adjudications if the juvenile was at least 16 years of age when the offense was committed (*People v. Davis*).[34]

Two other issues regarded the discretion retained by the court under the law, given its clear mandatory sentencing language. One of these issues concerned what are known as "wobblers." A "wobbler" offense is one where the judge, by statute, has discretion to sentence either as a felony or misdemeanor. Taking a case in which one court of appeals had overturned a trial court's decision to declare a charge in a strike case a misdemeanor (several other courts of appeals had affirmed that a trial court retained the right to do this under the three strikes law), the supreme court ruled in *People v. Superior Court (Alvarez)* that nothing in either the legislature's or the electorate's version of the law limits the judge's statutory discretion regarding wobblers. The court did state, however, that it would be an abuse of discretion on the part of a trial judge to reduce a felony to a misdemeanor just to avoid the two or three strike penalty. The trial court must consider the defendant's background and the nature of the offense in exercising this discretion.[35]

The other issue relating to the court's discretion arose when a trial court decided, over the prosecutor's objections, to discount a prior felony conviction in a three strike case and sentenced the defendant to six years in prison. The prosecution appealed, arguing that the court had no authority under the three strikes law to discount prior convictions—that such discretion rested solely with the prosecution. The court of appeals agreed and overturned the trial court's decision. The California supreme court, in *People v. Superior Court (Romero)*, sided with the trial court, ruling that nothing in the law denies judges this authority. The supreme court also suggested, but did not rule, that any law that would deny judges this authority would violate the separation of powers.[36]

The first three of these decisions drew little concern about changing the way the law was being applied throughout the state, since there was little division on the issues presented in these cases in the lower courts. But the *Romero* decision, which was issued in June 1996, had the potential to create an enormous impact. The appellate courts, which published more than twenty opinions on the issue of judicial authority to disregard prior convictions, were sharply divided. Many ruled that judges had no authority to disregard prior convictions, several that such authority did exist, and some that such authority existed, but in very limited circumstances.[37] By the time the supreme court's decision was announced, the law had been in effect for over two years and 16,000 offenders had been sentenced under its provisions. The decision in *Romero* was met with concerns that many of these offenders would have to be brought back to court from prison for resentencing. Concern was also expressed by many political leaders that the supreme court was substantially "watering down" the three strikes law by giving judges back the discretion that the law originally was intended to limit. In the aftermath of *Romero*, the actions of trial judges have quieted these concerns. Judges have not been

TABLE 9-3 Felony Jury Trials in Superior Court

Fiscal Year	Preliminary Hearings	Felony Cases Filed	Felony Trials	Trials per 100 Preliminary Hearings	Trials per 100 Cases Filed
Pre Three Strikes and You're Out Law					
FY 88/89	75,615	132,635	5,386	7	4
FY 89/90	80,596	151,115	5,481	7	4
FY 90/91	79,907	159,419	5,389	7	3
FY 91/92	85,375	164,635	5,716	7	3
FY 92/93	87,742	163,432	5,740	7	4
FY 93/94	79,439	154,959	5,485	7	4
Post Three Strikes and You're Out Law					
FY 94/95	85,119	158,959	6,167	7	4
FY 95/96	73,487	153,394	6,397	9	4

SOURCE: California Administrative Office of the Courts, Judicial Council of California.

bringing offenders back in large numbers for resentencing, and they have been using their authority to strike priors sparingly.[38]

Given the broad scope of the strike law, state agencies in California began analyzing the impact the law was having on local systems statewide soon after the law went into effect. A survey done by the Administrative Office of the California Courts approximately a year and a half after the strike law took effect showed the impact that the law was having on the work of the municipal and superior courts.[39] The survey found that 67 percent of responding municipal courts noted an increase in the number of preliminary hearings due to the three strikes law. Forty-six percent of the courts noted an increase in the length of the preliminary hearing, and 40 percent reported more pre-preliminary hearing appearances.[40]

More recent data, however, show that the number of superior court preliminary hearings are actually decreasing statewide (see Table 9-3).[41] There was a 13 percent increase in the number of felony trials between FY 1993–94 and FY 1994–95, the first full year that the law was in effect, even though there was only a 2 percent increase in felony filings during the same period. Moreover, the felony trial rate grew by 4 percent the following year, while felony filings decreased by 3 percent.[42] However, the following fiscal year showed declines in the number of preliminary hearings, felony cases filed, and felony trials. If one looks just at the rate of trials per 100 felony cases filed, there has been no change since FY 1988.

As expected, the trial rate for felony nonstrike cases is 4 percent, compared to 9 percent for second strike cases, and 41 percent for third strike cases.[43] But because the two and three strike cases represent such a small percentage of all trials, the law has not had a major impact on the overall trial rate.

TABLE 9-4 Comparison of Selected Counties on Use of Second and Third Strikes

County	Resident Population	Violent Crime 1997		Property Crime 1997		Two Strike Prison Admissions 1998		Three Strike Prison Admissions 1998	
		N	Rate	N	Rate	N	%	N	%
San Diego	2,763,400	18,006	651.6	39,891	1,443.5	4,250	10.9	441	9.0
Alameda	1,398,500	13,428	960.2	26,367	1,885.4	489	1.3	67	1.4
Los Angeles	9,524,600	106,673	1,120	156,356	1,641.6	16,715	42.8	2,062	42.2
San Francisco	777,400	8,608	1,107.3	14,706	1,891.7	346	0.9	24	0.5
Sacramento	1,146,800	8,938	779.4	32,896	2,868.5	1,719	4.6	277	5.7
Kern	634,400	4,094	645.3	11,161	1,759.3	1,017	2.8	243	5.0
Statewide totals	31,211,000	336,381	1,078	1,678,884	5,379	27,051	100.0	3,281	100.0

Note: Violent crimes consist of murder, forcible rape, robbery, and aggravated assault, while property crimes consist of burglary, larceny theft, and motor vehicle theft.

SOURCE: U.S. Department of Justice, Federal Bureau of Investigation, *Uniform Crime Reports: Crime in the United States, 1998.*

VARIATION BY COUNTIES
IN THE APPLICATION OF THE LAW

One of the major findings was that the application of the law by county prosecutors varied considerably. As noted earlier, the law's provision that allowed prosecutors to drop charges or not request application of the two or three strikes provision in the "interest of justice" afforded them great discretion in deciding whether to charge defendants with a two or three strike provision in the "interest of justice." Table 9-4 shows the use of the two and three strikes law in five major but diverse California counties. Alameda and San Francisco counties are "low-use" counties, while San Diego and Kern counties are "high-rate" users. Los Angeles is included simply because it dominates all the other counties in California.

The use of this discretion was most dramatic in San Francisco. From the outset, application of the law was controversial. When the strike law was on the ballot as Proposition 184 in November 1994, San Francisco voters were the only ones to reject the measure. Due to this public sentiment against the law, the San Francisco district attorney's office ran into several problems in obtaining strike convictions in the months immediately following the enactment of the law. For example, in the first strike case that was set to be prosecuted, the victim, a 71-year-old woman whose car was broken into, refused to testify against the defendant when she learned that the defendant was facing a mandatory life sentence as a third striker.[44] Just days later, a municipal court judge, in a case involving a wobbler, reduced a felony charge to a misdemeanor, exposing the defendant to a maximum sentence of one year in jail, rather than the twenty-five-year to life sentence that the district attorney's office was seeking.[45] As a result of these early and highly publicized cases, the district attorney's office began discounting prior convictions in a number of cases.

In his successful 1995 campaign to become district attorney, former defense lawyer Terence Hallinan openly criticized the strike law and its interpretation by the current district attorney. Once in office, one of Hallinan's first actions was to announce a new policy on strike cases: using the discretion conveyed by the law to the district attorney to discount prior strikes "in the furtherance of justice," strike penalties would no longer be sought for persons charged with nonviolent offenses.[46] Cases of strike defendants—that is, those with the requisite history of convictions for strikeable offenses—who were charged with violent crimes were reviewed by a committee of assistant district attorneys to determine whether strike penalties would be sought.

The same phenomenon was noted by Malcolm Feeley and Sam Kamin in their early study of the effects of the California law in San Francisco and Alameda counties:

> The Alameda County prosecutor's office is even more direct [than San Francisco's] in its adaptive response to the law it did not want. According to Chief Deputy Richard Igelhart, a case will not be brought as a third

strike unless the current felony is either serious or violent despite the fact that the language of the statute mandates the charging of any felony as a third strike.[47]

The opposite political sentiments surfaced in the high three strikes counties. Unlike those in San Francisco and Alameda counties, the local district attorneys in these three counties vowed to strictly enforce the law and charge all defendants as second and third strike offenders if their prior records so indicated. For example, the written policy of the Los Angeles district attorney's office on filing and prosecuting strike cases read: "Only in *rare* [emphasis in original] instances should the prosecution move to dismiss a prior felony conviction allegation under the 'in the furtherance of justice' standard" of the strike law. Furthermore, such action should only be taken when the sentence that would be imposed under the strike law "would result in a miscarriage of justice." Dismissing a prior could be done only with the written approval of the head deputy in charge of the branch district attorney's office.[48]

The initial decision to adhere to the law in some counties resulted in some pressures within the courts to cope with the added workloads. In Los Angeles County, officials reported that both the number of preliminary hearings held in strike cases and the length of time required to conduct them had increased. As more defendants facing strikes were demanding preliminary hearings, and prosecutors and defenders were litigating more vigorously at these hearings, judges and attorneys reported that it could take longer to move those cases out of municipal court and onto a superior court calendar. It was also reported that more motions tended to be filed in strike cases in municipal court.

IMPACT ON STATE PRISON SYSTEMS

California officials and others overestimated the impact of its strike law on the prison system. Although the sheer number of cases sentenced under the law is significantly higher than for any other state, the numbers are not as great as originally projected.[49] The first CDC population projection considered the impact of the strike law when it was still being considered by the state legislature and projected that the institutional population would more than double within a six-year period, from 120,379 in January 1994 to 245,554 inmates by December 1999 (Table 9-5).[50]

Very quickly, the CDC began to adjust downward the projected impact of the strike law. When revised figures were calculated in the Spring of 1995, the five-year projection was reduced by over 50,000 inmates. As seen in Table 9-5, with each successive biannual population projection, the CDC has lowered its estimation of the impact of the strike law. The 1998 projection was equivalent with the original 1993 projection, with both of them showing a projected inmate population of approximately 170,000 by 1999.

TABLE 9-5 California Prison Population Projections, 1994–1998

Year	Fall 1993 Projection[a]	Spring 1994 Projection[a]	Spring 1994 Projection with Impact of AB 971[b]	Spring 1995 Projection[c]	Spring 1996 Projection[d]	Spring 1997 Projection[e]	Spring 1998 Projection[f]	Difference: Spring 1998 – Earliest Projection with AB 971
1/31/94	121,432	120,379*	120,379*					
12/31/94	126,323	123,996	123,996	126,140*				
12/31/95	134,981	131,552	137,737	128,553	137,588*			
1996	142,865	138,821	157,680	142,551	143,170	145,565*		
1997	151,721	147,097	184,706	159,992	158,684	149,682	155,276	−29,430
1998	161,144	156,159	215,732	176,013	172,694	158,002	161,366	−54,366
1999	170,834	165,685	245,554	192,814	188,038	166,733	170,101	−75,453
2000				210,422	203,593	177,614	179,065	
2001					219,795	188,236	188,033	
2002					236,514	198,435	196,901	
Net increase	**49,402**	**45,306**	**125,175**	**84,282**	**93,344**	**42,671**	**41,625**	

*Actual institutional population at the time of the projection.

SOURCES: [a]California Department of Corrections, *Spring 1994 Population Projections, 1994–1999* (including update for three strikes law).
[b]California Department of Corrections, *Spring 1994 Population Projections, 1994–1999* (including update for three strikes law).
[c]California Department of Corrections, *Spring 1995 Population Projections, 1995–2000*.
[d]California Department of Corrections, *Spring 1996 Population Projections 1996–2001*.
[e]California Department of Corrections, *Spring 1997 Population Projections, 1997–2002*.
[f]California Department of Corrections, *Spring 1998 Population Projections, 1998–2003*.

Table 9-6 shows the number of CDC admissions for second and third strike offenders by month. As expected, there was a dramatic increase in the first twelve months that the law was in effect, but the number of admissions has leveled off and even declined slightly. This parallels the pattern of declining prison admissions for other offenders that the CDC had experienced prior to the implementation of the strike law.[51]

The primary cause of the missed projections appears to be that planners miscalculated how judges would sentence second strikers. Under California law, when sentencing an offender, the court can choose a sentence that falls within three ranges: low, mid, and high. If the sentencing range for an offense is five to ten years, the low end of the range would be five to six years, the mid-range seven to eight years, and the high end nine to ten years. In making its projections, the CDC originally assumed that judges would sentence second strikers at the midpoint of the sentencing range provided for each crime within the California Penal Code. However, CDC analysis of the sentences imposed on second strikers has shown that approximately 60 percent are being sentenced at the low end. The result has been shorter than expected sentence lengths and, consequently, shorter lengths of stay.[52]

WHO ARE THE STRIKERS?

Contrasting the attributes of inmates sentenced under the strike laws in California with those sentenced under more "traditional" three strikes laws like those in Washington state and Georgia illustrates more clearly how each state's strike zone, as defined by its laws, has produced very different types of offenders sent to prison (Table 9-7). As expected, in Washington, all but 7 of the 115 strike inmates have been sentenced for crimes against persons. In Georgia, only 88 cases have been sentenced under the two strikes provision, while over 3,000 have been sentenced under the one strike statute.

However, the vast majority of California second and third strike inmates have been sentenced for nonviolent crimes. Approximately 80 percent of the California two strikers and 60 percent of the three strikers were committed for a nonviolent offense. The fact that so many of these offenders have committed nonviolent crimes is a reflection of California's law that allows for a second or third strike to be imposed for "any felon" if the first or second prior conviction was a strikeable offense. The fact that Washington's and Georgia's inmates are older is reflective of both states' more narrow strike zone.

Table 9-8 presents a more detailed analysis of the types of offenses for which California inmates have been convicted as either two or three strikers.[53] The most frequent crime for these inmates is drug possession, with over 10,000 prison admissions. Over 600 inmates have been sentenced to

TABLE 9-6 Number of Second and Third Strike Cases Admitted to CDC by Month

Month	1994 Two Strikes	1994 Three Strikes	1994 Totals	1995 Two Strikes	1995 Three Strikes	1995 Totals	1996 Two Strikes	1996 Three Strikes	1996 Totals	1997 Two Strikes	1997 Three Strikes	1997 Totals	1998 Two Strikes	1998 Three Strikes	1998 Totals
January				562	36	598	822	102	924	729	120	849	694	83	777
February				602	55	657	785	123	908	776	98	874	703	82	785
March				848	73	921	836	95	931	850	110	960	877	130	1,007
April	25	0	25	775	78	853	854	96	950	874	131	1,005	835	129	964
May	99	0	99	859	79	938	930	129	1,059	736	122	858	786	107	893
June	168	0	168	823	90	913	732	112	844	741	121	862	789	92	881
July	259	5	264	710	61	771	799	131	930	788	113	901	897	109	1,006
August	334	12	346	906	93	999	903	139	1,042	749	117	866	768	75	843
September	408	16	424	840	79	919	771	126	897	696	88	784	636	80	716
October	488	31	519	760	80	840	843	128	971	808	91	899	849	101	950
November	546	21	567	805	98	903	681	100	781	650	95	745	702	88	790
December	567	49	616	761	84	845	728	145	873	785	109	894	715	88	803
Totals	2,894	134	3,028	9,251	906	10,157	9,684	1,426	11,110	9,182	1,315	10,497	9,251	1,164	10,415

Total two strike cases all years   40,262

Total three strike cases all years   4,945

Total striker cases   45,207

SOURCE: California Department of Corrections, "Monthly Three Strikes Statistical Reports."

TABLE 9-7 Comparison of Washington, California, and Georgia Prison Admissions

Characteristic	Washington Three Strikes		California Two Strikes		California Three Strikes		Georgia Two Strikes		Georgia One Strikes	
	N	%	N	%	N	%	N	%	N	%
Prison Admissions	115	100.0%	37,271	100.0%	4,613	100.0%	88	100.0%	3,046	100.0%
Average Age	38 years		33 years		36 years		40 years		29 years	
Gender										
Male	113	98.3%	35,474	95.2%	4,561	98.9%	88	100.0%	2,951	96.9%
Female	2	1.7%	1,797	4.8%	52	1.1%	0	0.0%	95	3.1%
Race/Ethnicity										
Black	41	35.7%	13,704	36.8%	2,025	43.9%	67	76.1%	2,168	71.2%
Hispanic	3	2.6%	12,200	32.7%	1,202	26.1%	0	0.0%	0	0.0%
White	67	58.3%	9,908	26.6%	1,202	26.1%	21	23.9%	878	28.8%
Other	4	3.5%	1,459	3.9%	179	3.9%	0	0.0%	0	0.0%
Current Offense										
Person	108	93.9%	7,265	19.5%	1,785	38.7%	88	100.0%	3,046	100.0%
Property	7	6.1%	13,662	36.7%	1,483	32.1%	0	0.0%	0	0.0%
Drugs	0	0.0%	11,728	31.5%	888	19.3%	0	0.0%	0	0.0%
Other	0	0.0%	3,895	10.5%	400	8.7%	0	0.0%	0	0.0%

Note: Due to missing data on current offense for California cases, the numbers do not total to 37,271 and 4,613 two and three strike inmates.

SOURCE: California Department of Corrections, Washington Department of Corrections, and Georgia Department of Corrections.

TABLE 9-8 Type of Crime for California Two and Three Strikers Admitted to Prison as of September 1998

Offense	Two Strikers N	Two Strikers %	Three Strikers N	Three Strikers %	Total N	Total %
Totals	37,271	100.0%	4,613	100.0%	41,884	100.0%
Person Crimes	7,265	19.5%	1,785	38.7%	9,050	21.6%
Homicide	325	0.9%	174	3.8%	499	1.2%
Robbery	2,816	7.6%	827	17.9%	3,643	8.7%
Assault	2,949	7.9%	432	9.4%	3,381	8.1%
Rape	98	0.3%	71	1.5%	169	0.4%
Kidnapping	84	0.2%	44	1.0%	128	0.3%
Other sex crimes	697	1.9%	237	5.1%	934	2.2%
Property Crimes	13,662	36.7%	1,483	32.1%	15,145	36.2%
Burglary	4,981	13.4%	860	18.6%	5,841	13.9%
Grand theft	1,017	2.7%	53	1.1%	1,070	2.6%
Petty theft with prior	3,932	10.6%	246	5.3%	4,178	10.0%
Receiving stolen property	1,221	3.3%	115	2.5%	1,336	3.2%
Vehicle theft	1,640	4.4%	151	3.3%	1,791	4.3%
Forgery/fraud	616	1.7%	39	0.8%	655	1.6%
Other property	255	0.7%	19	0.4%	274	0.7%
Drug Crimes	11,728	31.5%	888	19.3%	12,616	30.1%
Possession	9,494	25.5%	635	13.8%	10,129	24.2%
Sales/manufacturing	2,234	6.0%	253	5.5%	2,487	5.9%
Other Crimes	3,895	10.5%	400	8.7%	4,295	10.3%
Possession of weapon	2,484	6.7%	263	5.7%	2,747	6.6%
DUI	344	0.9%	19	0.4%	363	0.9%
Other	1,067	2.9%	118	2.6%	1,185	2.8%
Missing	721	1.9%	57	1.2%	778	1.9%

SOURCE: California Department of Corrections.

twenty-five years to life as three strikers for drug possession, and another 1,500 have received such sentences for property crimes.

Finally, we offer the case studies presented in Table 9-9 to further illustrate the types of crimes the strikers are committing. These five cases were drawn from the interviews with inmates, and in our estimation, here again, the pattern is the same. Inmates sentenced under this law for property crimes had committed relatively minor crimes where little if any harm was inflicted upon the victim. Furthermore, these cases were drawn from the three striker population, which is expected to reflect the more serious offender. Both the qualitative and quantitative data show that most inmates receiving the second and third strike sentences do not fit the profile of a violent and habitual offender for whom lengthy imprisonment is required.

TABLE 9-9 Selected Descriptions of the Current Offenses by Three Strikers

Case Descriptions

Case 1. Person Offense: Car Jacking

While attempting to steal a parked truck, the offender reportedly held the owner at bay with a buck knife. He fled on a freeway and was apprehended. No physical injuries or vehicle damage was reported. The offender was sentenced to 27 years to life with a minimum term of 22.95 years. The offender was employed at the time of arrest, earning between $300 and $500 per week net.

Case 2. Property Offense I: Possession of Cellular Telephone to Defraud Telephone Company

The offender was in possession of a cellular phone that when used would be associated with a different number and individual. Telephone calls billed to the victim represent the harm imposed in this case. The offender will serve at least 25.6 months. The offender was employed, earning $873 each week.

Case 3. Property Offense II: Petty Theft

The offender received a sentence of 27 years to life for attempting to sell stolen batteries to a retail merchant. The loss to the victim (cost of batteries) is $90. The offender was collecting disability pay at the time of arrest.

Case 4. Drug Offense: Sale of Marijuana

The offender sold a $5 bag of marijuana to an undercover police officer. The offense did not involve harm to person or to property. The offender will be incarcerated for at least 5 years.

Case 5. Other Offense: Reckless Driving, Evading the Police

The offender reportedly rolled his vehicle through a stop sign, panicked when police responded, and led police on a one-hour chase. He "decided to ride it out . . . [to] smoke [his] cigarettes and run out of gas." Police apprehended the offender after blowing out the tires on his vehicle. No victim was involved in this case. The offender received a sentence of 25 years to life of which he must serve 20 years. He was employed, earning $1,000 per week net.

IMPACT ON CORRECTIONAL COSTS

IN CALIFORNIA

It is difficult to directly assess the impact of the law on correctional costs. We have already noted that the impact on prison population growth has not been as great as expected, thus suggesting that there has been minimal costs to the CDC. However, the question of what would have been the sentences of the second and third strikers had the law not been adopted remains to be answered.

It is possible to make some gross estimates as follows. First, we can project the incarceration costs for those now being sentenced to the CDC. These costs are shown in Table 9-10. Here, one can see that a three striker convicted of a crime against the person is receiving an average sentence of forty-eight years (or life). Should he or she live so long, the cost to the CDC in 1996 dollars will be over $1 million. We estimated the cost of incarcerating offenders sentenced under the California three strikes law by comparing the operational costs for confining the typical violent and nonviolent third striker to

TABLE 9-10 California Correctional Costs for Strikers and Nonstrikers, 1996

Offense Type	CDC Cost per Year	Mean Minimum Time to Serve in Years		Total Costs per Offender	Inmates Admitted to Date	Estimated New Law Costs	
		New Law	Old Law			New Law	Old Law
Three Strikers							
Personal	$21,509	48.2	2.5	$1,036,519	1,785	$1,850,185,880	$38,393,565
Property	$21,509	31.1	1.3	$669,360	1,483	$992,660,999	$31,897,847
Drugs	$21,509	22.0	1.2	$471,477	888	$418,671,825	$19,099,992
Other	$21,509	24.9	1.0	$535,144	400	$214,057,568	$8,603,600
Three Strikers—All Offenses					4,556	$3,475,576,271	$97,995,004
Three Strikers—Property, Drugs, and Other Crimes Only				2,771	$1,625,390,391		$59,601,439
Two Strikers							
Personal	$21,509	9.0	2.5	$193,151	7,265	$1,403,240,707	$156,262,885
Property	$21,509	3.7	1.3	$80,013	13,662	$1,093,144,164	$293,855,958
Drugs	$21,509	3.5	1.2	$75,712	11,728	$887,946,583	$252,257,552
Other	$21,509	3.1	1.0	$65,602	3,895	$255,521,543	$83,777,555
Two Strikers—All Offenses					36,550	$3,639,852,997	$786,153,950
Two Strikers—Property, Drugs, and Other Crimes Only					29,285	$2,236,612,290	$629,891,065
Difference Between Three and Two Strike Costs and Old-Law Costs for Property, Drugs, and Other Crimes							$3,172,510,177

nonstrikers who have committed similar or more serious offenses. The average minimum time to serve was computed per offense category (person, property, drug, and other) for the second and third strikers. For the CDC nonstrikers, the average time served per offense category reflects the mean time served by felons released from the CDC during calendar year 1996.[54]

These data show that the costs of imprisonment of the second and third strikers are, as expected, significantly higher than for the nonstriker cases. The comparisons for the violent crimes are probably unfair, as they do not account for some of the very serious crimes that are embedded in that category (for example, simple assault, simple robbery, and so on). However, the other comparisons for property, drugs and "other" crimes are more telling and realistic. These are the types of crimes for which one would expect to receive a shorter or "normal" sentence had the law not been implemented. By just calculating the incarceration costs for these crimes and comparing the three and two strike costs with the prelaw incarceration costs, the total difference is approximately $3.2 billion. Again, these costs are in 1996 dollars and do not include capital costs associated with any new facilities that may need to be constructed to accommodate these inmates.

IMPACT ON CRIME RATES
WITHIN CALIFORNIA

As discussed earlier, three strike laws were expected to help reduce crime rates by incapacitating habitual offenders, who cannot be deterred or rehabilitated, and/or by deterring would-be offenders from committing new crimes. Already, we have observed a strong variation in how the law has been applied within California since its enactment in 1994. Although the number of post-implementation years is a relatively short (three to four years) time period with which to perform a time series analysis, a preliminary analysis of a natural experiment allows one to make some preliminary but tentative analyses of the relative effects of three strikes legislation on public safety. Two counties (San Francisco and Alameda) are clearly more lenient jurisdictions that have chosen not to apply the law as designed. The other three counties (Los Angeles, Sacramento, and San Diego) have conformed more to the law and have applied it far more frequently than the other two. If the law has crime control effects, one would hypothesize that crime rates would fall more quickly or sharply in the latter three counties as compared to the other two.

Figure 9-1 shows the rate of reported crimes per 100,000 persons for the five California counties and statewide, based upon the California Crime Index (CCI) from 1990 to 1996.[55] Consistent with national- as well as state-level trends, each of the five counties experienced decreasing crime rates over the six-year period. The largest reductions in overall crime rates have occurred in San Diego, Los Angeles, and San Francisco, with crime rates dropping by over 30 percent during the six-year period. In Alameda County, total crime also

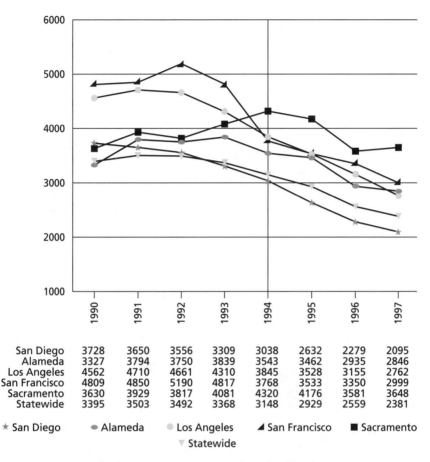

	1990	1991	1992	1993	1994	1995	1996	1997
San Diego	3728	3650	3556	3309	3038	2632	2279	2095
Alameda	3327	3794	3750	3839	3543	3462	2935	2846
Los Angeles	4562	4710	4661	4310	3845	3528	3155	2762
San Francisco	4809	4850	5190	4817	3768	3533	3350	2999
Sacramento	3630	3929	3817	4081	4320	4176	3581	3648
Statewide	3395	3503	3492	3368	3148	2929	2559	2381

★ San Diego   ● Alameda   ● Los Angeles   ▲ San Francisco   ■ Sacramento
▼ Statewide

FIGURE 9-1 Reported Crime per 100,000 Across Selected California Counties, California Crime Index: 1990–1996

SOURCE: *California Uniform Crime Reports 1990–1996.*

dropped (from 3,327 per 100,000 in 1990 to 2,935 in 1996), but at a far slower rate. Sacramento County, on the other hand, experienced increases in crime rates between 1991 and 1993, but by 1996 had returned to levels comparable to 1990. These data suggest no clear pattern of crime reduction occurring in relation to the application of California's three strike laws. Crime rates are being driven by factors other than the aggressive strike prosecution policies pursued in Los Angeles, San Diego, and Sacramento counties.

The same conclusion can be stated by looking only at violent crime rates. Overall, there was an 18.5 percent reduction in violent offenses reported to police between 1990 and 1996 statewide. As shown in Figure 10-1, Los Angeles and San Francisco counties posted substantial declines in their rates of violent crime. Alameda County was the only county in our sample that recorded a net increase (from 907 to 1,016) in violent acts reported to police

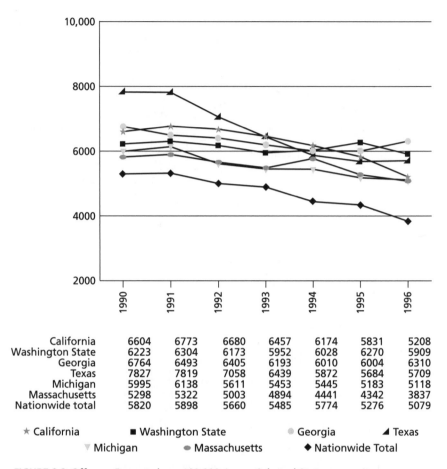

	1990	1991	1992	1993	1994	1995	1996
California	6604	6773	6680	6457	6174	5831	5208
Washington State	6223	6304	6173	5952	6028	6270	5909
Georgia	6764	6493	6405	6193	6010	6004	6310
Texas	7827	7819	7058	6439	5872	5684	5709
Michigan	5995	6138	5611	5453	5445	5183	5118
Massachusetts	5298	5322	5003	4894	4441	4342	3837
Nationwide total	5820	5898	5660	5485	5774	5276	5079

★ California   ■ Washington State   ● Georgia   ▲ Texas
▼ Michigan   ● Massachusetts   ◆ Nationwide Total

FIGURE 9-2 Offenses Reported per 100,000 Across Selected States, FBI Index of Crimes: 1990–1995

Note: California, Washington state, and Georgia are all states with three strikes and you're out laws. Michigan, Texas, and Massachusetts do not have three strikes and you're out laws.

SOURCE: *Uniform Crime Reports for the United States 1990–1995.*

between 1990 and 1996. However, violent offenses have been declining in Alameda County since 1994.

IMPACT ON CRIME RATES
AMONG THE STATES

The Uniform Crime Reports (UCR) index crime data from six strike states—California, Georgia, Massachusetts, Michigan, Texas, and Washington—were also collected and analyzed. California, Georgia, and Washington have adopted three strikes laws and have had them in place since 1993 or 1994. The other three states have not adopted three strikes legislation but had similar crime rates at the time that California, Georgia, and Washington adopted their bills. As shown in Figure 9-2, all six states showed trends in their crime rate patterns that are not consistent with the argument that adoption of these laws would produce independent effects on crime reduction. Admittedly, this analysis is simplistic from a methodological perspective, as it does not control for all of the factors that have been shown to be related to crime rates. It could also be that the non–three strike states had adopted other legislative reforms that served the same purpose of targeting habitual offenders. Moreover, there is no reason for Washington and Georgia to even assume that their laws would have an impact, as they were largely symbolic to begin with. Only California could possibly argue that three strikes might have an impact on its crime problem.

It has now been well established that the overall rates of crime as well as the violent crime rate in the United States declined during the period from 1990 to 1995. This downturn in crime was evident as early as 1993; in many states, crime rates were dropping well before then. Many social, economic, and public policy factors have been cited as contributing to changes in crime rates.[56] The bottom line is that California, which is the only state to aggressively implement a three strikes law, has shown no superior reductions in crime rates as compared to other states. Furthermore, within California, counties that have vigorously implemented the law have shown no superior decreases in crime rates as compared to other counties.

SUMMARY

The national movement toward "three strikes and you're out" legislation has been a symbolic campaign that has had little if any effect on the criminal justice system or public safety. With the noted exception of California, all of the states followed the initial lead of the state of Washington by carefully wording their legislative reforms to ensure that few offenders would be impacted by the law. Contrary to the perceptions of the public and policy makers, there are very few offenders who have a prior conviction for very serious crimes who then repeat the crime. In those rare instances in which an offender fits this profile, states already had the capacity to and were sentencing such offenders to very lengthy prison terms. Only California has tried to expand the "strike zone" so that thousands of offenders could be sentenced under the new law.

But even under California's ambitious law, the impact was not nearly as severe as projected. The California experience has also served to demonstrate how the enormous amount of discretion held by prosecutors can be used to apply any law to offenders as they see fit. Indeed, California has provided a clear example of "justice by geography," where similarly situated offenders have received very dissimilar sentences. Ironically, although the California law may have been designed to limit discretion by system officials in handling repeat offenders—through the ban on plea bargaining and the provisions for mandatory sentencing—it had the opposite effect, as district attorneys vary in their interpretation and application of the law. As Feeley and Kamin note:

> Thus, ironically, this [California] law like so many other laws designed to restrict discretion, has the effect of enlarging the discretionary powers—and hence sentencing powers—of the prosecutor at the expense of the judge.[57]

With regard to crime reductions, the law has had minimal impact. In those states that passed largely symbolic laws, one cannot link the three strikes reform to crime reduction, since the laws do not affect a significant portion of the criminal population. In California, crime was going down before the strike law took effect, and has continued its decline at the same rate as in states that not did pass three strike laws. More significantly, when we examined California counties that reflected differential application of the law, we found similar changes in pre- and post-reform crime rates, regardless of the county's policies on prosecuting strike cases. The failure of this reform to either deter or incapacitate the so-called "high-rate" offender is linked to an inability to target high-risk offenders (selective incapacitation) or to create the perception of imposition of the law in a swift and equitable manner. This is not to say that in California, and perhaps elsewhere, there are not many unfortunate offenders who have been severely punished using a very unfair strike zone.

NOTES

* The research presented here was supported by Grant No. 96-CE-VX-0009 awarded by the National Institute of Justice, Office of Justice Programs, U.S. Department of Justice. Points of view in this chapter are those of the author and do not necessarily represent the official position or policies of the U.S. Department of Justice.

1. Ted Gest, "Reaching for a New Fix to an Old Problem," *U.S. News & World Report* (February 7, 1994): 9.

2. Ray Surette, "News from Nowhere, Policy to Follow: Media and the Social Construction of 'Three Strikes and You're Out,'" in David Shichor and Dale K. Sechrest (eds.), *Three Strikes and You're Out: Vengeance as Public Policy* (Thousand Oaks, CA: Sage Publications, 1996).

3. For a summary of this literature, see J. P. Gibbs, *Crime, Punishment, and*

Deterrence (New York: Elsevier, 1975); and F. E. Zimring and G. J. Hawkins, *Deterrence: The Legal Threat in Crime Control* (Chicago: University of Chicago Press, 1973).

4. M. Klein, "Street Gangs and Deterrence Legislation," in David Shichor and Dale K. Sechrest (eds.), *Three Strikes and You're Out: Vengeance as Public Policy* (Thousand Oaks, CA: Sage Publications, 1996).

5. J. Petersilia, P. W. Greenwood, and M. Lavin, *Criminal Careers of Habitual Felons* (Washington, DC: National Institute of Law Enforcement and Criminal Justice, 1978); and P. W. Greenwood and A. Abrahamse, *Selective Incapacitation* (Santa Monica, CA: Rand Corporation, report prepared for the National Institute of Justice, 1982).

6. A. Blumstein, J. Cohen, J. A. Roth, and C. Visher (eds.), *Criminal Careers and "Career Criminals"* (Washington, DC: National Academy Press, 1986), p. 15.

7. D. Shichor and D. K. Sechrest (eds.), *Three Strikes and You're Out: Vengeance as Public Policy* (Thousand Oaks, CA: Sage, 1996).

8. P. W. Greenwood et al., "Estimating Benefits and Costs of Calculating New Mandatory-Sentencing Law," in D. Shichor and D. K. Sechrest (eds.), *Three Strikes and You're Out: Vengeance as Public Policy* (Thousand Oaks, CA: Sage, 1996).

9. John Clark, James Austin, and D. Alan Henry, "Three Strikes and You're Out: A Review of State Legislation," in *Research in Brief* (U.S. Department of Justice, National Institute of Justice, September 1997).

10. Indiana, Louisiana, and California include some drug charges; Florida includes escape; Washington treason; and South Carolina embezzlement and bribery.

11. The eight states are Arkansas, California, Georgia, Kansas, Montana, Pennsylvania, South Carolina, and Tennessee.

12. A strike-out in Georgia, Indiana, Louisiana, Maryland, Montana, New Jersey, North Carolina, South Carolina, Tennessee, Virginia, Washington, and Wisconsin results in a mandatory sentence of life in prison without the possibility of parole, while in three other states—California, Colorado, and New Mexico—parole is possible after a lengthy period of incarceration.

13. Virginia law does provide for the release of prisoners 65 years of age and older who have served a specified period of imprisonment; and a North Carolina law, separate from the three strikes statute, entitles those sentenced to life without parole to a review of their sentences after serving twenty-five years.

14. Washington Department of Corrections.

15. J. Austin, J. Clark, D. A. Henry, and P. Hardyman, *The Impact of Three Strikes and You're Out in Three States* (Washington, DC: National Institute of Justice, forthcoming).

16. Unless specific reference is being made to the legislative version of the law or the voter initiative version, any discussion of the law is meant to apply to the provisions that both versions share.

17. California law provides for several sentence enhancements, based on either the circumstances of the offense or the offender's prior criminal record. For example, any person convicted of a serious felony who has prior convictions for serious felonies is to receive a five-year sentence enhancement for each such prior conviction. This enhancement is added on after the strike sentence has been calculated, and must be served consecutively. California Penal Code § 667(a).

18. Clark et al., "Three Strikes and You're Out: A Review of State Legislation."

19. Penal Code § 667(b).

20. Penal Code § 667(g).

21. Penal Code § 667(c)(2) and (c)(4).

22. Penal Code § 667(f)(2).

23. A version of a "three strikes and you're out" law was in effect in California prior to March 1994, although it was not labeled as such and was substantially less severe than the new law. The preexisting version mandated a life sentence with no parole eligibility for twenty years for persons convicted for the third time of specified violent offenses when separate prison terms were served for the first two. The law also provided for a life sentence with no parole eligibility upon the fourth such conviction in which three separate prison terms had been served. In addition, the preexisting law contained sentencing enhancements related to repeat offending.

24. James Austin, "'Three Strikes and You're Out': The Likely Consequences on the Courts, Prisons, and

Crime in California and Washington State," *St. Louis University Public Law Review* XIV, One (1994).

25. California Department of Corrections.

26. P. W. Greenwood et al., "Estimating Benefits and Costs of Calculating New Mandatory-Sentencing Law."

27. When a sentence of twenty-five years to life was imposed on an offender who broke into a restaurant and stole four cookies and on another who stole a slice of pizza, the national news media was there to report it.

28. These cases are compiled and summarized in: Judge J. Richard Couzens, *The Three Strikes Sentencing Law* (Auburn, CA: Placer County Superior Court, 1997).

29. *People v. Sipe,* 36 Cal. App. 4th 468; *People v. Hamilton,* 40 Cal. App. 4th 1615; *People v. Kinsey,* 40 Cal. App. 4th 1621; and *People v. Askey,* 49 Cal. App. 4th 381.

30. *People v. Ayon,* 46 Cal. App. 4th 385; *People v. Cartwright,* 39 Cal. App. 4th 1123; *People v. Askey,* 49 Cal. App. 4th 381; *People v. Bailey,* 37 Cal. App. 4th 871; *People v. Campos,* 38 Cal. App. 4th 1669; *People v. Cooper,* 43 Cal. App. 4th 815; *People v. Diaz,* 41 Cal. App. 4th 1424; *People v. Gore,* 37 Cal. App. 4th 1009; *People v. Ingram,* 40 Cal. App. 4th 1397; *People v. Kinsey,* 40 Cal. App. 4th 1621; *People v. Patton,* 40 Cal. App. 4th 413; *People v. Reese,* 42 Cal. App. 4th 1113; *People v. Rodriquez,* 44 Cal. App. 4th 583; and *People v. Ruiz,* 44 Cal. App. 4th 1653.

31. *People v. Cooper,* 43 Cal. App. 4th 815; *People v. Applin,* 40 Cal. App. 4th 404; *People v. Brantley,* 40 Cal. App. 4th 1538; *People v. Kilborn,* 40 Cal. App. 4th 1325; *People v. McCain,* 36 Cal. App. 4th 817; *People v. Sipe,* 36 Cal. App. 4th 468; and *People v. Spears,* 40 Cal. App. 4th 1683.

32. *People v. Hatcher,* 33 Cal. App. 4th 1526; *People v. Reed,* 33 Cal. App. 4th 1608; *People v. Anderson,* 35 Cal. App. 4th 587; *People v. Sipe,* 36 Cal. App. 4th 468; *People v. Green,* 36 Cal. App. 4th 280; *People v. Hill,* 37 Cal. App.

4th 220; *Gonzales v. Superior Court,* 37 Cal. App. 4th 1302; *People v. Murillo,* 39 Cal. App. 4th 1298; *People v. Cartwright,* 39 Cal. App. 4th 1123; *People v. Ingram,* 40 Cal. App. 4th 1397; *People v. Hamilton,* 40 Cal. App. 4th 1615; *People v. Kinsey,* 40 Cal. App. 4th 1621; and *People v. Nelson,* 42 Cal. App. 4th 131.

33. *People v. Hazleton,* No. S051561 (Cal. Sup. Ct.).

34. *People v. Davis,* No. S053934 (Cal. Sup. Ct.). The dispute before the court centered around language in the law that also required that the juvenile was found to be a "fit and proper subject to be dealt with under juvenile court law" (§ 6679(d)(3)(C)). This phrase refers to the process of determining whether a juvenile should be prosecuted in adult court. Under California law, a juvenile can be prosecuted in adult court if the juvenile court waives jurisdiction by finding the juvenile to be unfit for the juvenile justice system. In the case before the Supreme Court, the defendant, Davis, had a prior juvenile adjudication for felony assault, but there was never any effort to waive that case to adult court, thus there was never a hearing to determine his fitness for juvenile court. Davis contended that since there was never a determination that he was fit for juvenile court, the juvenile adjudication for assault should not be counted as a prior strike. The Supreme Court disagreed, ruling that adjudication of a case in juvenile court is an implicit finding of fitness.

35. *People v. Superior Court (Alvarez),* No. S053029 (Cal. Sup. Ct.).

36. *People v. Superior Court (Romero),* No. S045097 (Cal. Sup. Ct.).

37. Judge J. Richard Couzens, "To Strike or Not to Strike; That Is the Question," in *Court News* (Judicial Council of California, February–March 1996).

38. For example, in Santa Clara and Contra Costa counties, judges were discounting priors in about 5 percent of strike cases. In Los Angeles County, the discount rate has been

approximately 14 percent. "The '3 Strikes' Crisis That Didn't Happen," *The San Francisco Recorder,* January 23, 1997.

39. Trial courts in California are comprised of the municipal courts and the superior courts. The municipal courts are responsible for all matters, including trial and sentencing, of persons charged with misdemeanors. Municipal courts also set bail and conduct preliminary hearings in the approximately 250,000 felony cases filed in municipal court each year, and have jurisdiction in cases involving infractions, in civil cases where the matter in dispute is no greater than $25,000, and in small claims cases not exceeding $5,000. There are 109 municipal courts statewide, with approximately 675 municipal court judges.

40. Administrative Office of the Courts, *The Impact of the Three Strikes Law on Superior and Municipal Court: Survey #2, July–December 1995.*

41. There are 58 counties in the state, each with its own superior court. There are approximately 800 superior court judges in the state, who handle approximately 160,000 felony cases each year, as well as probate, juvenile proceedings, and civil matters over $25,000.

42. Judicial Council of California, *1996 Annual Report.*

43. Administrative Office of the Courts, *The Impact of the Three Strikes Law on Superior and Municipal Court: Survey #2, July–December 1995.* These figures represent the medium trial rates for nineteen California superior courts that could provide the AOC with these data.

44. *San Francisco Daily Journal,* April 25, 1994.

45. *San Francisco Daily Journal,* April 28, 1994.

46. *San Francisco Daily Journal,* February 25, 1996.

47. M. M. Feeley and S. Kamin, "The Effect of 'Three Strikes and You're Out' on the Courts," in David Shichor and Dale K. Sechrest (eds.), *Three Strikes and You're Out: Vengeance as Public Policy* (Thousand Oaks, CA: Sage Publications, 1996).

48. Special Directive 94-04 of the Los Angeles County District Attorneys Office, May 2, 1994.

49. This analysis is not intended to be a criticism of CDC population projections methodology. The CDC projections are used to illustrate the gross overestimation of the impact of the California strike law.

50. California Department of Corrections, *Population Projections, 1994–1999 (Including Update for Three Strikes Law)* (Spring 1994).

51. Ibid.

52. This may be an explanation for why second strikers have a much lower trial rate than third strikers. Second strikers may be agreeing to plead guilty in exchange for an agreement that the prosecutor will seek a sentence at the low end of the sentencing range.

53. The California law requires two strikers to receive sentences twice as long as normally expected and to serve 80 percent of their sentences less pretrial custody credits. Three strikers must serve their entire sentences. Prior to the law's enactment, inmates served slightly less than 50 percent of their sentences.

54. Among the strikers, personal offenders must serve at least 85 percent of the imposed sentence, while all others must serve at least 80 percent of the imposed sentence. Therefore, for the personal crime offender, for example, we multiplied the average sentence imposed on three strikers convicted of a personal offense (56.7 years) times 85 percent to obtain the "minimum time to serve." For the nonstrikers, the figures represent actual average time served in CDC for those first released to parole during 1996. While these figures ought to represent only nonstrikers, it is possible that a minimal number of strikers may have been paroled during this time and included

in this population. Time served data for the nonstrikers was obtained from CDC Report, "Time Served on Prison Sentence: Felons First Released to Parole by Offense, Calendar Year 1996" (May 1997).

55. California Crime Index includes the number of reported homicides, forcible rapes, robberies, aggravated assaults, burglaries, and motor vehicle thefts. The FBI Uniform Crime Reports (UCR) includes homicide, forcible rape, robbery, aggravated assault, burglary, larceny theft, motor vehicle theft, and arson. California Department of Justice, *California Criminal Justice Profile 1995* (Sacramento, CA: Division of Criminal Justice Information Services, Criminal Justice Statistics Center, 1995).

56. See J. Austin and R. Cohen, "Are Crime Rates Declining?" (San Francisco, CA: National Council on Crime and Delinquency Focus, November 1996).

57. Feeley and Kamin, "The Effect of 'Three Strikes and You're Out' on the Courts," p. 150.

10

■

It's About Time

Our study of the American prison system revealed that most of the unprecedented numbers of people sent to prison are guilty of petty property and drug crimes or violations of their conditions of probation or parole. Their crimes or violations lack any of the elements that the public believes are serious or that they associate with dangerous criminals. Even offenders who commit frequent felonies and who define themselves as "outlaws," "dope fiends," crack dealers, or "gang bangers" commit mostly petty felonies. These "high-rate" and "superpredator" offenders, as they have been mislabeled by policy makers and criminologists, are, for the most part, uneducated, unskilled (at crime as well as conventional pursuits), and highly disorganized persons who have no access to any form of rewarding, meaningful conventional life.[1] They usually turn to dangerous, mostly unrewarding, petty criminal pursuits as one of the few options they have to earn money, win some respect, and avoid monotonous lives on the streets. Frequently, they spend most of their young lives in and out of trouble and behind bars. With time, they either "grow out" of these behavioral patterns or transition to an even more desperate existence that often leads to alcoholism, drug addiction, chronic unemployment, homelessness, mental illness, bad health, and an early death.

What may be more surprising is that a majority of all persons sent to prison, even the high-rate offenders, aspire to a relatively modest conventional life and hope to prepare for that while serving their prison sentences. This point should be considered particularly important because very little in the way of equipping prisoners for a conventional life on the outside is occurring in our prisons. In preceding decades, particularly the 1950s and 1960s, a much greater effort was made to "rehabilitate" prisoners. Whatever the outcome of these efforts (and this is a matter of some dispute), rehabilitation has been all but abandoned. Prisons have been redefined as places of punishment. In addition, rapid expansion has crowded prisoners into physically inadequate institutions and siphoned off most available funds from all services other than those required to maintain control. Prisons have become true human warehouses often highly crowded, violent, and cruel.

THE FINANCIAL COST

We must consider the costs and benefits of increased imprisonment rates. The financial cost is the easiest to estimate. Most people are aware that prisons are expensive to build and operate. Few, however, understand just how expensive. Indeed, previous estimates routinely cited by public officials have dramatically underestimated the amounts of money spent on housing prisoners and building new prisons.

Operating Costs

Since 1991, the amount of money required to operate just the nation's prisons (excluding the massive jail system) has grown from $18.1 billion to $30.3 billion.[2] To determine the costs per inmate per day or year, prison administrators typically calculate operating costs by dividing their annual budget by the average daily prison population. Using this crude method, the daily costs are estimated at $56, or about $20,500 per year. There is wide variation among the states, with some reporting operational costs of over $30,000 and others under $15,000 per year. The most expensive prison systems tend to be relatively smaller and are in states that are more affluent, have low crime rates and low incarceration rates, and have organized labor. These have a predominantly white prisoner population. The states with prisons of this type are Minnesota ($37,825), Rhode Island ($35,739), Maine ($33,771), Alaska ($32,415), and Utah ($32,361). The least expensive prison systems are located in the South and tend to be in states that are less affluent, have high crime rates and high incarceration rates, and have a lack of organized labor. These prisoner systems, which house predominantly black inmates, are in Alabama ($7,987), Oklahoma ($10,601), Mississippi ($11,156), Texas ($12,832), and Louisiana ($12,304)[3] However, this accounting practice is misleading and produces patently low estimates of the true costs of imprisonment. For example, agency budgets often exclude contracted services for food, medical and mental health care, legal services, and transportation provided by other government agencies.

According to two studies conducted in New York, these additional expenses increased the official operating costs by 20 to 25 percent.[4] An independent audit of the Indiana prison system found that actual expenditures were one-third higher than those reported by the agency.[5] Besides these "hidden" direct expenditures, other costs are rarely included in such calculations. To name only a few: the state loses taxes that could be paid by many of the imprisoned, pays more welfare to their families, and maintains spacious prison grounds that are exempt from state and local real estate taxation. In the New York study conducted by Coopers and Lybrand in 1977, these costs amounted to over $21,000 per prisoner.[6] Because the $20,500 figure cited earlier does not include these other indirect costs, the true annual expenditure probably exceeds $30,000 per prisoner. This would increase the estimated total prison expenditure from $30 billion to $45 billion.

Construction Costs

The other enormous cost is prison construction. Because prisons vary dramatically in their "mission," construction (and operating) costs vary dramatically. Prisons are enclosed, "total" institutions in which prisoners are not only housed but also guarded, fed, clothed, and worked. They also receive some schooling and medical and psychological treatment. These needs require—in addition to cell blocks or dormitories—infirmaries, classrooms, laundries, offices, maintenance shops, boiler rooms, and kitchens. Dividing the total construction costs of one of these institutions by the number of prisoners it houses produces a per-bed cost as low as $5,000 for a minimum-security prison in Alabama and as high as $128,000 for a maximum-security prison in Washington state. As of 1998, there were approximately 83,500 new prison beds under construction, with another 86,500 being planned for construction, for a total of 170,000 new prison beds. Assuming an average construction cost of $50,000, we will be spending $8.5 billion in direct prison construction costs.

But these costs are just part of the costs associated with building a new prison. First, the prison construction often needs to be financed. Instead of using current tax revenues to pay directly for this construction, however, the state does what most citizens do when they buy a house—that is, it borrows the money, which must be paid back over several decades. The borrowing is done by selling bonds or using other financing instruments that may double or triple the original figure, depending on the prevailing interest rates.

Second, there are other costs associated with the construction costs themselves. These include architectural and legal fees, project management fees, prison equipment, and site improvement costs for removing existing structures and hazardous waste materials, and for landscaping.

Third, prison construction costs are further increased by errors in original bids by contractors and cost overruns caused by delays in construction, which seem to be the rule rather than the exception. A survey of fifteen states with construction projects revealed that cost overruns averaged 40 percent of the original budget projections.[7] Because of these almost predictable overruns, prison construction projects typically have "contingency fees" set aside to cover such expenses.

The Million Dollar Cell

From the previous discussion, it is obvious that states will spend a lot more than $25,000 per year to house a prisoner and to build a cell in which he or she can live. But just how much more? In a recent study conducted for the U.S. Department of Justice, estimates were made on the costs of operating and constructing new prison beds for the District of Columbia. Table 10-1 uses the assumptions made in that study for developing the likely costs of a typical prison bed that will cost at least $50,000 to build. The results show that in total, a state will likely spend over $1 million in operating and construction costs over the projected thirty-year life cycle of that prison bed. The vast majority of those costs will be operating costs.[8]

Prisons versus Education

The states are just beginning to feel these enormous increases in the cost of imprisonment. Budgetary battles in which important state services for children, the elderly, the sick, and the poor are gutted to pay for prisons have already begun. In coming years, great cutbacks in funds for public education, medical services for the poor, highway construction, and other state services will occur. A recent analysis of the "tradeoff" of prison beds for higher education was conducted by the Justice Policy Institute and the Correctional Association of New York. The study found that since 1988, spending for New York's public universities has dropped by 29 percent, while funding for prisons has increased by 76 percent. In terms of real dollars, the state's annual prison budget has increased by $761 million, while funding for the New York City and state university systems has declined by $615 million. Currently, the state is spending $275 million more per year on prisons than on state and city colleges. And these costs do not include the $300 million now approved to construct an additional 3,100 new prison beds (at $96,775 per bed).[9]

THE "INCARCERATION
REDUCES CRIME" DEBATE

Perhaps the most hotly debated topic today is whether the imprisonment binge has actually reduced crime rates. Those who are largely responsible for this state of affairs—elected officials who have harangued on the street crime issue and passed laws resulting in more punitive sentencing policies, judges who have delivered more and longer prison terms, and government criminal justice functionaries who have supported the punitive trend in criminal policies—promised that the great expansion of prison populations would reduce crime in our society.

Figure 10-1 shows crime rate and incarceration rate data from 1933 through 1998. As the chart indicates, prior to 1965, there were relatively low crime and incarceration rates. Thereafter, both measures have steadily grown. Only since 1995 have crime rates begun their steady decline while incarceration rates have

TABLE 10-1 The Million Dollar Cell—
Typical Thirty-Year Life Cycle Costs of a Prison Bed

Cost Item	Costs
I. Construction Costs	
A. Direct construction costs	$50,000
B. Twenty-year debt service costs at 7.15% per year	$45,000
C. Project management at 4% of construction costs	$2,000
D. Legal fees/testing and inspection at 2% of construction costs	$1,000
E. Architectural and engineering fees at 8% of construction costs	$4,000
F. Fixtures and equipment at 6% of construction costs	$3,000
G. Project contingencies at 5% of construction costs	$2,500
H. Site improvements at 8% of construction costs	$4,000
II. Total Construction and Debt Service Costs (Items A through H)	**$111,500**
III. Operating Costs	
Direct operating costs	$25,000
External indirect government support at 25%	$6,250
IV. Total Operating Costs	**$31,250**
V. Thirty-year Operating Costs in 1999 Dollars	**$937,500**
VI. Total Costs for One Prison Bed in 1999 Dollars	**$1,049,000**

SOURCE: Austin et al., *District of Columbia Department of Corrections Long-Term Options Study* (Washington, DC: National Institute of Corrections, U.S. Department of Justice, January 31, 1997).

continued to increase. However, reported crime rates are still well above the levels reported prior to 1965. And, as we have noted throughout the book, the continuing increase in the prison population is not due to more people being sentenced to prison but due to prisoners serving longer sentences.

Does the chart in Figure 10-1 prove or disprove the arguments for the "incarceration reduces crime" equation? In this section, we review the scientific basis that has been offered by criminologists in support of the imprisonment binge. In making our assessment, we maintain that there are two basic requirements for their argument to hold. First, there must be a steady and consistent association over time between incarceration rates and crime rates. Where departures exist from the basic relationship, they must be reported and explained. Second, changes in other factors known to be associated with crime rates must be controlled for or, at least, acknowledged. Failure to meet either of these two requirements would be sufficient reason to reject the pro-incarceration position.

The Argument in Favor of
"Incarceration Reduces Crime"

The pro-incarceration advocates have a very simplistic two-variable equation—as incarceration goes up, crime rates must go down. To provide the scientific basis for this argument, the U.S. Department of Justice has played a key role in both articulating this proposition as a reasonable policy and funding a

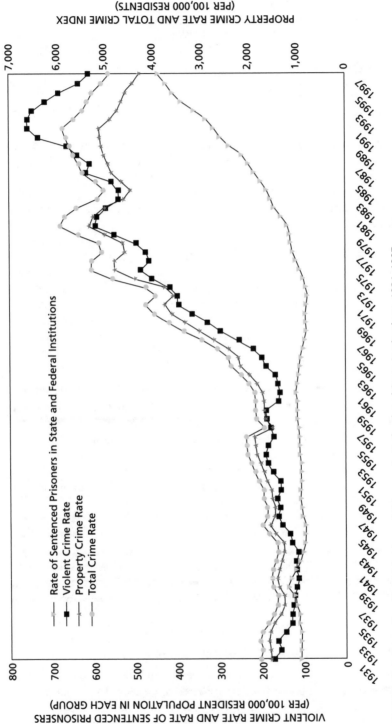

FIGURE 10-1 Crime Trends and Sentenced Prisoners in Federal and State Institutions, 1931–1997

Sentenced Prisoners Data Source: *Sourcebook of Criminal Justice Statistics, 1997,* Table 6.35. Crime Trends Data Source: Federal Bureau of Investigations, *Uniform Crime Reporting Program, 1931–1998.*

number of studies to demonstrate the causal relationship between imprisonment and crime. Beginning in the late 1980s, several key officials in President George Bush's administration's Department of Justice launched a major information campaign to solidify the scientific basis for supporting incarceration as the best means for reducing crime as follows:

> Statisticians and criminal justice researchers have consistently found that falling crime rates are associated with rising imprisonment rates, and rising crime rates are associated with falling imprisonment rates.[10]

Then Attorney General William Barr restated this position, arguing that the country had a "clear choice" of either building more prisons or tolerating higher violent crime rates. This view implied that increasing the government's capacity to imprison is the single most effective strategy for reducing crime. Barr listed twenty-four steps the government should take to reduce violent crime, including "truth in sentencing" that requires inmates to serve the full amount of their sentences, increased use of mandatory minimum prison sentences, relaxation of evidentiary rules to increase conviction rates, greater use of the death penalty, and higher numbers of police officers.[11] Similarly, President William Jefferson Clinton successfully campaigned for 100,000 police officers to be added to the streets to increase arrests. The 1994 Crime Bill, advocated by the then Democrat-controlled Congress and eventually adopted in 1996 by the Republican-controlled Congress, was designed to encourage states to increase the use of imprisonment by adopting "truth in sentencing laws" that would require inmates convicted of violent crimes to serve 85 percent of their sentences. States that adopted such laws were rewarded with federal funds to help pay for the construction of more prison beds. Clearly, both political parties have decided that we need to get even tougher with criminals.

During this period, a number of reports and studies were issued by the U.S. Department of Justice designed to support the proposition that increases in incarceration reduce crime. A primary tactic was to compare figures compiled by the Uniform Crime Reports (UCR) and the National Crime Survey (NCS, now referred to as the National Criminal Victimization Survey or NCVS) for violent crime rates (homicides, robbery, assault, rape, and kidnapping) with imprisonment rates between 1960 and 1990 in ten-year increments (see Figure 10-2).[12] By selectively using these ten-year increments, the Justice Department showed, as indicated in the bar chart in Figure 10-2, that during the 1960s, imprisonment rates dropped by 17 percent while reported violent crime rates increased 104 percent. During the 1970s, violent crime rates continued to increase, but only by 47 percent, whereas imprisonment rates increased by 39 percent. And in the 1980s, as imprisonment rates increased by 99 percent, violent crimes rates again increased, but by only 11 percent.

In other words, although violent crime rates have steadily increased over the past three decades, the rates of increase were lowest during the 1980s, when imprisonment rates were at their highest levels. These data led a Justice

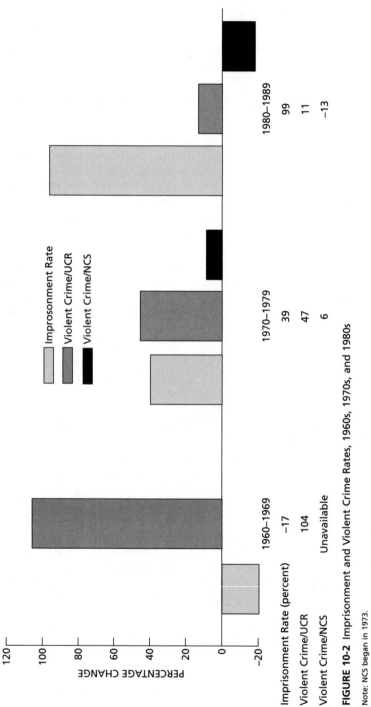

	1960–1969	1970–1979	1980–1989
Imprisonment Rate (percent)	–17	39	99
Violent Crime/UCR	104	47	11
Violent Crime/NCS	Unavailable	6	–13

FIGURE 10-2 Imprisonment and Violent Crime Rates, 1960s, 1970s, and 1980s

Note: NCS began in 1973.

SOURCE: William Barr, *Combating Violent Crime: 24 Recommendations to Strengthen Criminal Justice* (Washington, DC: U.S. Department of Justice, Office of the Attorney General), p. 5.

Department spokesperson to claim that violent crime will decline even more if more persons are imprisoned.

> No one knows for sure what the 1990s will bring. But my guess, based on the lessons learned over the past three decades, is this: If imprisonment rates continue to rise, overall violent crime rates will not increase and could actually fall in the 1990s. A big "if," of course, is whether imprisonment rates will continue their steady upward climb.[13]

Looking back at Figure 10-1, the "incarceration reduces crime" advocates believe their thesis has been validated. Although there are some inconsistencies over time, the basic pattern remains: as incarceration rates have increased, crime rates have declined.

The Argument Against "Incarceration Reduces Crime"

The major flaw in the "incarceration reduces crime" policy is its simplistic nature. For some reason, imprisonment advocates have completely rejected or ignored the long and rich history of criminology that has shown that many other social forces, in addition to the response of the criminal justice system, affect crime rates. It would be hard to find any credible social scientist or reasonable person who would agree that the rate of crime in any society is the sole product of how many of its citizens are incarcerated. Rather, crime is the product of a very complex set of individual, social, economic, political, and even random circumstances. The pro-incarceration advocates are asking the American people to exclude all other known factors associated with crime and to put all of their crime-fighting eggs in the incarceration basket. We believe, however, that a more careful examination of all available information demonstrates major inconsistencies in their argument and lends greater support to the conclusion that more imprisonment has little to do with crime rates.

Inconsistencies in the "Incarceration Leads to Lower Crime Rate" National Trend Returning to the argument set forth by the U.S. Department of Justice that crime rate increases were lowest in the 1980s and highest in the 1960s, a more careful year-by-year analysis of the same UCR data cited by the Justice Department shows that the nation's overall crime rates have had relative periods of stabilization in all four decades, usually during the initial part of the decade (1960 to 1962, 1970 to 1973, 1975 to 1978, 1980 to 1984, and 1990 to 1994), only to be followed by crime rate increases despite increases in the use of imprisonment (Figure 10-1). For the imprisonment theory to be valid, these countervailing trends either should not have occurred or should somehow be explained by the imprisonment theory. If there was a direct causal relationship between imprisonment and crime rates, stabilization in crime rates during these time periods should not have taken place.

The imprisonment advocates also claimed at one time that crime had been reduced since 1973 by over 30 percent, with most of the decline occurring since 1980. They based their case exclusively on the 1973 to 1992 NCVS household surveys (see Figure 10-3). During this same time period, imprisonment rates more than tripled, from 98 to 329 per 100,000. Like the UCR rates, the NCVS data also show a decline in household-reported crime beginning in 1980.

Beginning in 1985, however, both the UCR and NCVS violent crime rates began to increase despite the fact that the imprisonment rate continued to escalate. In fact, the overall violent victimization rate in 1995 is virtually the same as it was in 1973 when the number of people in prison was only 200,000 (see Figure 10-3).

Inconsistencies Among the States There are significant variations among the states with respect to their crime and incarceration rate trends. Perhaps most noteworthy is that states with the highest crime rates tend to have the highest incarcerations rates. In Figure 10-4, the states and the District of Columbia are plotted by their increases in rates of incarceration and changes in crime rates. If the plot converged on a line, it would indicate a relationship. It is apparent that there is no convergence and that greater increases in imprisonment did not produce decreases in crime. We analyzed this distribution by regression analysis, which establishes the line from which the points deviate the least (whether or not the distribution calls for a line) and measures to what extent the points deviate from it. This is indicated in a coefficient of correlation, R. When R is 1.0, the points are all on the line. In our case, R was 0.082 in the positive direction. This result suggests that in the twelve-year period, there was a very slight tendency for more incarceration to be related to increases in crime.[14] It would be simple-minded to conclude that this was a causal relationship. But it is very reasonable to recognize that this state-by-state comparison strongly indicates that the massive increases in incarceration failed to produce any reduction in crime rates. If incarceration rates were the principal driver of crime rates, the opposite result would occur.[15]

Inconsistencies Among Selected States Over Time If we were to pick three states to use in testing the imprisonment theory, California, New York, and Texas would be the obvious choices. As shown in Table 10-2, both California and Texas are the nation's leaders in increasing prison populations. In 1992, then Attorney General William Barr believed that California should serve as the model for the rest of the country. In fact, he was urging Texas to follow California's lead. "California quadrupled its prison population during the 1980s and various forms of violent crimes fell by as much as 37 percent. But in Texas, which did not increase prison space, crime increased 29 percent in the decade."

Under then Democratic Governor Ann Richards's leadership, Texas embraced Barr's advice and launched the largest prison construction program

Victimization rate per 1,000 persons
age 12 or older

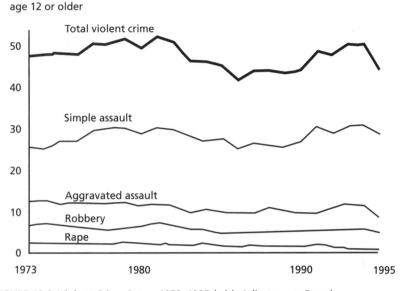

FIGURE 10-3 Violent Crime Rates, 1973–1995 (with Adjustments Based
on the Redesign of the National Crime Victimization Survey as of 1993)

Note: Collected under the National Crime Survey (NCS) and made comparable to data collected under the
redesigned methods of the National Crime Victimization Survey (NCVS).

SOURCE: U.S. Department of Justice, Bureau of Justice Statistics, *Criminal Victimization,
1973–1995* (April 1997).

in the state's history. As shown in Table 10-2, both states continued to increase
their imprisonment rates in the 1990s. California increased its imprisonment
rates by over 50 percent, while Texas tripled its rate. Both reported the same
decline in crime rates (about 35 percent) just as they have fallen nationally. Not
surprisingly, politicians in favor of imprisonment point to these two states as
examples of how imprisonment reduces crime. However, if we add New York
to the analysis we see how the greater "imprisonment lowers crime" thesis fails.
New York has only slightly increased its prison population and imprisonment
rates. Yet it has reported an even larger decrease in its crime rate. Furthermore,
the overall crime rate is significantly lower in New York than in California and
Texas despite its lower incarceration rate.

Inconsistencies Within States The pro-incarceration argument also fails to
explain why jurisdictions within a state that exercise very different sentencing
policies report similar declines in crime rates. The most recent example of this
situation was reported in Chapter 9 in the discussion of the effects of the "three
strikes and you're out" law in California. There we saw that counties that
largely ignored the "three strikes and you're out" law had declines in the crime
rates similar to those that had aggressively used the law to send more offenders to lengthy prison terms.

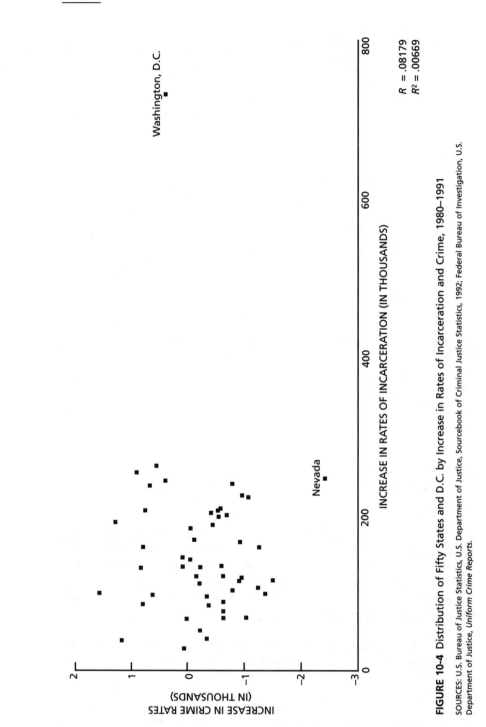

FIGURE 10-4 Distribution of Fifty States and D.C. by Increase in Rates of Incarceration and Crime, 1980–1991

SOURCES: U.S. Bureau of Justice Statistics, U.S. Department of Justice, Sourcebook of Criminal Justice Statistics, 1992; Federal Bureau of Investigation, U.S. Department of Justice, *Uniform Crime Reports*.

TABLE 10-2 Comparisons Between Crime Rates
and Incarceration Rates California, Texas, and New York 1990–1998

	CALIFORNIA		TEXAS		NEW YORK	
Year	Crime	Prison	Crime	Prison	Crime	Prison
1990	6,604	311	7,827	290	6,364	304
1991	6,773	318	7,819	297	6,245	320
1992	6,680	339	7,058	344	5,858	340
1993	6,457	368	6,439	385	5,510	354
1994	6,174	384	5,872	637	5,071	367
1995	5,831	416	5,684	677	4,560	378
1996	5,208	446	5,709	666	4,132	383
1997	4,865	475	5,481	717	3,911	386
1998	4,343	477	5,112	700	3,589	384
% Change	–34%	53%	–35%	141%	–44%	26%

However, there is even more direct evidence that altering the use of incarceration is unrelated to changes in crime rates. In San Francisco, a remarkable experiment in de-incarceration has occurred. As shown in Table 10-3, the county has reduced the number of offenders each year to state prison by over 60 percent. According to some, this would certainly produce a huge crime wave. But in fact, the crime rate went down by almost 40 percent—virtually the same decline reported for the state and Los Angles (Table 10-4).

Bad Math—The Numbers Do Not Add Up

There have been a number of criminologists and some major studies that have greatly contributed to the scientific basis for expanding the use of incarceration. Much of this "science" is grounded in a small number of studies funded by the U.S. Department of Justice in the 1970s conducted by the Rand Corporation and its leading researchers (Jan and Marcia Chaiken, Joan Petersilia, Peter Greenwood, and Alan Abrahamse).[16] These studies consisted of having newly admitted prisoners self-report how many crimes they had committed prior to being incarcerated. Based on these survey results, the Rand researchers concluded that a small number of prisoners admitted to having committed a very large number of crimes before they were incarcerated. Assuming they would continue to commit crimes at the same rate for an extended period of time, crime rates could be lowered by "selectively incapacitating" them. Lost in the discussion was the finding that most inmates sentenced to prison have very low or even nonexistent rates of criminal activity, suggesting that many prisoners pose little threat to public safety and need not be incarcerated. Nonetheless, policy makers were urged to adopt selective incapacitation sentencing strategies.[17]

A review by the National Academy of Sciences and Rand's own follow-up research later discovered that the selective incapacitation policy was incorrect

TABLE 10-3 San Francisco Crime and Sentencing Trends, 1990–1998

Year	Population	Serious Crime	Crime Rate	FELONY ARRESTS All	SENTENCES Prison	Jail	Jail/Probation
1990	724,100	34,810	4,807	7,355	1,239	1,146	2,973
1991	724,200	35,125	4,850	7,946	1,211	929	3,086
1992	744,500	38,642	5,190	8,740	1,314	1,051	3,690
1993	749,400	36,095	4,817	8,630	1,512	1,063	4,109
1994	753,400	28,389	3,768	7,941	953	656	3,465
1995	751,500	26,548	3,533	8,563	923	580	3,477
1996	768,200	25,737	3,350	8,244	816	775	4,305
1997	777,400	23,314	2,999	7,786	484	869	4,351
1998	789,500	20,990	2,659	7,301	NA	NA	NA
% Change	9.0%	−39.7%	−44.7%	−0.7%	−60.9%	−24.2%	46.4%

SOURCE: The Institute on Crime, Justice and Corrections, *San Francisco Jail Crowding Study.*

TABLE 10-4 California Crime Rates and Prison Sentences, 1990–1997

Year	STATEWIDE Reported Crime	STATEWIDE Prison Sentences	SAN FRANCISCO Reported Crime	SAN FRANCISCO Prison Sentences	LOS ANGELES Reported Crime	LOS ANGELES Prison Sentence
1990	3,443	32,265	4,807	1,239	4,596	13,083
1991	3,503	37,288	4,850	1,211	4,710	15,560
1992	3,492	43,199	5,190	1,314	4,661	16,532
1993	3,368	49,730	4,817	1,512	3,845	17,682
1994	3,148	42,388	3,768	953	3,528	12,105
1995	2,929	44,659	3,533	923	3,155	13,830
1996	2,559	47,283	3,350	816	2,762	17,574
1997	2,381	46,850	2,999	484	2,352	16,648
% Change	–45%	45%	–38%	–61%	–49%	27%

SOURCE: *Crime and Delinquency in California.*

for two reasons. The National Academy reanalysis of Rand's research found they had significantly overestimated the incapacitation effects of their proposed selective incapacitation policy. And then Rand itself found that its criteria for identifying high-risk inmates at the time of sentencing was invalid, but these findings did not deter others from arguing that incapacitation was a proven, cost-effective approach to fighting crime.

The first major effort to promote incapacitation was a report written by Edwin Zedlweski that was published with great fanfare by the U.S. Department of Justice, National Institute of Justice (NIJ), in 1987. Zedlweski argued that by incarcerating high-rate offenders, as defined by the Rand studies, crime would be significantly reduced and society would reap enormous economic benefits. Specifically, he states that although one year of incarceration would cost $25,000, society would avert $430,000 in social costs. Most of these averted costs were to be realized by assuming that each incarcerated offender would have committed 187 crimes per year, which would have cost victims and society, in responding to crime, about $2,300 per crime.[18]

In a related but later study, Mark Cohen and his colleagues tried to quantify the "true" costs of crime. The study, which was first published in 1988 and released in another version by the U.S. Department of Justice's NIJ in 1996, took the cost of crime one major step higher by adding the costs of "pain and suffering" to the cost-benefit equation. Remarkably, this piece of research claimed that the true cost of crime was actually $450 billion per year, with $345 billion being linked to so-called "quality of life" issues. These cost figures are well above the government's own estimates of $17.6 billion.[19]

These two studies have formed the basis for many politicians to argue that increased incarceration will significantly reduce crime and yet save money—in fact, hundreds of billions of dollars. Policies that served to reduce lengths of stay were criticized as "ineffective." Instead, "truth in sentencing," "three strikes and you're out," and other efforts to lengthen prison terms were advocated by many politicians who now had the scientific basis for their ideology. For example, John DiIlulio, using these data, claimed that "prisons were a bargain"; and California's then Governor Pete Wilson's chief economist promised that passing the "three strikes and you're out" legislation would cause the crime rate in California to drop by 20 percent and save the state $55 billion.[20]

These studies have been roundly criticized largely because the numbers presented do not add up to what is well known regarding the number and cost of crimes. With respect to the number of crimes associated with incarcerated felons, Zimring and Hawkins have simply noted that, assuming the prevention of 187 crimes per offender was accurate and given the large increase in the prison population, crime would have been eliminated in the United States many years ago.[21] A pointed example of the unfilled promise of a crime-free California by 1982 developed by Zimring and Hawkins is shown in Figure 10-5. Clearly, something is very wrong with the assumption that the average number of crimes committed per year for sentenced inmates is so high.

With respect to the cost-benefit claim made by Cohen and colleagues, Austin as well as Zimring and Hawkins have pointed out the inappropriateness of using rarely awarded jury awards for "pain and suffering" for all crimes regardless of their relative pettiness.

> These estimates are applied to all crimes despite the fact that virtually none then result in jury awards. . . . Even if one assumes that the $345 billion estimate of "quality of life" is accurate, what does it mean in real dollars? The answer is very little. The number is only a monetary symbol, it has nothing to do with real dollars, and has no economic significance.[22]

> The specific cost estimates are opportunistic, arbitrary, inconsistent, and too high. The schema lacks an articulated theory of either public or private cost. Moreover, Cohen's analysis reveals no relationship between its cost estimates and its conclusions about the cost-effectiveness of the investment in further crime control resources.[23]

Failure to Control for Other Factors
Known to Be Associated with Crime Rates

All of the data presented here point to an inescapable conclusion, namely, that crime rates are much more the products of other aspects of our society. Here, we return to the themes articulated in Chapter 8 on rehabilitation, namely, factors other than incarceration rates that are known to be linked to crime rates. In order for the "incarceration reduces crime" thesis to be valid, it must be shown that these other crime-related factors remained constant or were controlled in the analysis.

Demographics Since most crimes are committed by males between the ages of 15 and 24, as that population grows or subsides, one can expect associated fluctuations in the crime rates. Before changes in crime rates can be attributed

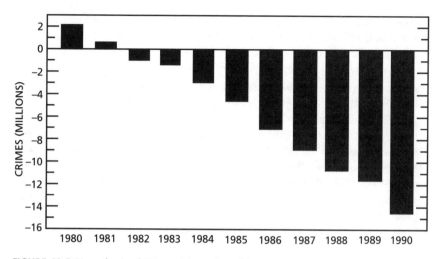

FIGURE 10-5 Hypothesized Crime Volume in California,
Using 1980 Crimes, the Zedlewski Model of Incapacitation,
and California Prison and Jail Trends

SOURCE: Zimring and Hawkins, *Incapacitation* (1995), p. 145.

to changes in imprisonment rates, the influence of demographic changes must be considered.

Beginning in the early 1960s and throughout the 1970s—the exact period of the rise in crime rates, this age group grew in size. By 1980, the growth had peaked, and the size of this group began to decline—just as the crime rate also began to decline. An article by Darrell Steffensmeier and Miles Harer found that most of the decline in crime rates observed from 1979 through 1985 was the direct result of a declining "at-risk" population.[24] Unlike the pro-incarceration rate analysis, this study controlled for changes in incarceration rates. When we take into account the influence of this demographic shift, reductions in the NCVS from 1980 to 1988 are largely attributable (60 percent of the crime reduction explained) to reductions in the high-crime rate population between the ages of 15 and 24. The same analysis, when applied to the UCR data, actually shows an increase in UCR during the same period.[25]

Demographics also influence how crime is reported in the NCVS rates. Since these surveys are based on the number, characteristics, and location of U.S. households, changes in the attributes of households over the past two decades will influence reported crime rates. For example, the Justice Department has acknowledged that since 1973, the size of the American household has (1) declined, (2) shifted from urban areas to suburban locations, and (3) shifted from the Northeast and Midwest to the South and the West.[26]

The first two conditions automatically reduce crime rate estimates because smaller households located in suburban areas are less likely than larger and urban households to experience crime. The third condition, relocation to the West where crime rates are highest, increases the likelihood of households being victimized. These trends in the NCVS must be more carefully analyzed before conclusions can be made that a tripling of the incarceration rate is solely responsible for declines in personal and household theft.

The Economy and Other Social Economic Indicators The 1990s also witnessed major improvements in a number of areas known to be related to crime rates (see Table 10-5). We have already noted the effects of demographics—namely, the aging of the U.S. population. The unemployment rate in general declined from 6.2 percent of the work-eligible population in 1990 to 4.1 percent in 1999. There are also indications that the number of teenage births and those on the public welfare rolls declined as well. And there are many more indicators of social well-being that also pointed in a positive direction. Many of these indicators are reflective of the earlier-cited study by Linsky and Strauss. As these indicators continue to improve, we can continue to expect further declines or at least stabilization in the crime rates. Clearly, these factors should be accounted for in assessing fluctuations in crime rates.

VOODOO CRIMINOLOGY

The failure of the massive expansion of prison populations to accomplish the most important objective of incarceration—the reduction of crime—should come as no surprise because the idea that increased penalties will reduce crime is based on a simplistic and fallacious theory of criminal behavior. It starts with the idea that every person is an isolated, willful actor who makes completely rational decisions to maximize his or her pleasure and to minimize his or her pain. Consequently, individuals only commit crimes when they believe it will lead to more pleasure, gain, or satisfaction and with minimal risk for pain or punishment. If penalties for being caught are small or nonexistent, then many persons who are not restrained by other factors (for example, strong conventional morals or the disapproval of close friends or family) will commit crimes—indeed, a lot of crimes. Only by increasing the certainty and severity of punishment, this thinking goes, will people "think twice" and be deterred.

The punishment/incapacitation/deterrence theory assumes that all individuals have access to the same conventional lifestyles for living out a law-abiding life. This is not true for most of the individuals who are caught up in our criminal justice system. For many, particularly young members of the inner-city underclass, the choice is not between conventional and illegal paths to the good life but between illegal and risky paths or no satisfaction at all. They are faced with a limited and depressing choice between a menial, dull, impoverished, undignified life at the bottom of the conventional heap or a life with some excitement, some monetary return, and a slim chance of larger financial rewards, albeit with great risks of being imprisoned, maimed, or even killed. Consequently, many "choose" crime despite the threat of imprisonment.

TABLE 10-5 Social Demographic Indicators Related to Crime Rates, 1990–1997

Year	Crime Rate	Median Age	% of Population 15–24	Unemployment Rate	AFDC Recipients	Abortions (in thousands)	Teenage Birthrate (per 1,000)
1990	5820	35.2	14.8%	6.2%	12,159	1,609	83.8
1991	5898	35.3	14.4%	7.0%	13,489	1,557	83.2
1992	5660	35.4	14.2%	7.4%	14,035	1,529	80.7
1993	5484	35.6	14.0%	6.6%	14,115	1,500	80.1
1994	5374	35.7	13.9%	5.6%	14,276	1,431	78.8
1995	5276	35.8	13.8%	5.4%	13,931	1,364	77.7
1996	5087	35.9	13.7%	4.8%	12,877	1,366	70.6
1997	4923	36.1	13.7%	4.6%	11,423	NA	NA
% Change	-15%	3%	-7%	-26%	-6%	-15%	-16%

SOURCES: U.S. Census Bureau, Poverty and Health Statistics Branch/HHES Division, *Current Population Survey* (March 1999); U.S. Census Bureau, Population Estimates Program, Population Division. Internet release date: December 23, 1999.

For many young males, especially African Americans and Hispanics, the threat of going to prison or jail is no threat at all but rather an expected or accepted part of life. Most minority males will be punished by the criminal justice system during their lifetimes. The federal government reports that an estimated 1 of every 20 persons (5 percent) can be expected to serve time in prison during their lifetime. The lifetime chances of a person going to prison are higher for men (9 percent) than for women (1 percent) and higher for blacks (16 percent) and Hispanics (9 percent) than for whites (2 percent). At current levels of incarceration, newborn black males in this country have a greater than 1 in 4 chance of going to prison during their lifetimes, while Hispanic males have a 1 in 6 chance, and white males have a 1 in 23 chance of serving time. These numbers do not include the probabilities of being arrested, jailed, or placed in a juvenile detention system.[27] Deterrence and punishment are effective only when the act of punishment actually worsens a person's lifestyle. For millions of males, imprisonment poses no such threat. As a young black convict put it when Claude Brown told him that his preprison life meant that there was a "60 percent chance he will be killed, permanently maimed, or end up doing a long bit in jail":

> "I see where you comin' from, Mr. Brown," he replied, "but you got things kind of turned around the wrong way. You see, all the things that you say could happen to me is dead on the money and that is why I can't lose. Look at it from my point of view for a minute. Let's say I go and get wiped [killed]. Then I ain't got no more needs, right? All my problems are solved. I don't need no more money, no more nothing, right? Okay, supposin' I get popped, shot in the spine and paralyzed for the rest of my life—that could happen playing football, you know. Then I won't need a whole lot of money because I won't be able to go no place and do nothin', right? So, I'll be on welfare, and the welfare check is all the money I'll need, right? Now if I get busted and end up in the joint [prison] pullin' a dime and a nickel, like I am, then I don't have to worry about no bucks, no clothes. I get free rent and three squares a day. So you see, Mr. Brown, I really can't lose."[28]

Voodoo criminology also espouses a fatalistic perspective that there is little one can do to change humans. This perspective has been argued most strongly by John DiIulio. In making his statements on crime and the criminal justice system, DiIulio has made use of the entire range of tactics employed by the academic apologists. He has uncritically accepted unverified, frequently outlandish statements of facts and built his own arguments upon them. He has drawn conclusions from a single case—an anecdote. He has selected facts or relationships, plucked them from their full context, and then twisted them to suit his conservative agenda. Sometimes, it appears he has just made things up.[29] Nonetheless, DiIulio and his fellow supporters (including former Drug Czar and Department of Education Secretary William Bennett) have argued that many wayward youthful offenders should be viewed almost as human garbage and dumped behind bars for as long as possible.

America is home to thickening ranks of juvenile "super-predators"—radically impulsive, brutally remorseless youngsters, including ever more pre-teenage boys, who murder, assault, rape, rob, burglarize, deal deadly drugs, join gun-toting gangs and create serious communal disorders. They do not fear the stigma of arrest, the pains of imprisonment or the pangs of conscience.[30]

This dark futuristic view of America has led others to warn of an impending crime wave. James Alan Fox, a criminologist who often appears before Congress to give advice on policy, has predicted that juvenile crime rates, especially crimes of violence, can only go up.

We are facing a potential bloodbath of teenage violence in years ahead that will be so bad, we'll look back at the 1990s and say those were the good old days.[31]

And DiIulio has recommended that the juvenile prison system be increased by threefold to handle the new wave of "superpredators."

Fortunately, like before, these dire predictions and calculations have been way off the mark. As noted in Chapter 3, juvenile crime, and especially juvenile violent crime, has been dropping—not increasing as forecasted.

AMERICA'S FARM SYSTEM
FOR CRIMINALS

We have a less deterministic view of human nature. Most people who engage in crime do so not as isolated individuals, but as participants (as we all are) in various social organizations, groups, or "social systems," each of which has its own rules and values. Some groups in our society (often because of subjection to reduced circumstances such as poverty, idleness, and incarceration over an extended period of time) develop preferences for deviant lifestyles. For example, young males who were abused as children, dropped out of school, lived in poverty, abused drugs, and served many juvenile jail and prison sentences have become immersed in deviant values and are distanced from any set of conventional values. They are most satisfied when engaging in specialized deviant practices related to their unique culture—wild partying involving drug use and sex along with extremely risky behavior involving extreme displays of machismo.[32]

Since crime is not the sole product of individual motives, efforts, especially by the state, to punish the individual without addressing the social forces that produced that individual will fail. Individuals do not decide to sell drugs, purchase drugs, and set up single-proprietor operations on their own. Most street crime involves groups, organizations, and networks. Drug dealers are persons who have been involved in groups and networks of people who use drugs, have connections, and know or are dealers. The same is true of gang bangers, hustlers, and thieves.

In effect, America has created a lower-class culture designed to produce new cohorts of street criminals each generation. Similar to organized sports, most of these criminal operations have major leagues, minor leagues, and a bench. Children come up through the ranks, learn the game, and finally move into the starting lineup once they reach their adolescent years. When they are temporarily or permanently removed (that is, arrested, imprisoned, or killed), they are replaced by others from the bench to continue the game. When the bench is depleted, someone comes up from the minors. Much as in professional and college sports, the span of their career is short, with their most active crime years taking place between the ages of 15 and 24. Our impoverished inner-city neighborhoods (or what is left of them as neighborhoods) have almost unlimited reserves milling about who are kept out of the starting lineup by managers and first-string players. As soon as the police arrest the "kingpin" drug dealer, the leaders of a gang, or some of the top pimps or hustlers, new recruits move in to take over these positions.

This characterization of criminal operations also explains why the War on Drugs, which has been going on for two decades, has failed. During the 1980s, the government spent billions of tax dollars and arrested millions for drug possession or drug trafficking. Regularly, the media reported that a new large-scale drug operation and some kingpin drug dealers had been caught. Drugs continued to be at least as available as they were before the new arrests, however, as "new" kingpins quickly and often violently replaced the recently departed leaders.

Even if a particular type of criminal operation dies out, new crime games appear. In the late 1980s, the news media and government officials were blaming crack cocaine dealing for unprecedented numbers of homicides in Los Angeles inner-city neighborhoods. However, sociologist Jack Katz discovered that, contrary to the media's reports, homicide rates in the crack neighborhoods had not changed over the last decade.[33] Earlier in the 1980s, rival gangs were killing each other over territory. It seems, using the sports analogy, that the number of players available for crime games is related to broader social conditions, such as the existence of a large underemployed population of young males who have the ordinary youthful desires for respect, excitement, and gratification but are confronted with extremely limited access to legitimate means of acquiring them. Thus, the number of potential players remains constant over an extended period. Only the types of games being played change from season to season.

OUR PRISON SYSTEM
IN THE TWENTY-FIRST CENTURY

Where Are We Headed?

In a previous edition of this book, written in 1995, we presented a scenario, based on policies that were being proposed by the Clinton administration, Congress, and many states. The key components of that plan were as follows:

Policy 1: Add 100,000 police officers.

Policy 2: Increase the proportion of adult arrests resulting in a felony conviction.

Policy 3: Increase the proportion of convictions resulting in a prison sentence.

Policy 4: Adopt a "truth in sentencing" policy that would require offenders convicted of violent crimes to serve 85 percent of their prison terms.

We predicted that the net result of these proposed reforms would be to create a prison population of 2.3 million in the twenty-first century.

Fortunately, only two of the policies have been partially adopted. Congress has funded the 100,000 police officers that are now being hired throughout the nation's police forces. However, there has been much criticism that the funds allocated for this program have not resulted in police hires but in the subsidy of existing officer positions.

The area of change has been in sentencing policy. Prior to 1993, twenty-two states had adopted "truth in sentencing" laws. Fortunately, only five more states have adopted these laws since then. It now appears that the remaining states are less likely to adopt such draconian laws, as they recognize the substantial prison operating and construction costs associated with such sentencing policies. Nonetheless, the damage has been done. The Bureau of Justice Statistics now estimates that newly sentenced inmates will serve a minimum of forty-two months in prison as opposed to the previously reported figure of twenty-five months. The long-term consequences of longer prison terms coupled with higher parole violation rates will require further continuation of the imprisonment binge. Table 10-6 shows the likely consequences if we continue to sentence inmates to longer prison terms and maintain very high parole violation rates. This projection is actually conservative, as it assumes no increase in prison admissions and that most inmates will be released at their earliest release date. Under such policies, the prison population will increase by another 260,000 inmates over the next few years. And those numbers do not include the nearly 120,000 inmates in federal prison and another 665,000 in the local jails.

The Continued Cost of the Imprisonment Binge

Unless we find a way to reverse the trends that have been set in motion, we will continue to pay a heavy price. Based on the data presented in Table 10-1, the additional 260,000 prison beds will have to be constructed at a cost of nearly $30 billion. Another $8 billion will be required each year to fund the additional prisoners. To do this constitutionally while preserving a semblance of our civil rights will require an expansion of the other parts of the criminal justice system—the jails, courts, and police departments. Assuming that the use of probation and parole will be reduced, there will be limited savings on the least expensive components of the correctional system.

Unless we want to strip down or abandon many other government enterprises such as education, welfare, transportation, and medical services, we will

TABLE 10-6 Long-Term Projection of State Prison Populations

Prison Growth Factor	Admissions	Length of Stay	Population
New court commitments	334,630	42 months	1,171,205
Parole violators	206,118		
New sentences	76,264	32 months	203,370
Technical violators	129,854	6 months	64,927
Totals	540,748		1,439,502
Current state prison population			1,178,978
Net increase			260,524

have to greatly increase state taxes to pay for this massive experiment in imprisonment. In many ways—for example, in terms of the financial costs, the social disruptions, and the removal of a very large percentage of our young male population—this current policy will lead to a situation like World War II, but prolonged for decades.[34]

Of course, other consequences will arise. Since a large percentage of the current prison population is black, most of the nation's 5.5 million black males between the ages of 18 and 39 will be incarcerated or under the criminal justice system, and we will look a lot like South Africa of the 1950s and 1960s.[35]

It is now clear that this increase will have little if any impact on the crime rate. The prison population will become increasingly older, and the prisons will be filled with hundreds of thousands of aging adults who pose a minimal threat to public safety. We will have removed such a large portion of young males and perhaps reduced the forms of street crime we are presently experiencing, but it is impossible to anticipate what new forms of social problems, crime, and upheavals this extremely punitive experiment will cause. The massive social disruptions—such as the removal of most young, black males—might result in unanticipated new types of violent, criminal activities. Each year hundreds of thousands of prisoners are being released to society—many of them with no parole supervision. Many of them will be socially crippled and embittered by their long prison terms.

For the most part, their chances of pursuing a merely viable, much less satisfying, conventional life after prison are small. The contemporary prison experience has converted them into social misfits; and cripples, and there is a growing likelihood that they will return to crime, violence, and other forms of disapproved deviance. They will at least be an enormous nuisance and burden, and some also may engage in a lot of crime.

This ultimate cost of imprisonment—that which society must suffer when prisoners are released—continues to be confirmed by research. The Rand Corporation found that convicted felons sent to prison or granted probation had significantly higher rates of rearrest after release than those on probation.[36] The Linsky and Strauss study cited earlier found that states with higher rates of incarceration have higher rates of violence and suicide.

Sampson and Laub found persons who experienced incarceration had higher rates of criminality.

> One clear possibility is that current [sentencing] policies are producing unintended criminogenic effects. From our perspective, imprisonment may have powerful negative effects on the prospects of future employment and job employment. In turn, low income, unemployment, and underemployment are themselves linked to heightened risks of family disruption. Through its negative effects on male employment, imprisonment may thus lead indirectly through family disruption to increases in future rates of crime and violence. The extremely high incarceration rate of young black males renders this scenario very real.[37]

Even if we assume that crime will eventually decline, how long will we have to maintain such a large prison system to continually deter and incapacitate each successive generation of potential criminals? We do not believe Americans are ready for this costly, inhumane, and racist solution to the crime problem through massive imprisonment, but we will be left with its failure.

Our Vindictive Society

Crime has incurred another profound cost: the increase of general vindictiveness in our society. Historically, Americans (as compared to Europeans and Japanese, for example) have been highly individualistic, which means, for one thing, that they are prone to blaming individuals for their actions. In America, according to the dominant ideology, everyone is responsible for his or her acts, and every act is accomplished by a willful actor. Consequently, every undesirable, harmful, "bad" act is the work of a blameful actor. This belief has resulted in our being the most litigious people in the world and has given us the world's largest legal profession. It has also led us to criminalize more and more behavior and to demand more and more legal action against those who break laws. Today many Americans want someone blamed and punished for every transgression and inconvenience they experience.

Social science should have taught us that all human behavior is only partially a matter of free will and that persons are only partially responsible for their deeds. Everyone's actions are always somewhat influenced or dominated by factors not of one's own making and beyond one's personal control (with economic situation being the most influential and obvious).

Moreover, seeking vengeance is a pursuit that brings more frustration than satisfaction. It has not only been an obstacle in solving many social problems and in developing cooperative, communal attitudes (the lack of which is one important cause of the crime problem), but it is in itself a producer of excessive amounts of anxiety and frustration. Ultimately, vindictiveness erects barriers between people, isolates them, and prevents them from constructing the cooperative, communal social organizations that are so necessary for meaningful, satisfying human existence. Ironically, it is just these social structures that contain the true solution to our crime problem.

The Crime Problem as a Diversion

Our tendency toward vindictiveness is greatly nurtured by the media, politicians, and other public figures who have persistently harangued on the crime issue. They do this largely because the crime issue is seductive. It is seductive to politicians because they can divert attention away from larger and more pressing problems, such as the economy and pollution, whose solutions would require unpopular sacrifices, particularly for them and other more affluent segments of the society.[38] Street crime is seductive to the media because it fits their preferred "sound bite" format of small bits of sensational material. Likewise, it is deeply seductive to the public, who, though they fear crime, possess at the same time deep fascination for it.

IT'S ABOUT TIME

We *must* turn away from the excessive use of prisons. The current incarceration binge will eventually consume large amounts of tax money, which will be diverted from essential public services such as education, child care, mental health, and medical services—the very services that will have a far greater impact on reducing crime than will building more prisons. As we continue to imprison millions of people under intolerably cruel and dangerous conditions, we will accumulate a growing number of ex-convicts who are more or less psychologically and socially crippled and excluded from conventional society, posing a continuing nuisance and threat to others. We will severely damage some of our more cherished humanitarian values, which are corroded by our excessive focus on blame and vengeance. And we will further divide our society into the white affluent classes and a poor nonwhite underclass, many of whom will be convicts and ex-convicts. In effect, we are gradually putting our own apartheid into place.

We believe that these trends can be reversed without jeopardizing public safety. But how should we accomplish a turnaround of this magnitude? First, we must recognize that crime can only be, at best, marginally reduced by escalating the use of imprisonment. If we are to truly reduce crime rates, we as a society must embark on a decade-long strategy that reverses the social and economic trends of the previous decade. In particular, we must jettison the overly expensive and ineffective criminal justice approach and redirect our energies on the next generation of youth, who already are at risk for becoming the next generation of criminals.

The "crime reduction" reforms we have in mind have little to do with criminal justice reform. Rather, these reforms would serve to reduce poverty, single-parent families headed by females, teenage pregnancies and abortions, welfare dependency, unemployment, high drop-out rates, drug abuse, and inadequate health care. These are the social indicators that have proven to be predictive of high crime rates.

The programs and policies that will work—such as better prenatal health care for pregnant mothers, better health care for children to protect them against life-threatening illnesses, Head Start, Job Corps, and Enterprise Zones—have been well documented and may well be contributing to the current decline in crime.[39] But we also need a level of commitment from our major corporate leaders to reduce the flight of jobs, especially the so-called blue-collar and industrial jobs, from this country to Third World nations where cheap labor can be exploited for profits but at tremendous cost to this country.

So how do we go about cutting our losses? We begin by reducing, or at least reducing the rate of growth in, the prison population and reallocating those "savings" to prevention programs that target at-risk youth and their families. But is it realistic to assume that prison populations and their associated costs can be lowered without increasing crime? How, exactly, should we proceed?

Reduce Prison Terms

Many methods of reducing prison populations have been advocated. Some argue that certain classes of felony crimes should be reclassified as misdemeanors or decriminalized completely. In the late 1960s, there was a great deal of support to do this for many minor drug offenses. Others claim that a significant number of those convicted of felonies could be diverted from prison to probation or to new alternatives to prison, including intensive probation, house arrest, electronic surveillance, and greater use of fines and restitution.

We are persuaded, however, that these "front-end" reforms will not substantially reduce prison crowding. Historically, well-intentioned alternatives have had marginal impact on reducing prison populations. Instead, they have had the unintended consequence of widening the net of criminal justice by imposing more severe sanctions on people who otherwise would not be sentenced to prison.[40] They have little support with public officials, who, like the public, are increasingly disenchanted with probation and other forms of community sanctions. Moreover, the current problem is not increasing prison admissions but increases in the length of stay and the number of parole violators.

For alternatives to work, legislators, prosecutors, police, judges, and correctional agencies will all have to agree on new laws and policies to implement them. Such a consensus is unlikely to occur in the near future, since these measures are replete with controversy and disagreement. Even if the forces that are presently driving the punitive response to crime abated considerably, it would take several years to work through these disagreements and effect changes in the laws and policies that would slowly produce an easing of prison population growth. Such a slow pace of reform would not allow states to avoid the catastrophe that is rapidly developing in our prisons.

Even diversion of a substantial number of offenders from prison would not have a major impact on prison population growth. Front-end diversion reforms are targeted for those few offenders who are already serving the shortest prison terms (usually less than a year). The recent flood of tougher sentencing laws has greatly lengthened prison terms for offenders charged with more serious crimes and repeat property or drug offenders. Consequently, it is this segment of the prison population that is piling up in the prisons. The problem is that inmates with long sentences are unlikely to be candidates for diversion from prison.

For these reasons, we believe the single most direct solution that would have an immediate, dramatic impact on prison crowding and would not affect public safety is to shorten prison terms. This reform can be done swiftly and fairly through a number of existing mechanisms, such as greater use of existing good-time credit statutes, accelerating parole eligibility, developing reentry programs for inmates, and altering existing parole revocation policies.

Indeed, many states have launched such programs with no impact on crime rates. Between 1980 and 1983, the Illinois director of corrections released more than 21,000 prisoners an average of 90 days early because of severe prison crowding. The impact on the state's crime rate was insignificant, yet the program saved almost $50 million in tax dollars. A study of the program found that the amount of crime that could be attributed to early release was less than 1 percent of the total crime of the state. In fact, the state's crime rate actually declined while the early release program was in effect. Based on these findings, the state expanded its use of "good time" by another 90 days. A recent study of that expanded program found that the state is now saving over $90 million per year in state funds, even taking into account the costs of early release crimes (which represent less than 1 percent of all crimes committed in Illinois) to crime victims.[41]

An earlier demonstration of how swiftly and easily prison populations can be reduced occurred in California from 1967 to 1970. When Ronald Reagan became governor, he instructed the parole board to reduce the prison population. The board began shortening sentences, which it had the power to do within the indeterminate sentencing system, and in two years lowered the prison population from 28,000 to less than 18,000.

Many other states are following these examples. A study of the Oklahoma preparole program found that inmates could be released earlier by three to six months without influencing the state's crime rate and at considerable savings to the state. Specifically, that study found that for each inmate released early, the state saved over $9,000 per inmate, even when taking into account the costs of crimes committed by these offenders had they remained in prison.[42]

For such a policy to work, prison terms would have to be shortened across the board, and include inmates serving lengthy sentences for crimes of violence who, because of their age, no longer pose a threat to public safety. Because the average prison stay in the United States is approximately two years, even marginal reductions in the length of stay for large categories of inmates would have substantial effects on population size. Using the 1997 figure of approximately 540,748 prison admissions, and assuming that 80 percent of those inmates (representing those who are nonviolent and have satisfactory prison conduct records) had their prison terms reduced by thirty days, we can see that the nation's prison population would have declined by about 36,000 inmates. A ninety-day reduction would result in nearly 110,000 fewer prisoners. Assuming a conservative average cost of $25,000 per inmate, the nation would avert as much as $2.8 billion a year in operating costs and virtually eliminate the need to construct new prisons except for replacement purposes.

Humanize Our Prisons

Whether or not we make any progress toward rational sentencing policies and succeed in dramatically reducing our prison populations, we must confront another issue. Our prisons are, at best, warehouses where prisoners stagnate and are rendered less and less capable of coping with outside society or, at worst, cruel and dangerous maxiprisons where prisoners are damaged and suffer severely. As a civilized people, we must not tolerate this.

The consequences to our society of supporting or even tolerating inhumane prisons are varied and profound. There is the obvious consequence of having to receive back into our society released prisoners who have been critically damaged by their imprisonment. Less obvious is that the general society itself is polluted by the mistreatment of its prisoners. In the first place, guards and other staff persons who must work in the inhumane prison environment are contaminated by it, as are their families and the townsfolk near the prison. It is virtually impossible to be part of or witness to the systematic mistreatment of other human beings without experiencing some deleterious effects. More generally, support for an inhumane prison system requires that citizens embrace the simplistic concept that prisoners are less worthy beings who deserve their extreme punishment. This belief, which is advanced by unscrupulous and self-serving politicians for their self-gain, rests on and then in turn, in a looping process, promotes invidiousness, hate, fear, and other emotions that are inimical to the functioning of a cohesive, orderly, beneficent society.

Prisons where prisoners are systematically treated as less than human; denied dignity, basic human rights, and life necessities; and are physically and mentally mistreated are festering sores that poison the entire society. The state does not have to make prisons into country clubs or "molly-coddle" felons to treat prisoners humanely. Prisons are inherently punitive and can operate efficiently and effectively while treating prisoners in a manner consistent with the minimum standards and rights for prisoners that have been formulated by many private and public bodies.[43] Many of these were proposed in the late 1960s and early 1970s, when considerable concern and effort to reform the prison system were manifest. Some have been realized in many prison systems. But many have not; and at present, most people who decide or influence prison policy completely ignore prisoners' rights and welfare. The courts, particularly the U.S. Supreme Court, after almost completely ignoring the plight of prisoners (the "hands-off" policy), began ruling in the early 1960s on issues regarding prisoners' rights, cruel and unusual punishment, and due process. However, after the mid-1970s, the Supreme Court effectively returned to the hands-off policy.[44]

Given the anti–prison reform climate, we believe that presenting an argument in support of a full prisoners' rights agenda would be futile at this time.

However, several features of a system of incarceration should be acceptable to anyone interested in accomplishing the prison's dominate goals—punishment and incapacitation—and not engaging in unnecessary and counterproductive punitive practices. These are as follows:

1. *No cruel and unusual punishment.* Prison overcrowding, the adoption of control practices in reaction to prison violence, and the lack of concern on the part of the public have resulted in an increase in extremely punitive policies and practices. These include denial of adequate medical services, the excessive use of physical punishment in the management of prisoners, and housing prisoners in extremely punitive arrangements, all of which, when delivered maliciously, have been ruled in violation of the Eighth Amendment of the Constitution.[45]

2. *Safety.* Prisoners should be able to avoid being attacked, raped, and murdered and in other ways being preyed on by other prisoners and staff. Effective strategies such as adequate surveillance, voluntary access to safe living areas within prison systems, housing prisoners in small units, and single celling should be introduced.

3. *Health.* Prisoners should have access to the resources and services required to maintain their physical and mental health. These include access to medical and psychiatric services, adequate diet, and recreation. It also means that they should not be subjected to incarceration regimens that are physically and mentally deleterious, such as extended periods of isolation and restriction on mobility.[46]

4. *Rehabilitation.* As suggested earlier, there has been considerable disagreement on whether rehabilitative programs as they have been practiced have been effective in reducing recidivism. However, it appears obvious to us and certainly consistent with a rational system of punishment that prisoners should have access to programs that, according to their and appropriate experts' judgment, improve their chances to adjust to life after prison. This approach would include education, vocational training, and a wide variety of treatment programs that have been experimented with in the past or will be created in the future.

5. *Re-entry assistance.* Given the large number of inmates being released and the high rate of parole violations, it will be increasingly important to start building supportive re-entry programs for these inmates. Most inmates receive little if any preparation for their release or assistance in the three areas they require help the most: employment, residence, and family support. Certainly it makes little sense to simply dump inmates out of prison with no more than $20 to $50 and expect them to make it on the outside as an ex-convict with few, if any, marketable or social skills. Community-based programs operated in particular by nonprofit organizations are needed to help facilitate the re-entry process.

This is a minimum list of features that would serve as a foundation for a humane and rational system of incarceration. Many other characteristics should be introduced to achieve a truly effective and humane system.[47] But these listed features are crucial. Without them we will continue to deliver excessive and irrational punishment to our prisoners and dump them back out into the "streets," damaged and handicapped, ready to descend into the growing urban pit called the "underclass" or to be recycled once again through prison.

NOTES

1. See Peter Elikann, *SuperPredators: The Demonization of Our Children* (New York: Insight Books, Plenum Publishing, 1999).

2. Criminal Justice Institute, *The 1998 Corrections Yearbook* (1999), p. 87.

3. In addition to the data provided by the Criminal Justice Institute on daily operating costs, the U.S. Department of Justice reported that in 1996, the operating costs were $20,100. The state-by-state comparisons are located in the DOJ report. See *State Prison Expenditures, 1996* (Washington, DC: U.S. Department of Justice, Bureau of Justice Statistics, Office of Justice Programs, August 1999).

4. See D. McDonald, *The Price of Punishment* (Boulder, CO: Westview, 1989); and Carl Loeb, "The Cost of Jailing in New York City," *Crime and Delinquency* (October 1978): 446–452.

5. See Bruce Cory and Stephen Gettinger, *Time to Build? The Realities of Prison Construction* (New York: Edna McConnell Clark Foundation, 1984).

6. See Loeb, "The Cost of Jailing."

7. See Cory and Gettinger, *Time to Build?*

8. James Austin, Darlene Grant, David Bogard, and Curtiss Pulitzer, *District of Columbia Department of Corrections Long-Term Options Study* (Washington, DC: U.S. Department of Justice, National Institute of Corrections, January 31, 1997).

9. Robert Gangi, Vincent Schiraldi, and Jason Ziedenberg, *New York State of Mind?: Higher Education vs. Prison Funding in the Empire State, 1988–1998* (New York: Justice Policy Institute and the Correctional Association of New York, 1999).

10. See Steven D. Dillingham, director, Bureau of Justice Statistics, *Remarks: The Attorney General's Summit on Law Enforcement Responses to Violent Crime: Public Safety in the Nineties* (Washington, DC: March 4–5, 1991).

11. William Barr, *Combating Violent Crime: 24 Recommendations to Strengthen Criminal Justice* (Washington, DC: U.S. Department of Justice, Office of the Attorney General, July 22, 1992).

12. Crime in the United States is measured by two different methods. The first is the Uniform Crime Reports (UCR), which includes all crimes reported to the police and tabulated by the FBI. The UCR only captures a limited number of crimes (homicide, rape, aggravated assault, robbery, burglary, larceny theft, and motor vehicle theft). A second method involves annual surveys conducted by the Census Bureau of persons living in households to determine how many households have been victimized by one of seven crimes (rape, robbery, assault, personal theft, household theft, burglary, and motor vehicle theft) each year. This crime reporting system, known as the National Crime Victim Survey, or NCVS, began in 1973. The NCVS does not include crimes against businesses (shoplifting, commercial burglaries), drug crimes, homicides, or crimes against children under the age of 12. Furthermore, the NCVS tends to record a large number of trivial crimes that are ordinarily not reported to the police. The UCR, unlike the NCVS, does include homicides, crimes committed against

businesses or commercial properties, and crimes committed against children under the age of 12 and those not living in households. For these reasons, most criminologists believe that the UCR is a more reliable measure of crime.

For a review of the methodological merits of the UCR and NCVS, see Darrell Steffensmeier and Miles Harer, "Did Crime Rise or Fall During the Reagan Presidency?" *Journal of Research in Crime and Delinquency* 28, 3 (1991): 330–359.

13. See Dillingham, *Remarks.*

14. National Council on Crime and Delinquency, *Why Is Crime Going Down? A Congressional Briefing* (Washington, DC: National Council on Crime and Delinquency, 1996).

15. This same analysis was performed by Franklin E. Zimring and Gordon Hawkins in their recent book *Incapacitation: Penal Confinement and the Restraint of Crime* (New York: Oxford University Press, 1995), p. 106.

16. For a review of the Rand research, see Zimring and Hawkins, *Incapacitation: Penal Confinement and the Restraint of Crime.*

17. Richard B. Abell, "Beyond Willie Horton: The Battle of the Prison Bulge," *Policy Review* (Winter 1989): 32–35; William P. Barr, "Speech to California District Attorney's Association," *Federal Sentencing Reporter* 4, 6 (1992): 345–346; John DiIulio and Anne Morrison Piehl, "Does Prison Pay? The Stormy National Debate over the Cost-Effectiveness of Imprisonment," *The Brookings Review* (Fall 1998): 28–35.

18. Edwin W. Zedlweski, *Making Confinement Decisions* (Washington, DC: National Institute of Justice, 1987).

19. Mark A. Cohen, "Pain, Suffering, and Jury Awards: A Study of the Cost of Crime to Victims," *Law and Society Review* 22, 3 (1988): 537–555; Ted R. Miller, Mark A. Cohen, and Brian Wiersema, *Victim Costs and Consequences. Research Report* (Washington, DC: U.S. Department of Justice,

National Institute of Justice, 1996); *Criminal Victimization in the United States, 1992* (Washington, DC: U.S. Department of Justice, Bureau of Justice Statistics, 1994), Table 91.

20. Phillip J. Romero, *How Incarcerating More Felons Will Benefit California's Economy* (Sacramento, CA: California Governor's Office of Planning and Research, March 31, 1994).

21. Franklin E. Zimring and Gordon Hawkins, "The New Mathematics of Imprisonment," *Crime and Delinquency* 34 (1988): 425–436.

22. James Austin, "Are Prisons Really a Bargain?," *Spectrum* (1996), p. 10.

23. Zimring and Hawkins, *Incapacitation: Penal Confinement and the Restraint of Crime,* p. 138.

24. Darrell Steffensmeier and Miles Harer, "Did Crime Rise or Fall During the Reagan Presidency?" *Journal of Research in Crime and Delinquency* 28, 3 (1991): 330–359.

25. U.S. Department of Justice, *Crime and the Nation's Households, 1991* (Washington, DC: Bureau of Justice Statistics, Office of Justice Programs, July 1992), pp. 5–6.

26. Ibid.

27. Bureau of Justice Assistance, "Lifetime Likelihood of Going to State or Federal Prison" (Washington, DC: U.S. Government Printing Office, March 1997).

28. Claude Brown, "Manchild 1984," *This World* (September 23, 1984): 7–8.

29. The most blatant display of DiIulio's use of these tactics appeared in a *Readers Digest* article titled "Crime in America, It's Going to Get Worse" (1995). He begins his piece with a story about a guy, a "career criminal," who shot a man strolling on the street in a robbery attempt. According to DiIulio, the shooter had thirteen previous convictions for robberies, burglaries, theft, and drug possession, but had slipped past "forgiving" judges for years.

This case is far out of line with what is happening in Florida, and DiIulio misplaces the "blame" for this situation on liberal judges. Florida has had a habitual offender law for many years that allows for life sentences on the third conviction of a serious felony (including property or drug violations). It is up to the prosecutor to apply this extremely tough sanction on defendants. Judges have little control once the prosecutor decides to file charges a certain way. DiIlulio knows very well that making points from a single case, an anecdote, is fudging. This case, if it did happen anything like DiIlulio contends, is a weird anomaly, and no conclusions about criminal justice policy can be drawn from it.

30. See Peter Elikann, *SuperPredators*, p. 4.

31. See ibid., p. 25.

32. Jack Katz, in a study of street criminals, found that the excitement of criminal behavior was one of the strong attractions it holds for many offenders. See *Seductions in Crime* (New York: Basic Books, 1990). In a much earlier study, Joan Moore documents the culture of urban Chicanos in Los Angeles and how their involvement in gangs inevitably leads to drugs, arrests, and prison. See *Homeboys: Gangs, Drugs and Prison in the Barrios of Los Angeles* (Philadelphia: Temple University Press, 1978).

33. "If Police Call It Gang Crime, That Doesn't Make It True," *Los Angeles Times,* September 28, 1989, part 11, p. 7.

34. Todd R. Clear has presented evidence that this is in fact occurring already with great increases in incarceration of some categories of the population, particularly African Americans. See "The Unintended Consequences of Incarceration," paper presented to the National Institute of Justice Workshop on Corrections Research, February 14–15, 1996.

35. Bureau of Prisons, *1990 Census, Race and Hispanic Origin by Age and Sex for the United States, Regions, and States* (Washington, DC: Bureau of the Census, Racial Statistics Branch, 1992); and Bureau of Justice Statistics, *Sourcebook of Criminal Statistics, 1991,* Table 6.82 (Washington, DC: U.S. Government Printing Office, 1993).

36. Joan Petersilia and Susan Turner, *Prison Versus Probation in California: Implications for Crime and Offender Recidivism* (Santa Monica, CA: Rand Corporation, 1986).

37. Sampson and Laub, *Crime in the Making: Pathways and Turning Points Through Life* (London: Harvard University Press, 1993), p. 255.

38. When he was U.S. attorney general under Ronald Reagan, Edwin Meese was one of the best examples of a powerful politician who made great use of the crime issue to divert attention. Throughout his public career, he barely avoided prosecution on various charges involving his and his friends' receiving money illegally. All the while he persistently harangued about the crime problem, defined it as a problem of career criminals, and called for more punitive action, even suspension of constitutional procedures to keep career criminals in prison. In April 1988, the press reported on his possible involvement in the Wedtech scandal, which led to the conviction of several persons, one a very close personal friend of Meese. In the midst of all this, he delivered a speech to the nation's mayors in which he again fulminated against the new dangerous criminals, drug users.

39. See Lisbeth Schorr and Daniel Schorr, *Within Our Reach* (New York: Anchor Books, 1990), for an exhaustive list of such programs and policies.

40. See James Austin and Barry Krisberg, "The Unmet Promise of Alternatives to Incarceration," *Crime and Delinquency* 28, 3 (1983): 374–409.

41. James Austin and Melissa Bolyard, *The Effectiveness of Shorter Prison Terms* (San Francisco: National Council on Crime and Delinquency, March 1993). See James Austin, "Using Early Release to Relieve Prison Crowding," *Crime and Delinquency* 32: 404–502.

42. See James Austin and Patricia Hardyman, *The Use of Early Parole with Electronic Monitoring to Control Prison Crowding* (San Francisco: National Council on Crime and Delinquency, 1992).

43. As early as 1955 at Geneva, the United Nations Congress on the Prevention of Crime and the Treatment of Prisoners adopted a set of Standard Minimum Rules for the Treatment of Prisoners. See *Human Rights: A Compilation of International Instruments* (United Nations publication, Sales No. E.88.XIV 1), section G.

44. See Jack E. Call, "The Supreme Court and Prisoners' Rights," *Federal Probation* (March 1995): 36–46, for a discussion of the Court's shift in prisoners' rights matters.

45. The Federal District Court of Northern California ruled that treatment of prisoners at Pelican Bay SHU (segregated housing unit) was cruel and unusual in these regards. See *Madrid v. Gomez,* 889 F. Supp. 1149 (N.D. Cal. 1995).

46. In the opinion delivered by the Federal District Court regarding the conditions of confinement in the SHU at Pelican Bay, the court found that "many, if not most, inmates in the SHU experience some degree of psychological trauma in reaction to their extreme social isolation and the severely restricted environmental stimulation in the SHU." See *Madrid v. Gomez.*

47. In *The Struggle for Justice* (New York: Hill & Wang, 1971), the Working Party for the American Friends Service Committee, which consisted of persons with a variety of experiences with prison systems, produced one of the best-thought-out lists of these. See pp. 168–169.

Index

Abbott, Jack, 111–12
Abraham, Nathaniel, 54
Abt Associates study, 65
Adams, Linda, 60–61
Adjustment centers, 120
Administrative breakdown, 95–96
Administrative confusion, 96–97
Administrative segregation, 100
  consequences of lockup, 131–37
  history of, 119–20
  official program, 120
  and protective custody populations, *118 table*
  reality of lockup, 121
  Texas population, 129–31
  turmoil in lockup, 121–25
Admissions. *See* Prison admissions
Adult correctional populations, *4 table*
African-Americans:
  expectations of going to prison, 238
  incarceration rates, 3–5, 94–95
  staff and inmates at private state prisons, 79

Age
  and crime, 162–63
  of jurisdiction, 55
  of youthful offender population, *59 table*
Alabama, 47
Alcatraz, 125
Alienation, 111–12
American Civil Liberties Union, 95
Amity Right Turn (Calif.), 176
Amnesty International, 61
Arbitrary disciplinary punishment, 106
Arkansas, 99
Assaults, 81
Asset sale, 65
Atlanta federal prison, 125
Attributes of prison programs, *104 table*
Austin, James, 41, 60–61, 234

Ballasiotes, Diane, 184
Banishment, 12
"Barn bosses," 99
Barr, William, 7, 225, 228

Bennett, William, 238
Berk, Richard, 163
"Big house" prisons, 91
Black Muslims, 95, 122
Black Panthers, 122
Blumstein, Alfred, 18
Boot camps, 160–62
  argument for, 167
  research on, 167–69
Bosket, Willie, 134–35
Breed, Allen, 126–27
Bronx Community College, 105
Brown, Claude, 238
Bunker, Edward, 109
Bureaucratic prison, 97–100
Burke, Peggy, 60–61
Burt, Martha, 156
Bush, George, 5, 225

California, 13, 47, 93, 100, 120, 124,
  228–29, 246
  correctional costs for strikers and
    nonstrikers, 1996, *209 table*
  crime rates and prison sentences,
    1990–1997, *233 table*
  current offenses by three strikers,
    208 table
  felony jury trials in superior court,
    199 table
  hypothesized crime volume in,
    235 figure
  impact of three strike laws on crime
    rates in, 210–12, *211, 212 figure*
  parole failures, 142, 148, 150
  prison population projections,
    1994–1998, *203 table*
  strike law
    description and legislative history,
      195–97
  super-max prisons in, 127–28
  type of crime for two and three
    strikers admitted to prison,
    207 table
California Crime Index, 210
California Department of
  Corrections, 197
Career criminals, 18–19, 31–38, 185
CCA Youngstown, 84

Cell extraction, 97
*Census of State and Federal Correctional
  Facilities,* 77, 81
Center for Studies in Criminology
  and Criminal Law (U. of Penn.), 25
Chambliss, Bill, 4–5
Characteristics of three state prison
  systems: Nevada, Illinois,
  Washington, *25 table*
"Chickenshit rules," 106–7
Christiansen, Robert, 107
Classification systems, 99
Clemmer, Donald, 119
Clinton, William Jefferson, 5, 184,
  225, 240
Cohen, Mark, 233–34
College programming, 105–6
Colonial era, 9
Colorado, 85
Community corrections, 110
Consortium of Niagara Frontier, 105
Construction costs, 221
Contemporary prison, 91–92
Contract prisons, 94
Convict labor, 68–69
Coopers and Lybrand study, 221
Corcoran facility, 124
Correctional Association of New York
  studies, 38–41, 222
Correctional facilities, 65
Corrections Corporation of America,
  65, 70, 72, 78
Costs:
  construction, 221
  continuing, 241–43
  of imprisonment binge, 13, *14 table*
  operating, 220–21
  of a prison bed, typical thirty-year
    life cycle, *223 table*
Crack cocaine, 5, 7
Crime Bill (1994), 225
Crime committed by released
  prisoners with drug problems,
  projected, *172 table*
Crime episode, 33–34
Crime trends and sentenced prisoners
  in federal and state institutions,
  224 table

Criminal behavior:
  and drugs, 163–64
  and gender/age, 162–63
  and incarceration, 165
  and job stability, 163
  and marriage, 163
  and social/economic structure,
    164–65
Criminal Justice Institute, 38, 139
Criminal justice system expenditures,
  14 table
Cripe, Clair, 67–68, 73
Crowding, 93–94
Cruel and unusual punishment, 76,
  248
Cunningham, Dennis, 71–72

Deaths, 81, 83
Delaware, 47
Demographics, 234–36
Dependency, 153–55
Dereliction, 36–37, 156–57
Detachment, 112
Determinate sentencing, 24
Deterrence, 185, 238
Deukmejian, George, 128
Dickens, Charles, 135
DiIlulio, John, 234, 238–39
The Discovery of the Asylum
  (Rothman), 9
District of Columbia, 85
Drift, 155–56
Drug dealers, 239
Drug possession, 204, 207
Drug testing, 150
Drug treatment. *See* Prison drug
  treatment
Drug treatment programs, how many
  inmates can participate in?,
  174 table
Drug use, 7
  and crime, 163–64
Due process, 76
Dukakis, Michael, 5
Durham, Alexis, 70, 75

Economic trends, 1980s, 10–11
Economy and crime, 164–65
Education, 105–6, 222

Electronic monitoring, 151
Employee characteristics of private
  facilities, *82 table*
Employees in public and private state
  facilities, *81 table*
Employment, 147–48
England, 12
Escapes, 81
Excessive use of force, 97
Ex-convicts, 111

Farm system for criminals, 239–40
Fear of crime, 4–8
Federal Adoption Assistance and Child
  Welfare Act, 61
Federal Bureau of Prisons, 125, 195
Federal Sentencing Guidelines, 5
Feeley, Malcolm, 67, 201–2, 214
Female inmates, 57–59
  abuse of, 61–62
  characteristics of, 59–61
  incarceration rates, *5 table*
Figlio, Robert M., 18
Florida, 70
  habitual sentencing laws, 41–46
Fowler, Lorraine, 59
Fox, James Alan, 239

Gaes, Gerald, 85
Gallup Poll, 5
Gang banging, 108
Gangs, 122–23, 134
Gender and crime, 162–63
General population, 117
George Washington University survey,
  56
Georgia, 195, 204, 213
Goshka, Mike, 93
Gottfredson, Michael, 19
Greenberg, David, 18–19
Greenwood, Peter, 18, 46, 185–86
Guards:
  abuse of female inmates by, 61–62
  pay of, 98

Habitual offenders, 38, 185
  Correctional Association of New
    York study, 38–41

Florida's habitual sentencing laws, 41–46
Hallinan, Terence, 201
Hamilton County Jail (Tenn.), 70
Hammer v. King County, 96
Harer, Miles, 235
Hawes-Cooper Act, 69
Hawkins, Gordon, 234
Health, 248
Higher education, lack of access to, 105–6
High-rate offenders, 18, 214, 219
Hirschi, Travis, 19
Hispanics:
    expectations of going to prison, 238
    incarceration rates, 3–5, 94–95
    staff and inmates at private state prisons, 79
Homicides, 30–31
Horton, Willie, 5
Huling, Tracy, 57
Humanizing prisons, 247–49

Idleness, 104
Illicit drug use, national estimates, 1979–1995, *165 table*
Illinois, 24, 50, 120, 142
Immigration and Naturalization Service, U.S., 70, 72
Imprisonment and violent crime rates, *226 figure*
Imprisonment binge:
    accomplishments of, 12–13
    costs of, 13, *14 table*
Incarceration rates, 1, *2 figure,* 3, *4 tables*
    increase in, *230 figure*
Incarceration reduces crime debate, 222
    argument against, 227
    bad math—numbers don't add up, 231–34
    failure to control for other factors, 234–36
    inconsistencies in the national trend, 227–31
    argument in favor of, 223–27

Incidents, by type, in CDC institutions, *101–2 table*
Indeterminate sentencing, 91–92, 120
Index crimes, 5
Informers, 132
Inmate characteristics at public facilities and private facilities, *79 table*
Institute on Crime, Justice and Corrections survey, 53
Intensive supervision programs, 150–51

Jackson, George, 123, 134
Jacobs, James, 97
Jail and prison populations by gender, *59 table*
Job:
    search, 147–48
    stability and crime, 163
Johnson, Lyndon, 5
Justice, U.S. Dept. of, 3, 139–40, 142, 222–23, 231, 233, 235
Justice Policy Institute, 222
Justice Statistics, Bureau of, surveys, 24, 47, 77–78, 141, 163, 241
Juvenile arrest rates, male and female, *51 table*
Juvenile correctional system:
    characteristics of population, 56, *57 table*
    conditions of confinement, 52
    history of, 50–52
    trends in numbers confined in adult facilities, 53
    waivers to adult court, 53–56
Juvenile delinquency, 52
Juvenile Justice and Delinquency Prevention Act (1973), 52
Juveniles in juvenile private and public facilities, *53 table*

Kamin, Sam, 201–2, 214
Katz, Jack, 240
Kennedy, Robert, 125
Kentucky, 70
Kirchheimer, 163–64
Klass, Polly, 184
Klein, Malcolm, 185

Kupers, Terry, 135–36

Laub, John, 165, 243
Leavenworth federal prison, 125
Length of stay, 140–42
Life sentences, 20
Linsky, Arnold, 164–65, 236, 242
Lipton, Douglas, 175
Lockup, 100, 108–9
  consequences of, 131–37
  official program, 120
  reality of, 121
  turmoil in, 121–25
Lompoc prison, 106–7
Los Angeles, 240
Louisiana, 85, 191
Luttwak, Edward, 11–12

Mackenzie, D.L., 168
Major incidents:
  in public and private facilities,
    83 table
  in public and private medium and
    minimum facilities, 84 table
Male incarceration rates, 4 table
Mandatory minimums, 20
Marijuana, 164
Marion prison (Ill.), 125–27
Marriage and crime, 163
Martin, Dannie, 106–7
Martinson, Robert, 165
Maryland, 191
Mauer, Marc, 57
Maximum-security prisons, 125–29
McCleery, Richard, 135
McDonald, Douglas, 70
Meaninglessness, 112
Michigan, 54
  prison population estimates of
    eligibility for TC-type programs,
    175 table
Michigan Department of Corrections,
  174
Minimum custody, 99
Moderate crimes, 27–29
Morash, Mary, 60
Morissey decision, 144

National Academy of Sciences, 231,
  233
National Center on Addiction and
  Substance Abuse (CASA), 170,
  172–73
National Council on Crime and
  Delinquency, 142–43
National Crime Survey, 225
National Crime Victim Survey, 13,
  225, 228, 235
National Institute of Justice, 175, 233
National Survey of State Prison
  Privatization, 78
Native Americans, incarceration rates,
  3–5
Nevada, 24, 145–46
New admissions, 20
New strike laws compared with
  preexisting sentencing provisions,
  192–94 table
New York, 13, 93, 128–29, 228–29
New York State Prison System, 105–6
New York Theological School, 105
New York Times, 128–29
Nineteenth century, 9
Normlessness, 112
Northeast Ohio Corrections Center,
  85
Numbers of inmates in prison, boot
  camps, and drug treatment,
  1994–1998, 162 table

Office of Juvenile Justice and
  Delinquency Prevention, 169
Office of National Drug Policy, 164
Okeechobee School for Boys (Fla.),
  70
Oklahoma, 128, 151, 246
One-shot crime, 37–38
Operating costs, 220–21
Oregon, 85
Overcrowding, 93–94

Parole. See also Release
  officers, 149–50
  selected conditions of, in effect in
    51 jurisdictions in 1988, 145 table
  violators, 20, 143–46
Pelican Bay prison (Calif.), 127–28

Pell grants, 105
Penitentiary, 9
People v. Davis, 198
People v. Hazleton, 197–98
People v. Superior Court (Alvarez), 198
People v. Superior Court (Romero), 198
Petersilia, Joan, 185
Petty crimes, 26–27
Phillips, Kevin, 10
Plea bargaining, 196
The Politics of Rich and Poor (Phillips),
    10
Pontiac Correctional Center (Ill.),
    109
Powerlessness, 112
Prison admissions, 46–47
    change in proportions that are
        nonwhite and for drug crimes,
        23 table
    habitual offenders, 38–46
    lifestyles of and types of crimes
        committed by prisoners, 22–25,
        43 table
    national trends on, 19–23
    patterns of crime, 31–38
    public misperceptions about, 17–19
    seriousness of crimes, 25–31
    Washington, California, and
        Georgia, compared, *206 table*
Prison drug treatment, 160–62
    argument for, 169–76
    problems with, 176, 179
    proposed cost effectiveness of,
        171 table
    summaries of studies on,
        177–78 table
Prisoner experience:
    arbitrary disciplinary punishment,
        106
    "chickenshit rules," 106–7
    lack of access to higher education,
        105–6
    reduced resources and contacts,
        103–4
    restricted freedom, 103
    violence, 100–103
Prisonization, 110
Prison Law Project, 95

Prison Litigation Reform Act, 95
Prison system:
    cost of imprisonment binge, 241–43
    crime problem as a diversion, 244
    vindictive society, 243
    where are we headed?, 240–41
Prison term reductions, 245–47
Private:
    adult correctional firms, *66 table*
    facility characteristics by level of
        security, *80 table*
    management firms outside the
        United States, by location,
        66 table
    prison market share of prison
        facilities, *67 table*
Privatization:
    advantages of, 71–75
    background of, 64–67
    future of, 85–86
    historical overview, 67–71
    legal issues, 75–77
    state prison survey
        inmate and facility characteristics,
            78
        inmate violations and deaths, 81,
            83–85
        methodology, 77–78
        staffing and employment, 78–82
Project New Vision (Texas), 176
Property crimes, 207
Proposition 184 (Calif.), 201
Protective custody, 108–9, 117–18
Psychological impairment, 135–36
Public:
    attitudes toward most important
        problem facing the country,
        8 table
    strategies for private prisons,
        72 table
Public Agenda Foundation surveys,
    12, 47
Punishment, 96–97, 238

Racial:
    hostility, 122–23
    skewing, 94–95

Rand Corporation studies, 18, 46, 142, 150–51, 197, 231, 233, 242
Rauma, David, 163
Reagan, Ronald, 246
Rearrest rates, 142–43
Recidivism, 167–69
  among probationers and matched prisoners, *143 figure*
Reentry:
  assistance, 248
  shock of, 146–47
Reforms, 244
  humanization of prisons, 247–49
  reduced prison terms, 245–47
Rehabilitation, 9, 12, 96, 149, 160, 248
  demise of, 92–93
Release:
  all states 1996, *140 table*
  dependency, 153–55
  dereliction, 156–57
  doing good, 152–53
  drift, 155–56
  drug testing, 150
  electronic monitoring, 151
  finding a job, 147–48
  intensive supervision programs, 150–51
  parole failures, 143–46
  parole officers, 149–50
  rates of rearrest after release, 142–43
  shock of reentry, 146–47
  time in jail and prison before parole, 139–42
  and time served—jail, prison, and parole 1996, *141 table*
Residential Substance Abuse Treatment (RSAT) program, 170
Retired convicts, 109
Richards, Ann, 228
Robberies, 29
Robbins, Ira, 73
Roosevelt, Theodore, 69
Rosenbaum, Marsha, 7
Rothman, David, 9
Rushe, 163–64

Safety, 248

Sam Houston University survey, 12
Sampson, Robert, 165, 243
San Francisco crime and sentencing trends, 1990–1998, 231, *232 table*
San Quentin, 68, 106, 124–25, 134
Scared Straight Shock Incarceration programs, 184
Schichor, D., 186
Sechrest, D.K., 186
Second and third strike:
  cases admitted to CDC by month, *205 table*
  selected counties compared on use of (Calif.), *200 table*
Security threat group, 129
Segregation, 95
Self-estrangement, 112
Sellin, Thorsten, 18
Serious crimes, 29–31
  proportion of convicted offenders sentenced for, *21 table*
Severity of crimes committed by persons admitted to prison, *27 table*
  Washington, Illinois, Nevada, *28 table*
Slater, Robert, 125
Social:
  demographic indicators related to crime rates, *237 table*
  impairment, 136–37
  structure and crime, 164–65
Soledad, 124
South Carolina, 85, 191
Special program units, 120
Staged fights, 124
State action, 76–77
State prison:
  admissions, *20 table*
  impact of strike laws on, 202–4
  inmate characteristics: offense charge, demographics, housing patterns, *58 table*
  long-term population projections, *242 table*
  populations, adult and juvenile, 1998, *57 table*
State strike law variations, *187–90 table*

Stay'n Out (New York), 176
Steffensmeier, Darrell, 235
Strauss, Murray, 164–65, 236, 242
Street crime, 34–36, 239, 244
Strikes laws. *See* Three strikes and
    you're out movement
Super Max, 100, 117–19
Supreme Court, U.S., 76–77, 247
Syracuse University, 105

Technical violations, 144
Tennessee, 70, 191
Texas, 85, 93, 99, 108, 228–29
    administrative segregation
        population, 129–31
    parole and probation violators,
        144–45
    sentencing patterns in, 21–22
    therapeutic community program,
        174–75
Therapeutic community model,
    173–76
Thomas, Charles, 70–71
Three strikes and you're out
    movement, 184–86, 213–14
    California's law
        description and history, 195–97
        impact on correctional costs,
            208–10
        impact on crime rates in
            California, 210–12
        impact on state prison systems,
            202–4
        impact on the courts, 197–200
        variation by county in applying,
            201–2
    diversity among states, 186–91
    impact on crime rates among the
        states, 212–13
    new laws compared with
        preexisting sentencing, 191–95
    offenders in California, Washington,
        Georgia compared, 204–8
Trends:
    in Texas administrative segregation
        populations, *130, 131 tables*
    in violent and property offenses,
        6 table

Truth-in-sentencing laws, 20, 225,
    241
Tuition Assistance Program (TAP),
    105
Turner, Susan, 18, 46
Type of offense for 1996 prison
    admissions, *22 table*

Uniform Crime Reports, 162, 212,
    225, 228, 235
*United States v. State of Florida: Florida
    Department of Corrections,* 96
*United States v. The Parish of Orleans
    Criminal Sheriff's Office,* 96
University of Maryland study, 167
U.S. Corrections Corporation, 70

Vindictiveness, 243
Violence, 100–103
    coping with, 108–9
Violent crime rates, 1973–1995,
    229 figure
Virginia, 191
Voodoo criminology, 236–39

Wackenhut, 65, 78
Waivers to adult court, 53–56
Ward, David, 126–27
Warehousing prisoners, 9–12, 90–91
War on Drugs, 5, 7, 59, 240
Washington, 24, 204, 213
The Washington Post, 62
Weaversville Intensive Treatment Unit
    for Juvenile Delinquents (Penn.), 70
Weld, William, 92–93
Wilson, Pete, 93
Wirthlin Group poll, 47
Withdrawal, 109
Wobbler offense, 198
Wolfgang, Marvin E., 18
Women inmates. *See* Female inmates
World War II, 9, 242

"Young Black Americans and the
    Criminal Justice System," 57, 59

Zedlweski, Edwin, 233
Zimring, Franklin, 234